MODERN JEWISH THOUGHT

MODERN JEWISH THOUGHT

A Source Reader

Edited by NAHUM N. GLATZER

SCHOCKEN BOOKS • NEW YORK

First published by SCHOCKEN BOOKS 1977

10 9 8 7 6 5 4 3 2   81 82 83 84

Copyright © 1977 by Schocken Books Inc.

For acknowledgments see pages 211–14.

Library of Congress Cataloging in Publication Data

Main entry under title:

Modern Jewish thought.

    Bibliography: p. 215
    1. Judaism—History—Modern period, 1750–
    —Sources. I. Glatzer, Nahum Norbert, 1903–

BM195.M6   296.3   76-9139

Manufactured in the United States of America

ISBN 0–8052–0542–X

To my grandchildren
JOHANNA and RINA
with love

Contents

Foreword

This source book is an attempt to introduce the reader to *one* aspect of modern thought and reflection on life and human existence: the Jewish aspect. Most of the personalities who speak here are best understood against the background of the civilization in which they are at home.

For many years I have been teaching a course on modern Jewish thought, first at Brandeis University, later at Boston University, and paid careful attention to students' reaction to this course; I was able to make use of their responses, both affirmative and critical. But only the urging of Theodore Schocken, publisher of Schocken Books, prompted me to start converting copious lecture notes and reading lists into organized book form. Alas, Theodore Schocken did not live to see the fruition of many of the projects he initiated, among them this one; he died March 20, 1975.

Arrangement of the book is by personality, encompassing those personalities who are significantly representative of the ideas, trends, movements, and tendencies in, roughly, the last two centuries. They include men who originated the scholarly-critical approach to Judaic materials; spokesmen for the Westernization of the Jews and for a historical view of Judaism; advocates of liberalism and of neo-Orthodoxy; representatives of the rationalist and of the mystical quest; men who lived by a vision of Zion and the realization of that vision; teachers who perceived both the need to preserve and the need to reconstruct tradition; men who hear the commanding voice of Auschwitz and keep the memory of the fallen alive.

There is an astounding variety of outlook, point of view, envisioned goals; an outburst of creative energy in a period usually characterized as an era of assimilation, acculturation, alienation, and worship of the idols of this world. Such characterization is only half the picture. The other half, especially in recent years, is an earnest attempt on the part of many to return, to acknowledge one's roots, to strive for a meaningful survival and a desire to acquire at least some knowledge of the meaning of Judaism.

I have been privileged to know at close range some of the personalities included in this volume. This circumstance has been of immense help in understanding their work and in attempting to evaluate their place in modern life and thought and in Western thought at large.

Needless to say, the list of personalities here presented is far from complete; economy of space demanded severe selectivity. In the modern period alone the following could have been included: Alexander Altmann, Salo W. Baron, Nathan Birnbaum, Eugene Borowitz, A. D. Gordon, Will Herberg, Louis Jacobs, Erich Kahler, Ludwig Lewisohn, Abram L. Sachar, Gershom Scholem, Steven S. Schwarzschild, and Ernst Simon. And there are others.

The fifteen chapters of the volume roughly correspond to the fifteen weeks of an average semester in an American university. Adjustments can easily be made to suit different academic calendars. Extra-academic study groups and institutes can safely disregard the division and simply select material that suits their purpose. The short prefaces preceding individual texts offer basic biographical and historical background information.

Students enrolled in a course such as Modern Jewish Thought—and there are many in the country—will do well to acquaint themselves with the territory at large, before deciding on which part to concentrate. In this respect, the bibliography should prove useful; it provides first a list of general books, then enumerates works by and on specific personalities.

Translations have been revised in places; a few of the texts have been abridged; omissions are, as a rule, indicated by three dots in brackets.

It is a distinct pleasure to record my gratitude to Peter Bedrick and Seymour Barofsky of Schocken Books for their good counsel, and to Tobie Atlas for her intelligent and gracious aid in the preparation of the manuscript, and to Bertha Katzenstein for her help in the preparation of the index.

N. N. Glatzer

Boston University
December, 1975

MODERN JEWISH THOUGHT

MOSES MENDELSSOHN

Letter to Johann Caspar Lavater

Johann Caspar Lavater (1741–1801), Protestant minister in Zurich, met Moses Mendelssohn (1729–1786), the Jewish philosopher and advocate of enlightenment and emancipation, and was impressed by Mendelssohn's religious liberalism. When the French philosopher Charles Bonnet (1720–1793) published his *La palingénésie philosophique* (1769), Lavater translated a part of the work (in which Bonnet argued for the truth of Christianity) and sent it to Mendelssohn, requesting him either to refute Bonnet's argument or convert to Christianity. The Swiss deacon did not realize that the Jewish thinker's respect for Jesus as a human being in no way implied his being ripe for conversion. On the other hand, Mendelssohn tried hard to avoid open polemic and therefore refused to criticize Bonnet's views. In his letter to Lavater, written on December 12, 1769, he reminded the pastor of the precarious position of the Jew in the gentile world and pleaded for tolerance.

Mendelssohn's major work is *Jerusalem, or On Religious Power and Judaism* (1783), an attempt at a synthesis of Jewish religion and philosophical rationalism. The attempt failed; Mendelssohn's definition of Judaism as revealed legislation (designating "religion," faith, as common possession of mankind) satisfied neither the orthodox believer nor the liberal. Still, Mendelssohn remained a symbol of a thinker who in his own life reconciled Judaism with western culture.

To Lavater he wrote:

Dear Friend:

You have found it advisable to dedicate your translation from the French of Bonnet's *Examination of the Proofs for Christianity* to me and to request me publicly and solemnly to refute this treatise if I felt that its arguments in support of the claims of Christianity were erroneous. Should I, however, find the arguments convincing, you ask me "to do what wisdom, love of truth, and honor require, and what a Socrates would have done had he read the treatise and found it irrefutable," namely, to abandon the religion of my fathers and to embrace the faith advocated by M. Bonnet. For even if I were ever tempted to stoop so low as to place expediency above my sense of truth and probity, my course of action would in this particular case obviously be dictated by all three elements.

I am convinced your motives are pure and reflect nothing but your loving concern for your fellowmen. Indeed, I should not be worthy of anyone's respect if I did not gratefully reciprocate the affection and friendship for me that are evident in your dedicatory inscription. Yet I must confess that your action has shocked me deeply. I should have expected anything but a public challenge from a Lavater.

Since you recall the confidential conversations I had with you and your friends in my home, you cannot have forgotten how often I attempted to shift the discussion from religious issues to more neutral and conventional topics and how strongly you and your friends had to prod me before I would venture to express my views on these matters [i.e., views on Jesus and Christianity], which touch upon man's deepest convictions. Unless memory betrays me, I was assured on these occasions that our conversations would be kept confidential. I would, of course, rather be mistaken in my recollection than accuse you of a breach of promise.

Nevertheless, you could easily have foreseen how repugnant it would be to me to issue a public statement about these matters after I had carefully tried to avoid discussing them even in the privacy of my own home and among just a few trusted men, of whose good will I was certain. The fact that the voice that now challenges me cannot easily be disregarded or dismissed only adds to my embarrassment. What could therefore possibly have motivated you to single me out against my will in order to drag me into the arena of public controversy, which I had hoped never to enter? Even if you had ascribed my reticence merely to timidity and shyness, should a loving friend not have shown some tolerance and leniency for such personal shortcomings?

My disinclination to enter into religious controversy has, however, never been the result of fear of folly. My study of the foundations of my religious faith does not date from yesterday. Very early in my life I had already become alare of the need to examine my views and actions. And the principal reason for which I have spent my leisure time since then in the study of philosophy and the humanities was precisely that I wanted to prepare myself for this task. I had no other motives. I knew that my studies could not possibly bring the slightest material advantage to someone in my situation. I realized there was no promising career for me in this field. And as for inner rewards? O, my dear friend! The civic status and position of my coreligionists are not conducive to the free development of our intellectual capacities. To ponder the true state of our affairs can hardly increase our happiness. Let me refrain from elaborating this point. Any person who knows our plight and who has a human heart will understand more than I can possibly say here.

If my decision, after all these years of study, had not been entirely in favor of my religion, I would certainly have found it necessary to make my convictions known publicly. I fail to see what could have kept me tied to a religion that is so severe and generally despised had I not, in my heart, been convinced of its truth. Whatever the result of my studies, I would have felt compelled to leave the religion of my fathers had I ever begun to feel that it was not true. And had my heart been captured by another faith, it would have been depravity not to admit to the truth. What could possibly cause me to debase myself [by not admitting it]? There is only one course, as I have already pointed out, that wisdom, love of truth, and honesty can choose.

If I were indifferent to both religions or mocked and scorned all revelations, I might indeed follow the counsel which expediency dictates while conscience remains silent. What could deter me? Fear of my fellow Jews? They lack the power to intimidate me. Stubbornness? Inertia? Blind adherence to familiar customs and conventions? Since I have devoted a large part of my life to the examination of my tradition, I hope no one will expect me to sacrifice the fruits of my studies to such personal failings.

You can, therefore, see that I would have been impelled to make a public statement about the results of my studies had they left me without the sincere conviction of the validity of my faith. However, inasmuch as my investigations strengthened me in the faith of my fathers, I was able to continue in it quietly, without feeling that I had to render an account to the world of my convictions.

I do not deny that I see certain human excesses and abuses that tarnish the beauty of my religion. But is there any friend of truth who can claim that his religion is completely free of man-made accretions and corruptions? All of us know that the search for truth can be impeded by the poisonous breath of hypocrisy and superstition. We wish we could dispel both without damaging the beauty and truth of the essentials of our religion. Nevertheless, of the validity of the essentials of my faith I am as firmly and irrefutably convinced as you or M. Bonnet is of his, and I declare before God, who has created and sustained both you and me—the God in whose name you have challenged me—that I shall adhere to my principles as long as my soul remains unchanged.

My inner remoteness from your religion has remained unchanged since I disclosed my views to you and your friends. And I would even now be prepared to concede that my respect for the moral stature of its founder has not diminished since then, were it not that you have clearly disregarded the reservation which I had attached to my views at that time. But there comes a moment in a man's life when he has to make up his mind about certain issues in order to be able to go on from there. This happened to me several years ago with regard to religion. I have read; I have compared; I have reflected; and I have made up my mind.

Still, I admit that I would never have entered into a dispute about Judaism, even if it had been polemically attacked or triumphantly held up to scorn in academic textbooks. There would have been no counterargument from me even against the most ridiculous notion which anyone, whether trained or merely semiliterate in the field of rabbinics, might have discovered in some literary trash that no serious-minded Jew bothers to read. I wanted to refute the world's derogatory opinion of the Jew by righteous living, not by pamphleteering. However, it is not only my station in life but also my religion and my philosophy that furnish me with the most cogent reasons why I wanted to avoid religious controversy and discuss, in my publications, only those religious verities which are of equal importance to all religions.

According to the principles of my religion, I am not expected to try to convert anyone not born into my faith. Even though many people think that the zeal for proselytizing originated in Judaism, it is, in fact, completely alien to it. Our rabbis hold unanimously that the written as well as the oral laws that constitute our revealed religion are binding only for our own people. "*Moses* had given *us* the law; it is the inheritance of the Hou e of *Jacob*" (Deuteronomy 33:4).[1] All other nations were enjoined by God to observe the law of nature and the religion of the patriarchs.[2] All who live in accordance with this religion of nature and of reason are called "the righteous among other nations"; they too are entitled to eternal bliss.[3] Far from being obsessed by any desire to proselytize, our rabbis require us to discourage as forcefully as we can anyone who asks to be converted. We are to ask him to consider the heavy burden he would have to shoulder needlessly by taking this step. We are to point out that, in his present state, he is obligated to fulfill only the Noahide laws in order to be saved but that upon his conversion he will have to observe strictly all the laws of his new faith or expect the punishment which God metes out to the lawbreaker. Finally, we are to paint a faithful picture of the misery and destitution of our people and of the contempt in which they are held, in order to keep him from a hasty decision he may later regret.[4] As you see, the religion of my fathers does not ask to be propagated. We are not to send missionaries to the two Indies or to Greenland in order to preach our faith to distant nations. [. . .] Anyone not born into our community need not observe its laws. The fact that we consider their observance incumbent upon us alone cannot possibly offend our neighbors. Do they think our views are absurd? No need to quarrel about it. We act in accordance with our convictions and do not mind if others question the validity of our laws, which, as we ourselves emphasize, are not binding on them. Whether they are acting fairly, peaceably, and charitably when they mock our laws and traditions is, of course, something else that must be left to their own consciences. As long as we do not want to convince or convert others, we have no quarrel with them.

If a Confucius or a Solon were to live among our contemporaries, I could, according to my religion, love and admire the great man without succumbing to the ridiculous desire to convert him. Convert a Confucius or a Solon? What for? Since he is not a member of the household of Jacob, our religious laws do not apply to him. And as far as the general principles of religion are concerned, we should have little trouble agreeing on them. Do I think he can be saved? It seems to me that anyone who leads men to virtue in this life cannot be damned in the next. [. . .]

It is my good fortune to count among my friends many an excellent man who is not of my faith. We love each other sincerely, although both of us suspect or assume that we differ in matters of faith. I enjoy the pleasure of his company and feel enriched by it. But at no time has my heart whispered to me, "What a pity that this beautiful soul should be lost. . . ." Only that man will be troubled by such regrets who believes that there is no salvation outside his church.

Every man, admittedly, has a duty to teach his fellowmen understanding and virtue and to seek to eradicate prejudice and error in every possible way. Consequently, one could assume that a man has the responsibility of taking a public stand against religious notions that he considers erroneous. Nevertheless, not every prejudice or weakness we seem to detect in our fellowmen is equally harmful. Nor should we react to all of them in the same manner. Some prejudices strike directly at the happiness of mankind. Their influence on morality is pernicious; we cannot expect even an incidental benefit from them. These prejudices must be attacked immediately and unhesitatingly by anyone who has the interests of mankind at heart. Any delay or detour would be irresponsible. Fanaticism, hatred of one's fellowmen and the wish to persecute them, levity, self-indulgence, amoral atheism—these are among the failings that disturb man's inner peace and happiness and destroy his latent capacity for truth and goodness before it can unfold.

But some of my fellowmen hold views and convictions which, although I may consider them wrong, do belong to a higher order of theoretical principles. They are not harmful, because they have little or no relationship to the practical concerns of daily life. Yet they frequently constitute the foundation on which people have erected their systems of morality and social order and are therefore of great importance to them. To question such notions publicly merely because we consider them biased or erroneous would be like removing the foundation stones of a building in order to examine the soundness of its structure. Any person who is interested more in man's welfare than in his own fame will refrain from public statements in such matters. He will proceed with the utmost care in order not to destroy someone else's ethical principles, even though he may suspect they are faulty, until the other person is prepared to accept the truth in their stead.

Therefore, I find it possible to remain silent despite the fact that may encounter racial prejudices and religious errors among my fellow citizens, as long as their views do not subvert natural religion or undermine natural law. In fact, these views may incidentally even produce some good. I admit that our actions do not deserve to be called moral if they are grounded in error and that the cause of the good will be advanced more effectively and lastingly by truth, where truth is known, than by prejudice and error. Nevertheless, as long as truth is not yet known or not yet sufficiently accepted to have the same impact upon the masses that their old prejudices did, their preconceived notions must be considered inviolate by any friend of true virtue.

We must show this kind of discretion especially where a people, though harboring seemingly erroneous beliefs, has otherwise distinguished itself intellectually and morally and has produced a number of great personalities who rank high among the benefactors of mankind. We should, with respectful silence, overlook the errors of so noble a member of the human family even if we think it is all too human on occasion. Is there really anyone among us who is entitled to ignore the excellent qualities of such a people and to criticize it for a single weakness he may have discovered?

These are the reasons, rooted in my religious and philosophical convictions, for which I carefully avoid religious controversy. If you add to them the circumstances of my life among my fellowmen, I am sure you will find my position justified. I am a member of an oppressed people which must appeal to the benevolence of the government for protection and shelter—which are not always granted, and never without limitations. Content to be tolerated and protected, my fellow Jews willingly forgo liberties granted to every other human being. Barred even from temporary residence in many countries, they consider it no small favor when a nation admits them under tolerable conditions. As you know, your circumcised friend may not even visit you in Zurich, because of the laws of your own home town. Thus, my coreligionists owe much grateful appreciation to any government that shows them humanitarian consideration and permits them, without interference, to worship the Almighty in the ways of their fathers. They enjoy a fair amount of freedom in the country in which I live. Should they therefore attack their protectors on an issue to which men of virtue are particularly sensitive? Or would it not be more fitting if they abstained from religious disputes with the dominant creed?

These considerations governed my actions and motivated my decision to stay away from religious controversies unless exceptional circumstances were to force me to change my mind. To the private challenges of some men whom I respect highly I was bold enough to react with silence, while for the little minds that think they can bait me publicly because of my religion, I have nothing but contempt. But when a Lavater solemnly calls upon me, I have no choice but to express my convictions in public, lest my silence be misconstrued as contemptuous disregard or acquiescence.

I have read your translation of Bonnet's essay with close attention. After everything I have already said, I hope there can no longer be any doubt as to whether I found his arguments convincing. In addition, however, I must confess that I do not consider his reasoning even adequate as a defense of the Christian religion, as you seem to do. [. . .]

I have given you the reasons for which I fervently wish to have nothing to do with religious disputes. But I have also intimated to you that I could easily present strong arguments in refutation of M. Bonnet's thesis. If you insist, I shall have to overcome my reservations and publish my arguments against M. Bonnet's apologia in the form of a "Counterinquiry." I hope you will spare me this disagreeable task and permit me to return to the peaceful stance which is so much more natural to me. I am sure you will respect my preference if you put yourself in my place and look at the situation from my point of view, not yours. I should not like to be tempted to go beyond the limits that I have set for myself after mature consideration.

I am, with sincerest respect,

your obedient servant,
M. M.

Berlin, December 12, 1769.

LEOPOLD ZUNZ

Scholarship and Emancipation

Leopold Zunz (1794–1886) was born in Detmold, Germany, eight years after Mendelssohn's death. He was educated at the Jewish school at Wolfenbüttel and at the Berlin university, and was one of the founders of *Wissenschaft des Judentums* (Science of Judaism). This movement applied the spirit and the methods of modern, objective, critical research to Jewish history and literature. It was Zunz's belief that scholarship based on these principles would demonstrate Judaism's deeply ingrained tendency to be an integral part of the world's literary history and to collaborate with the West in its intellectual and human growth. Furthermore, he thought that the modernization of Jewish studies would counteract anti-Jewish biases and promote civic equality. Zunz's own work exemplified the novel approach of *Wissenschaft*. His main field of research was medieval sacred poetry and the various Hebrew liturgies. His first major work was *Die gottesdienstlichen Vorträge der Juden* (The Liturgical Addresses of the Jews) issued in 1832. The selection that follows is from the introduction to this basic presentation of the historical development of midrashic literature. Zunz's hope that a German university would establish a chair for Judaic studies did not materialize. In the revolutionary war of 1848, and later, he was a resolute advocate of democracy and liberalism and demanded separation between church and state.

Permit me to preface the necessary information about the contents and the meaning of the book which is herewith presented to my readers with a few remarks about Jewish affairs in general and the problems to whose solution I should like to contribute in particular. In doing so I appeal the judgments of authorities which recognize prejudice and abuses to places where the verdict pronounced is truth and justice. For when all around us freedom, scholarship, and civilization are fighting for and gaining new ground, the Jews too are entitled to make claim to serious interest and untrammeled justice. Or shall the arbitrariness of club-law and of medieval madness retain a foothold only in the laws applying to Jews, at a time when clericalism and Inquisition, despotism and slavery, torture and censorship are on their way out?

It is high time that the Jews of Europe, particularly those of Germany, be granted right and liberty rather than rights and liberties—not some paltry, humiliating privileges, but complete and uplifting civil rights. We have no desire for stingily apportioned rights which are balanced by an equal number of wrongs; we derive no pleasure from concessions born of pity; we are revolted by privileges obtained in an underhanded manner. Any man should blu sh with shame whom a patent of nobility from the powers-that-be raises above his *brothers in faith*, while the law, with stigmatizing exclusion, assigns to him a place below the lowest of his *brothers in fatherland*. Only in lawful, mutual recognition can we find satisfaction, only irrevocable equality can bring our suffering to an end. However, I see no love or justice in a freedom which removes the shackles from the hand only to apply them to the tongue, in a tolerance which takes pleasure in our decline rather than our progress, in a citizenship which offers protection without honor, burdens without prospects. Such noxious elements can only produce serious sickness in the body politic, harming the individual as well as the community. [. . .]

The neglect of Jewish scholarship goes hand in hand with civil discrimination against the Jews. Through a higher intellectual level and a more thorough knowledge of their own affairs the Jews could have achieved a greater degree of recognition and thus more justice. Furthermore, much bad legislation, many a prejudice against Jewish antiquity, much condemnation of new endeavors are a direct consequence of the state of neglect in which Jewish literature and Jewish scholarship have been for about seventy years, particularly in Germany. And even though writings about the Talmud and against the Jews mushroomed overnight and several dozen Solons offered themselves to us as reformers, there was no book of any consequence which the statesmen could have consulted, no professor lectured about Judaism and Jewish literature, no German learned society offered prizes in this field, no philanthropist went traveling for this purpose. Legislators and scholars, not to mention the rabble among writers, had to follow in the footsteps of the 17th-century authorities, Eisenmenger,[5] Schudt,[6] Buxtorf,[7] and others like beggars, or had to borrow from the dubious wisdom of modern informants. Indeed, most people frankly admitted their ignorance of this area or betrayed it with their very first words. The (supposed) knowledge of Judaism has not progressed beyond the point where Eisenmenger left off 135 years ago, and philological studies have made almost no progress in 200 years. This explains the fact that even estimable writers assume an entirely different character—one is tempted to call it spectre-like—when the subject of the Jews comes around: all quotations from the sources are copied from the subsidized works of the 16th and 17th centuries; statements that were successfully refuted long ago are served up like durable old chestnuts; and given the lack of any scholarly activity, or any up-to-date apparatus, the oracle of the wretches is consulted. Out of ignorance or malice, some people have blended an imaginary Judaism and their own Christianity into a sort of system of conversion or concluded that regressive laws were necessary. Although excellent men have already spoken out in favor of Jewish studies and worked for them, on the whole there has been little improvement in this regard. [. . .]

In the meantime, however, the Jews have not been completely idle. Since the days of Mendelssohn they have worked and written in behalf of civil rights, culture and reform, as well as their trampled-upon ancient heritage. A new era has revealed its strength in life and scholarship, in education and faith, in ideas, needs, and hopes; good seeds have been sown, excellent forces have been developed. But what is still needed is a protective institution which can serve as a support for progress and scholarship and as a religious center for the community. The physical needs and public safety of Jewish communities are being met by hospitals and orphanages, poorhouses and burial grounds. However, religion and scholarship, civil liberty, and intellectual progress require schools, seminaries, and synagogues; they must enlist the efforts of capable community leaders, competent teachers, well-trained rabbis. If emancipation and scholarship are not to be mere words, not some tawdry bit of fancy goods for sale, but the fountainhead of morality which we have found again after a long period of wandering in the wilderness, then they must fecundate institutions—high-ranking educational institutions, religious instruction for everyone, dignified religious services, suitable sermons. Such institutions are indispensable for the needs of the congregational totality of the Jews; but to establish them we need religious zeal and scholarly activity, enthusiastic participation in the entire project, benevolent recognition from the outside.

Free, instructive words are something not to be denied. Mankind has acquired all its possessions through oral instruction, through an education which lasts a lifetime. In Israel, too, the words of teaching have passed from mouth to mouth in all ages, and any future flourishing of Jewish institutions may derive only from the words that diffuse knowledge and understanding. [. . .]

Apart from all present-day efforts in this field and any personal connection I may have with them, the institution of the liturgical addresses of the Jews seemed to me to deserve and require a strictly historical investigation. The substance of my research on the origin, development, and fortunes of this institution, from the time of Ezra[8] to the present, is now presented in this book. [. . .] I hope that in addition to their main purpose, the recognition of the right and the scholarship of the Jews, my investigations will stimulate interest in related studies and win for the nobler endeavors of our time the favor of the mighty, the benevolence of the prudent, the zeal of the pious. Such a reward will be sweeter to me than any literary acclamation.

NAHMAN KROCHMAL

The Cycles of Jewish History

Nahman Krochmal (1785–1840) was born in Brody, Galicia, Austria, and early became an exponent of the *Wissenschaft des Judentums* (Science of Judaism) trend and of the enlightenment (Haskalah). Kant, Schelling, and Hegel were his guides in philosophy and history. His scholarly aim was interpretation of Jewish history and literature by means of the historico-critical method. His thoughts in the areas of philosophy, history, and literature are presented in his *Moreh Nevukhe ha-Zeman* (Guide of the Perplexed of the Time) published by Leopold Zunz in 1851. In this work idealistic philosophy merges with the Judaic tradition. Krochmal speaks of the Absolute Spirit, but identifies it with the God of Israel. He considers philosophy to be the higher means of comprehending the truth of faith, but combines this tenet with the views of Maimonides that the Torah favors occupation with philosophy. Jewish history follows the pattern of history in general: growth, mature achievement, decline, and extinction. Yet, the history of Israel differs from that of other nations inasmuch as, upon completing a cycle, Israel, representing the Absolute Spirit, is permitted to enter into a new cycle. The selection that follows expresses this view in Krochmal's own words (from the *Guide*). As an enlightened traditionalist and tradition-minded modernist, Krochmal was greatly respected in his day.

> For I the Lord change not;
> And ye, O sons of Jacob, are
> not consumed.
> Malachi 3:6

According to the workings of the natural order there are three periods through which each primordial nation passes from the time it comes into being until it passes from the scene and perishes:

1. The period of first growth, during which the spirit is born. [. . .] This spirit transforms the material parts of the nation into organic units, integrated through all manner of ordered relationships, and it holds them together as a single entity, ready to receive every excellence and perfection. This period is called: *the stage of the nation's germination and growth.*

2. Thereafter, the spirit becomes fully actualized, all those beneficial institutions and spiritual attributes to which we have alluded reach their apogee, and after a longer or shorter lapse of time, the nation moves forward in all of them, gaining fame and glory. This period will be called: *the stage of power and achievement.*

3. However, in the case of every living thing, the cause of its withering and death is already contained within it. Thus, even during the course of the second stage, the seeds of corruption and degeneration begin to appear in the nation. Thereafter, they sprout, proliferate, and grow, dissolving all bonds and corrupting every beneficial usage, until gradually the nation's glory dwindles away, the nation declines and diminishes to the point of nonexistence. We shall call this period: *the stage of decomposition and extinction.*

This is the pattern for all the nations which possess a limited manifestation of spirit, one of which is therefore finite and destined for extinction. But in the case of our nation, although we too have succumbed to the above-mentioned natural course of events with regard to material and tangible externals, the fact is, in the words of the rabbis: "They were exiled to Babylon, exiled to Elam, and the Divine Presence was with them."⁹ That is to say, the universal spirit which is within us protects us and excludes us from the judgment that falls upon all mortals. And all this follows easily from what has been said above.

Even so, we have seen fit to mention the periods we have traversed since the nation's beginnings until this day in order to show clearly how the cycle of the three stages that we have mentioned repeats itself in our history, and how, when break-down, decomposition, and decay have become complete, a new and reviving spirit always takes shape within us; though we fall, we arise invigorated—the Lord, our God, has not forsaken us.

HEINRICH GRAETZ

The Diaspora: Suffering and Spirit

Heinrich Graetz (1817–1891) wrote the first monumental *History of the Jews*, published in eleven volumes from 1853 to 1876. Here the drama of the Jewish people is unfolded in its moments of glory and instants of defeat and degradation, from its biblical origins up to 1848. The elements of destruction are powerful indeed, but the reign of the spirit is stronger still. Israel appears on the scene of world history as a protest against idolatry and deification of nature. The Creator-God that it proclaims is free and good, and expects man to initiate the messianic kingdom for Israel and mankind. The *History* became a source of inspiration and of much needed information.

Graetz studied Talmud and rabbinics and introduced himself to general literature. His doctoral dissertation was *Gnosticismus und Judentum* (Gnosticism and Judaism), in 1846. For several years he was a close friend of Samson Raphael Hirsch, but the friendship did not endure. In 1853, he was appointed to the faculty of the newly established Jewish Theological Seminary at Breslau; he remained there to the end of his life. Graetz also wrote on biblical subjects. In the final period of his life, he had to defend himself—and Judaism—against anti-Semitic attacks.

Before starting to write his magnum opus, Graetz sketched out his views on the structure and concept of Jewish history. His "Construction of Jewish History" appeared in 1846. The piece that follows is taken from that essay.

This is the eighteen-hundred-year era of the diaspora,[10] of unprecedented suffering, of uninterrupted martyrdom without parallel in world history. But it is also a period of spiritual alertness, of restless mental activity, of indefatigable inquiry. In order to sketch a clear and appropriate picture of this period, one would have to draw a two-sided image. One aspect would show humbled Judah with the wanderer's staff in his hand, the pilgrim's bundle on his back, his features grave, his glance turned heavenward; he is surrounded by the walls of a dungeon, the implements of martyrdom, and the red-hot branding iron. The other aspect is of the same figure, bearing the earnestness of the thinker upon his luminous brow, the mien of a scholar in the radiant features of his face; he is in a study filled with a huge library in all the languages of mankind and dealing with all branches of divine and human knowledge. The external history of this era is a history of suffering to a degree and over a length of time such as no other people has experienced. Its inner history is a comprehensive *Literaturgeschichte*, a literary history of religious knowledge, which yet remains open to all the currents of science, absorbing and assimilating them; once again, a history unique to this one people. *Inquiring* and *wandering, thinking* and *enduring, studying* and *suffering*—these fill the long stretch of this era. Three times during this period world history changed its garb. Decrepit Rome languished and sank into the grave. Out of its decay the chrysalis of the European and Asiatic peoples took shape; these peoples in turn developed into the glistening, butterfly-like figures of Christian and Islamic knighthood; and, finally, from their incinerated castles arose the phoenix of civilized international relations.

World history was transformed three times, but the Jews remained the same; at most they merely altered their external appearance. Likewise the spiritual content of world history was transformed three times. From a developed but hollow state of civilization mankind submerged into barbarism and dismal ignorance, only to raise itself again from its ignorance into the bright spheres of a higher civilization. The spiritual content of Judaism remained the same; it only steeped itself in the substance and form of new ideas. While the Judaism of this era includes the most celebrated *martyrs*, compared to whom the persecuted sufferers of other nations and religions may almost be considered fortunate, it also produced towering thinkers who did not remain merely the pride of *Judaism* alone. There is likely no science, no art, no direction of the spirit in which Jews have not shared, in which they have not demonstrated equivalent ability. *Thinking* became as characteristic a feature of the Jews as did *suffering*.

On account of the largely forced, rarely voluntary, migrations of the Jews, the Jewish history of this era encompasses the entire inhabited earth: it stretches into the snowy regions of the north and into the blazing sun of the south; it traverses all oceans and establishes itself in the most remote corners of the world. As soon as a new part of the world is invaded by a new people, scattered Jews immediately appear, defying every climate and every hardship. If a new area of the world is discovered, Jewish communities are soon formed and grouped together here and there following an inner drive for crystallization which operates without worldly aid or external compulsion. Dispersed to all regions of the earth, the Jews form a huge circle that expands out of sight. Its periphery coincides with the ends of the inhabited world; at its center is the Temple, still sacred even in ruins. These migrations brought the Jewish people new experiences; homeless, they exercised and sharpened their gaze. Thus even the plenitude of their suffering contributed to broadening the horizons of Jewish thinkers. The Jewish history of this era witnessed, was affected by, and to an extent participated in all the overwhelming events of world history from the time when the full terror of the barbarians exploded upon the overrefined Roman Empire until the spark of culture was struck anew from the hard anvil of barbarism. Every storm upon the sea of world history also had an effect on Judaism, shaking it to its foundations without shattering it. The Jewish history of eighteen centuries presents a microcosm of world history even as the Jewish people has become a universal people; being nowhere at home, it is at home everywhere.

What prevented this ever-wandering people, these truly eternal Jews, from degenerating into brutish vagrants or a vagabond horde of gypsies? The answer is self-evident. During its desolate history of eighteen hundred years the Jewish people carried with it the Ark of the Covenant which placed an ideal striving in its heart and even transfigured the badge of shame on its garment with an apostolic radiance. The proscribed, outlawed Jew, pursued over the entire earth, felt an exalted, noble pride in bearing, and in suffering for, a doctrine which reflected eternity and by which the nations would eventually be educated to the knowledge of God and to morality, a doctrine from which the salvation and redemption of the world would go forth. The lofty consciousness of his glorious apostolic task kept the sufferer erect, even transformed his sufferings into an aspect of his 'exalted mission. Such a people for which the present meant nothing while the future meant everything, which seemed to exist by virtue of its hope, is for that very reason as eternal as hope itself. The Law and the messianic hope were two protecting and consoling angels at the side of the humbled Jews, saving them from despair, from stupefaction, and loss of identity. The Law for the present, the messianic hope for the future, both mediated by scholarship and the effusions of poetic art—these poured balm on the grieved hearts of the unfortunate people. Since for this subjugated nation the world at large was reduced to a gloomy, filthy dungeon in which it was unable to satisfy its urge to act, the more talented among its members retreated to the inner world of ideas which expanded proportionately as the restraints of the outside world were drawn more narrowly around its mangled body. Thus appeared a doubtless rare phenomenon: the persecuted proved more than a match for his oppressor, the tormented almost pitied his tormentor, the prisoner felt freer than his jailer.

Jewish literature reflects this serious intellectual life and was bound to become the richer as it not only served the needs of the highly talented, but acted as a salve for the entire suffering people. As the Jewish people made itself at home all over the inhabitable earth, Jewish literature became truly a world literature. It makes up the kernel of Jewish history which the history of suffering has surrounded with a bitter husk. The entire people has deposited its treasure of ideas and its inner being in this immense literature. The teachings of Judaism are contained in it, refined, glorified, visible to the weakest eye. Only someone accustomed to reducing a lofty, imposing wonder of the world to the category of an everyday phenomenon will regard it as of little account. The consecutive data and events of Jewish history must be connected with the thread of this literature. It provides the pragmatic continuity and therefore must not be treated incidentally, as a mere appendix to the main history. The appearance of a new significant book is not just an interesting detail, but within its circle becomes a *deed* which has consequential ramifications. Jewish literature was born in pain and spasms of death; it is as manifold as the countries of its origin, variegated as the dress of the nations among whom it blossomed, rich and polymorphic as the recollection of its millennial experiences; it bears the unmistakable traces of a *single* progenitor, of Judaism. A single trait is imprinted upon all its configurations, every surface and edge reflecting the ideal whose rays they capture. Jewish literature thus constitutes the basic possession of this era which with regard to its active aspect can therefore justly be termed the *theoretical-religious* era. It stands in contrast to the era after the first exile, which had a *political-religious* character, and to the pre-exilic era, which was predominantly *political*. [. . .]

MOSES HESS

Political Rebirth

Moses Hess (1812–1875), unacknowledged "father of modern socialism" and an early pioneer of the Zionist idea, was born in Bonn, Germany, and lived for many years in Cologne and Paris. In 1841 he published *Die europäische Triarchie* (The European Triarchy), advocating a United States of Europe composed of England, France, and Germany, as a means of preventing Russia from Russianizing a divided Europe. Political reform, however, should go hand in hand with social reform. Hess developed a social theory favoring the working class, befriended young Karl Marx and Friedrich Engels (an association that did not last), and founded a socialist journal. The failure of the revolutions of 1848 did not diminish his faith in the ultimate emergence of a classless society. But, according to Hess, Marx's *Communist Manifesto* (1848) was an annulment of "true socialism," the socialism of free, ethical labor leading to human brotherhood.

Hess, who originally advocated the assimilation of the Jews, later realized the futility of such an act; Europeans always regarded the Jews as an anomaly. What was needed was an end to Jewish homelessness and the establishment of an independent society. "Here I am again after twenty years of estrangement in the midst of my people." With these words Hess started his *Rome and Jerusalem*, published in 1862—the document of his newly won faith in the future of Judaism. "My nationality [is] inseparable from the heritage of my fathers, from the Holy Land and the eternal city, the birthplace of the belief in the divine unity of life and in the future brotherhood of all men."

The work—in some of its aspects visionary and prophetic—betrays the influence of Heinrich Graetz's *History of the Jews*. Its tenets were debated by the Western European intellectuals of the period; socialists observed a conspiracy of silence. Soon the book was forgotten; it was rediscovered by Zionists and at the First Zionist Congress at Basel in 1897 it was hailed as herald of socialist Zionism. The selection that follows is from *Rome and Jerusalem.*

What we have to do at present for the regeneration of the Jewish nation is, first, to keep alive the hope of the political rebirth of our people, and next, to reawaken that hope where it slumbers. When political conditions in the Orient shape themselves so as to permit the organization of a beginning of the restoration of a Jewish state, this beginning will express itself in the founding of Jewish colonies in the land of their ancestors, to which enterprise France will undoubtedly lend a hand. You know how substantial was the share of the Jews in the subscriptions to the fund raised for the benefit of the Syrian war victims. It was Crémieux[11] who took the initiative in the matter, the same Crémieux who twenty years ago traveled with Sir Moses Montefiore to Syria in order to seek protection for the Jews against the persecutions of the Christians.[12] In the *Journal des Debats*, which very seldom accepts poems for publication, there appeared, at the time of the Syrian expedition, a poem by Léon Halévi, who at the time, perhaps, thought as little of the rebirth of Israel as Crémieux, yet his beautiful stanzas could not have been produced otherwise than in a spirit of foreseeing this regeneration. When the poet of the *Schwalben* mournfully complains:

> Where tarries the hero? Where tarries the wise?
> Who will, O my people, revive you anew;
> Who will save you, and give you again
> A place in the sun?

The French poet answers his query with enthusiastic confidence:

> Ye shall be reborn, ye fearsome cities!
> A breath of security will always hover

O'er your banks where our colors have fluttered!
Come again a call supreme!
Au revoir is not *adieu*—
France is all to those she loves,
The future belongs to God.

Alexander Weill sang about the same time:

There is a people stiff of neck,
Dispersed from the Euphrates to the Rhine,
Its whole life centered in a Book—
Ofttimes bent, yet ever straightened;
Braving hatred and contempt,
It only dies to live again
In nobler form.

France, beloved friend, is the savior who will restore our people to its place in universal history.

Allow me to recall to your mind an old legend which you have probably heard in your younger days. It runs as follows:

"A knight who went to the Holy Land to assist in the liberation of Jerusalem, left behind him a very dear friend. While the knight fought valiantly on the field of battle, his friend spent his time, as heretofore, in the study of the Talmud, for his friend was none other than a pious rabbi.

"Months afterward, when the knight returned home, he appeared suddenly at midnight, in the study room of the rabbi, whom he found, as usual, absorbed in his Talmud. 'God's greetings to you, dear old friend,' he said. 'I have returned from the Holy Land and bring you from there a pledge of our friendship. What I gained by my sword, you are striving to obtain with your spirit. Our ways lead to the same goal.' While thus speaking, the knight handed the rabbi a rose of Jericho.

"The rabbi took the rose and moistened it with his tears, and immediately the withered rose began to bloom again in its full glory and splendor. And the rabbi said to the knight: 'Do not wonder, my friend, that the withered rose bloomed again in my hands. The rose possesses the same characteristics as our people: it comes to life again at the touch of the warm breath of love, in spite of its having been torn from its own soil and left to wither in foreign lands. So will Israel bloom again in youthful splendor; and the spark, at present smoldering under the ashes, will burst once more into a bright flame.' "

The routes of the rabbi and the knight, dear friend, are meeting today. As the rabbi in the story symbolizes our people, so does the knight of the legend signify the French people which in our days, as in the Middle Ages, sent its brave soldiers to Syria and "prepared in the desert the way of the Lord" [Isaiah 40:3].

Have you never read the words of the prophet Isaiah: "Comfort yet, comfort ye, my people, saith your God. Speak ye comfortably to the heart of Jerusalem, and cry unto her, that the appointed time has come, that her iniquity is pardoned; for she hath received at the Lord's hand double for all her sins. The voice of one that crieth in the wilderness, prepare ye the way of the Lord, make straight in the desert a highway for our God. Every valley shall be exalted, and every mountain and hill shall be made low, and the crooked shall be made a straight place, and the rough places a plain. And the glory of the Lord shall be revealed, and all flesh shall see it together: for the mouth of the Lord hath spoken it" [Isaiah 40:1–5].

Do you not believe that in these words, with which the second Isaiah opened his prophecies, as well as in the words with which the prophet Obadiah closed his prophecy,[13] the conditions of our own time are graphically pictured? Was not help given to Zion in order to defend and establish the wild mountaineers there? Are not things being prepared there and roads leveled, and is not the road of civilization being built in the desert in the form of the Suez Canal works and the railroad which will connect Asia and Europe? They are not thinking at present of the restoration of our people. But you know the proverb, "Man proposes and God disposes." Just as in the West they once searched for a road to India, and incidentally discovered a new world, so will our lost fatherland be rediscovered on the road to India and China that is now being built in the Orient. Do you still doubt that France will help the Jews to found colonies which may extend from Suez to Jerusalem, and from the banks of the Jordan to the Coast of the Mediterranean? Then pray read the work which appeared shortly after the massacres in Syria, by the famous publisher, Dentu, under the title *The New Oriental Problem*. The author hardly wrote it at the request of the French government, but acted in accordance with the spirit of the French nation when he urged our brethren, not on religious grounds, but from purely political and humanitarian motives, to restore their ancient State.

I may, therefore, recommend this work, written, not by a Jew, but by a French patriot, to the attention of our modern Jews, who plume themselves on borrowed French humanitarianism. I will quote here [. . . from . . .] this work, *The New Eastern Question*, by Ernest Laharanne.[14]

"In the discussion of these new Eastern complications, we reserved a special place for Palestine, in order to bring to the attention of the world the important question, whether ancient Judea can once more acquire its former place under the sun. [. . .]"

ABRAHAM GEIGER

Revelation

One of the fathers of religious reform in Central Europe, Abraham Geiger (1810–1874) was born in Frankfurt am Main, Germany, received a traditional education, and was trained in Greek and Semitic languages. He served as a rabbi in various cities, and finally in Berlin. He was instrumental in convening synods of liberal rabbis, in initiating the (conservative) Jewish Theological Seminary in Breslau, and in establishing the liberal *Hochschule für die Wissenschaft des Judentums* (Academy for Jewish Research) in Berlin. As a scholar he contributed to research in Bible and Jewish history; he intended his religious reforms to be based on solid scholarship. His main work was *Urschrift und Übersetzungen der Bibel* (The Original Text and Translations of the Bible), 1857, and the better known *Allgemeine Einleitung in die Wissenschaft des Judenthums* (General Introduction to the Science of Judaism) based on lectures in the Academy. He felt the need to reform Judaism in the direction of prophetic ethics, humanism, and universalism, and to consider ideas such as Return to Zion and Resurrection as outmoded. The following piece is taken from *Das Judenthum und seine Geschichte* (Judaism and Its History), 1864.

There are facts of such an overwhelming power that even the most stubborn opinion must yield to them. Such a fact is the origin of Judaism in the midst of rude surroundings, like a vigorous growth out of a barren soil. We have essayed to draw, in a few scanty outlines, a comparison between the convictions, presentiments and assertions that prevailed in antiquity in general, and those presented by Judeism. Even that incomplete sketch must convince the unprejudiced mind that we behold an original energy which has preserved its significance for all times and has proven to be a creative force. Let us for a few more moments, dwell upon the principal representatives, the organs of that religious idea, upon the prophets. In them we perceive characters of quiet greatness, of simple sublimity; of fervor with moderation; of boldness with humble submission—traits that are imposing and make us feel the very breath of a higher spirit. Our ancient teachers observe: "No two prophets deliver the prophetic message in the same strain and expression. Each one of them is complete within himself, each has a peculiar, distinct character of his own, and yet all have the same general characteristics and are animated by one great idea. Isaiah, bold, noble, severely serious, and yet lovingly indulging in the most joyful and glorious hopes, full of the most cheerful confidence; hence hurrying from gloomy predictions and threats of severe chastisement over to a description of a most brilliant future. Jeremiah, tender-hearted, looking sad into the tangled and desperate condition of his time; hence plaintive and reproving his contemporaries with severity, yet never despairing, yet full of cheerful conviction that the idea he proclaims must prevail, if not in his time, certainly in the future. Ezekiel, as if overwhelmed by the idea that animates him, as if dazzled by the light surrounding him, indulges in bold figures in the effort to represent the glory of his visions, yet clearly and fully conscious whenever moral precepts are to be distinctly emphasized to his people; and withal, endowed with that clear, comprehensive vision which penetrates the very heart of man and calls attention to his faults and virtues.[15] Our ancient teachers finely describe that difference: "Isaiah appears as a man of the palace, familiar with the manners and the pomp of a court, with the divine appointments, speaks only in general terms of its brilliancy; standing on an eminence, he draws the sublime in his own light. Ezekiel appears as a villager who is suddenly brought into brilliant city life, and in his excitement does not know where to stop in his picturing of both the detail and the whole of his impressions. [46] They differ, but all are devoted to one great idea, all are sustained by the same higher spirit.

They love their country with intense fervor; their speeches and admonitions are addressed to the people at widely different times, to uplift them, to strengthen and encourage them, to support their country and the national life. They love their country, take profound pleasure in describing it as a land flowing with milk and honey, a land in which a man "may eat bread without stint," "whose stones are iron, out of whose hills thou mayest dig brass" [Deuteronomy 8:9]; joyfully they describe it as a land that has been favored by God with the most various blessings, but the most essential matter to them always remains: "For from Zion goeth forth the Law, and the word of God from Jerusalem" [Isaiah 2:3]. "Mountains around about Jerusalem, but God round about His people [Psalm 125:2]."

And with naïvete and affection, the condition of that land in comparison with Egypt is described: "The land whither thou goest in to possess it is not like the land of Egypt from whence you came out; there ye sowed seed and watered it with your own labor, as a garden of herbs: but the land whither ye go to possess it, is a land of hills and valleys, and drinketh water of the rain of heaven: a land which God forever careth for: His eyes are always upon it, from the beginning of the year even unto the end of the year."

Egypt, it is true, is a garden of God in the eyes of the Israelites, a land which, by the annual overflowing of the Nile and by canals, carries water everywhere; which may be cultivated with the sure hope of success; which exhibits, with but rare exceptions, its fertility from year to year and offers its rich treasures in abundance; but nevertheless, Palestine is prized more highly: a land of valleys and mountains, needing rains, depending upon nature's moods, so that the eye of God has to be upon it from the beginning of the year to its end [Deuteronomy 11:12]: and therein consists the glory and the excellence of the country.

They glorify that land as an especially favored and gifted one; and even when it has vanished from them, when it has been taken from them, their strength is not broken, they are not bound to its soil; their love for their earthly country rests upon their love for a higher one from which a ray descends upon the former. The poet, after bewailing the destruction of the city, the banishment of its inhabitants, after having indulged in lamentations, exclaims: "Thou, O God, remainest forever; Thy throne, from generation to generation" [Lamentations 5:19]—a thought which runs through thousands of years, even after the national life has disappeared. Can it be wondered that such a cheerful confidence exerted a powerful influence also on later generations? You hear the same words centuries thereafter. The state was destroyed a second time, every hope blasted, the last flickering light, kindled by Ben Koziba,[17] was put out, and Roman oppression lay heavy upon the people. Rabbi Akiba with some friends visited Jerusalem, and they saw a jackal running out from where formerly the Holy of Holies had been standing. Akiba's companions wept and rent their clothes; Akiba remained silent, almost cheerful. His friends asked, "Since when have you become so indifferent to the misfortunes of our people? Do you not see the second fulfillment of the words: 'Yea, for this do we weep, because of the mountain of Zion, which is desolate, jackals walk about upon it?' " [*Ibid.*, 5:18]. "Well, my friends," replied Akiba, "indeed those words have again been verified; but the other will also come true: 'Thou O God, remainest forever, Thy throne from generation to generation.' I live in unshaken, firm confidence."[18]

That the prophets did not look for security of their persons when the interests of the cause demanded their devotion; that they labored with entire unselfishness, regardless of appreciation or glory or praise, is attested by every word uttered by them. It appears as though the words spoken by one of them resounds through all their sermons:

"I gave my back to the smiters and my cheeks to them that plucked off the hair, I hid not my face from the shame and spitting, for God the Lord will help me; therefore shall I not be confounded, therefore have I set my face like a flint, I know I shall not be ashamed" [Isaiah 50:6–7].

And though from different sides they heard cries such as these: "Prophesy to us of wine and strong drink" [Micah: 2:11], "Foolish is the prophet, the man of the spirit raveth" [Hosea 9:7], they did not yield, they did not desecrate their lips, they did not keep silent: "The Lord God hath spoken, who can out prophesy?" [Amos 3:8]. A higher force impelled them, would not suffer them to keep silent, to grow weary of preaching; it was a moral and spiritual enthusiasm that placed them on an eminence to which we, in later days, must ever look up.

Thus Judaism is a grand phenomenon in history; and thus its representatives and organs are men of such dignity and spiritual greatness that we must pay them the tribute of our admiration. They entered the lists without being encouraged, without having patterns before them; on the contrary, in a discouraging environment, encircled by nations addicted to idolatry, amidst priests and proclaimers of other nations who did homage to sensuality which degraded human nature. Whence, then, came that force which all at once enters the scene as something original? We arrive here at the consideration of the very depth and bottom of the human soul, beyond which it can not go, of an energy creating of its own apprehension, without being impelled thereto by any external impulse.

We discriminate, in general, a two-fold intellectual operating ability in man, a two-fold distinguishing endowment—we discriminate *talent* and *genius*. They touch upon each other in many points, so that a distinct line of demarcation can not be drawn between them; yet they preserve each its own particular peculiarity; they are not only separate, but they differ in their whole nature, in their foundation. Talent is an endowment with the ability of easily and quickly receiving, digesting, and reproducing with taste and skill; but talent leans upon something that has been achieved, upon results that are present before it, upon treasures already acquired—it creates nothing new. Genius works quite differently. It is independent, it creates, it discovers truths heretofore hidden, it discloses laws heretofore unknown; it is as though the forces that work in the depth of nature bared themselves to it in greater clearness according to their connection and legitimate co-operation; as though they presented themselves to it to be grasped, as though the mental and spiritual movements in the individual as well as in mankind as a whole, unveiled themselves before it, that it may behold the deepest foundation of the soul and may be able to dissect the motives and impulses hidden away there. Talent may be practiced, it may even be acquired by laborious application; genius is a free gift, a gift of grace, a mark of consecration stamped upon man, that can never be acquired, if it be not in the man. Talent, therefore, can not overcome impediments and obstacles if they present themselves with overwhelming force, it can not thrive under unfavorable circumstances. Genius, on the other hand, advances its conquering force against the most untoward conditions, it opens a way; it must expand its force, for it is a living impulse, a power that is stronger than its possessor, a touch of the energy dispersed into nature but condensed in him, linking him with the spirit of all spirits who manifests Himself to him by higher illumination. Talent propagates the knowledge which has been stored up, perfects it also now and then, and makes it the common property of all. Genius enriches humanity with new truths and perceptions, it gives the impulse to all great things that have come and are still to come to pass in this world.

When Columbus discovered the New World, he had not been specially prepared for it, nor fitted thereto by superior geographical knowledge, by greater experience gained on his voyages; nor could those justify any conclusion that India was to the west of Spain. It was the light of genius that caused him to see the surface of the earth, he was favored with a look into the nature of the globe and to feel that the land must be across the ocean which had been thought to be boundless; and thus what had been as knowledge, but imperfect, in him, turned into living conviction whose truth he made every effort to prove. Copernicus was probably not the greatest astronomer of his time; others may have made more correct calculations and may have been far superior to him in the science, but it was as if the whole working of the natural forces of attraction and repulsion and the entire movement of the world had been revealed to his vision; as though the veil which dark tradition had thickened, had been drawn aside from before him; as though he had looked with bold eye into the mechanism of the universe and held fast to what he had seen as a rapidly grasped truth which he afterwards with deep insight tried to substantiate, in which he did not fully succeed, because it had to be more clearly explained and more firmly established than he was able to do then. Newton is said to have been induced to establish the law of gravitation by the falling of an apple observed by him while sitting near an apple tree. Many people before him had seen apples falling, but not with the eye of genius; for that beholds in the single phenomenon the great, comprehensive law which causes that phenomenon; it looks through that external manifestation into the invisible working from which everything proceeds.

Such instances could be added to by others from every field. The historian who deserves the name as such, is not made by the profundity and care in research, the full knowledge of all incidents; he is perhaps often compelled to refuse a mass of burdensome material in order not to be perplexed and crushed by a crowd of details. But this affords him his favored position, that his vision is sharper and sees into the character of the time, that the entire working of the wheels of the ideas moving in the depths of the period, is laid bare before him. It is as if the period as a whole with its deepest foundations uncovered, stood before his mental vision, as if he had actually listened to the most secret intentions of its chief actors. In that way, all that was before known is put into its proper place, because the connection between the events and the actors has only become perfectly clear. You may perhaps call that good sense, acumen, a happy faculty of combination. When the acute thinker does not run into error, when his combination knows how to connect the proper parts, then it is the work of genius. And what is it that enables the poet to look so deep into the soul that he recognizes the temperament, the desires, the passions so clearly, as though the chambers of the heart were opened for him? What enables him to grasp and present all complications and combinations in the most various relations and conditions, however much they may be entangled and hidden to ordinary vision, and to fathom and picture a character in its unity? Is it the great experience he has had? Is it that, perchance, he himself has passed through all that? Certainly not! It is the vision that more surely and sharply receives the picture of the whole life of the human soul from the individual phenomenon and knows how to represent it. In fact, it is only genius that enables an individual to interfere with might in the movements of the mind and spirit and to give him a forward impulse for centuries to come—and as it is in individuals, so it is in whole nations as well.

The Greeks boasted of being autochthons, of having risen and sprung from their own soil. We shall not examine whether that claim is justified; but another claim, which is the real meaning of it, will surely be admitted; namely, the autochthonic character of the mind, the aboriginal nature of their national talent. The Greeks had neither pattern nor teacher in art or science, they were teacher and master to themselves, they speedily attained such perfection in art as makes them instructors of mankind almost for all time. It is as though a higher living sense for the beautiful, the harmonious, the symmetrical, and the pleasing had been innate in that nation—we observe a national genius through the possession of which masters in every art and science made their appearance. Therefore, even later centuries willingly listened to the words of that nation, hastened thither, where they could see the works of the plastic art, where they could enjoy, as it were, a rejuvenating bath in the spiritual fountain that parts thence and runs through the centuries. Is not the Jewish people, likewise, endowed with such a genius, a religious genius? Is it not, likewise, an aboriginal power that illuminated its eyes so that they could see deeper into the higher life of the spirit, could feel more deeply and recognize more vividly the close relation between the spirit of man and the supreme spirit, that they could more distinctly and clearly behold the real nature of the moral in man, and then present to the world the result of that inborn knowledge. If this be so, we may speak of a close touch of the individual spirit with the supreme spirit, or the light thrown into individual spirits by the power that fills everything, so that they could break through their finite barrier; it is—let us not hesitate to speak the word—it is *revelation*, and that too, as manifested in the whole nation.

The Greeks were not all artists; each one of them was not a Phidias or a Praxiteles, but yet the Greek nation alone was capable of producing such great masters. The same was the case within Israel. Surely not all its men were prophets, and the exclamation, "Would that all the people were prophets" was but a pious wish;

the other: "I shall pour out My spirit upon all flesh [Joel 3:1], is a promise, it had not become the reality. Nevertheless, Israel is the people of revelation within which the favored representatives appeared; it is as if the sparks of light had been scattered and had been gathered into a blaze in the more favored ones. A thorn-bush produces no grapevine; a neglected people produces no prophets such as the Jews gave to the world. The historical books of the Bible are full of reproach about the morals and the depravity of the people of Israel at the time of their kings; the authors want to prepare us for the devastation that came on later as a punishment for their sins. Yet, noble forces in great number must have existed within that nation; there must have been a native endowment and disposition, when men of such significance could rise and develop out of the people. Judaism was not a mere voice crying in the wilderness, and though it did not prevail in all, it was still an energy which existed, though weaker in many, yet to such an extent that, concentrating in individuals, it could produce such heroes of the spirit. Nor does Judaism claim to be the work of individuals, but that of the whole people. It does not speak of the God of Moses or of the God of the prophets, but of the God of Abraham, Isaac, and Jacob, of the God of the whole race, of all the patriarchs who were equally endowed with the gift of prophetic vision, the genius of revelation which was latent in the whole people and found concentration and expression in individuals. The fact that the greatest prophet left his work unfinished contains a great truth: he must not be regarded as the Atlas who bears the world on his shoulders, who completes the work without the cooperation of others from beginning to end. "No man knoweth of his sepulchre unto this day" [Deuteronomy 34:6] and our ancient teachers remark, "His grave should not serve for a place of pilgrimage whither people go to do honor to *one* and thus raise him above the level of man." Moses did his part of the work according to his great capacity as one of the whole people. Judaism arose within the people of revelation. And why then should we not use the word where we touch bottom rock, an illumination pro-ceeding from a higher mind and spirit, which can not be explained; which is not a compound produced by a process of development even if it is further developed afterwards; which all at once appears in existence as a whole, like every new creation proceeding from the original spirit? We do not want to limit and define the word in any dogmatic manner; it may be understood in different ways, but as to its essence it remains the same: the point of contact of human reason with the fundamental source of all things. High as the ancient teachers estimated revelation, they never denied that it is connected with human ability. The Talmud teaches: "The spirit of God rests only on a wise man, on a man possessing moral power, who is independent because he is frugal and contented by having conquered all ambition, greed, and desire;"[19] a man who bears his importance within him, who feels the divine within him. Only such a one is capable of receiving the divine, not a mere speaking trumpet through which the spoken word passes without his being conscious of it; no, a man in the true sense of the word, who touches close upon the divine and is therefore susceptible to it. A deep thinker and great poet of the Middle Ages, Judah ha-Levi, emphatically designated revelation as a disposition that was present in the whole people. Israel, he says, is the religious heart of mankind which in its totality always preserved its greater susceptibility, and its individual distinguished men were the heart of that heart.[20] Maimonides speaks of a flash-like illumination as which revelation must be regarded; to one the light lasted but for a short time, to another it occurred repeatedly, and with Moses, it was a lasting one, an illumination which lights up the darkness, affords man a look into the hidden recesses, which reveals to him what remains concealed for others.[21]

Judaism is such a religion, has grown out of such divine visions and has connected into a whole all that it did behold; Judaism is a religion of truth, because the view into the essence of things is infallible, beholding the unchangeable and the everlasting: That is its everlasting message.

SAMSON RAPHAEL HIRSCH

The Jewish Calendar

Samson Raphael Hirsch (1808–1888), born in Hamburg, Germany, was trained by his father, grandfather, and by the enlightened orthodox Hakham Isaac Bernays of Hamburg. In 1830 he became a rabbi and founder of neo-Orthodoxy, a form of Judaism that combines classical Jewish learning and living with openness toward worldly culture, strict religious practice with active citizenship. Hirsch conceived Judaism to be fulfillment of what was initiated in classical antiquity and in modern humanism. It stands for justice, love, and self-perfection, he argued. We live in a divine world; everything is to be in the service of God. He detected a system of symbolic implications in Jewish ritual, liturgy, and custom. Israel was established as a people (a term Jewish reformers avoided), not as a religious sect, he maintained. For the cultivation of his ideas Hirsch demanded formation of separate congregations, a demand that entailed withdrawing from existing local communities. He assumed the rabbinate of the separatist congregation in Frankfurt am Main in 1851 and the leadership of a school system in the spirit of neo-Orthodoxy.

Hirsch wrote *Neunzehn Briefe über Judentum* (Nineteen Letters on Judaism) 1836; *Horeb* (1837), which is a systematic presentation of "Israel's Duties in the Dispersion"; commentaries on the Pentateuch (1867–1878), Psalms (1882), and the Prayer Book (1895); and six volumes of essays (1902–1912). The section that follows is an interpretation of parts of the Jewish calendar, i.e., the months *tishri* (roughly, September), the month of "beginning" and "redemption," and the month that follows, *heshvan*.

The catechism of the Jew consists of his calendar. On the pinions of time which bear us through life, God has inscribed the eternal words of His doctrine, making days and weeks, months and years the heralds to proclaim His truths. Nothing would seem more fleeting than these elements of time, but to them God has entrusted the care of His holy things, thereby rendering them more imperishable and more accessible than any mouth of priest, any monument, temple or altar could have done. Priests die, monuments decay, temples and altars fall to pieces, but time remains for ever, and every new-born day emerges fresh and vigorous from its bosom. The priest can visit only a few—priests and monuments, temples and altars must wait till you come to them—and you are most in need of them precisely when you do not come to them, when you do not feel yourself drawn to the Sanctuary, or when misery dooms you to isolation. Not so the children of Time. They do not wait till you come to them; they come to you unannounced and you cannot refuse them; they are able to find you when immersed in the busy mart of life or in the full career of enjoyment, in the lonely stillness of the prison or on the painful bed of sickness; and everywhere they hand to you the word of God, admonishing and warning, inspiring, comforting. Ubiquitous like the deity who sends it, time approaches all contemporaneously and in one moment in the East and the West, in the South and the North; it fills millions of ages and all stations with one and the same feeling and thought.

Consider the month *tishri*, this month of "beginning" and "redemption"! How it stands before you like a divine herald, what a store of thoughtfulness and joy, of trepidation and peace, of warning and comfort it will bring to you!

The Jewish calendar has a dual year, and it also recognizes a dual day. One year commences with autumn, and after ploughing its way through winter to spring and summer it closes again with autumn. The other year starts with spring, and although summer is followed by autumn and winter, it leads back again to smiling and rejuvenated spring. In the same way there is one day which begins with night, when the veil of night is spread over the cradle of creation, a day which, however great the promise of the rosy dawn and the midday brightness which follows, nevertheless ends again with night; and another day which breaks with the morning and advances to midday and after traversing the shadows of the night leads again to morning.

The night-day, which leads from night to night, is the day of the creation by which in all places you reckon the periods of your earthly pilgrimage. But in the temple of God, in the *mikdash*, the day of light, the day which leads you from morning to morning is the unit; everything there begins with the morning and everything ends with the morning.

The autumnal year, the year which begins with *tishri*, entering with the harvest and closing with the harvest, is year of the creation of the earth. By it you count the years of the world, the years of your world, of your doings, of your occupation with the things of the earth. But the spring-year, which commences with the spring month *nisan*, and ends with the same month of spring, is the year of Judaism, the year of the redemption of Israel and mankind; by it you count your Jewish life, your Jewish months and festivals.

This dual reckoning of years and days, does it not strike you as the trumpet call of death and life, of annihilation and resurrection, of transitoriness and eternity? Must it not ever awaken in you the living consciousness of your dual existence, of the combination of the earthly and the transitory with the divine and enduring in your own nature, in all your relationships, in the whole life of man upon earth.

Eliminate from your life everything which makes you a Jew, strike out from the life of mankind everything which Judaism has given to it, everything which ripens at the call of Judaism—then you count in fact from night to night, and the history of mankind counts from night to night with you. All existence is a blossomless autumn, and in a cheerless autumn it fades away and dies. No matter how high the sun of prosperity climbs above the earth, the shadow of night finally envelops everything in its veil; and no matter how brilliantly the tree of the earthly life bedecks itself, the most fertile summer is followed by the autumn, the stormy season comes and the richest foliage is stripped away. What has sprung from the dust becomes dust again, "all goes to the pasture of death," and the flotsam and wreckage of Time proclaims all to be transitory.

[Do not] let this transitory life deceive you, if you believe that youth will last for ever, that the blossoms will endure, that strength will never wane, that greatness is permanent, that joy and pleasure are unassailable, that wealth is secure, that earthly greatness is eternal! [Do not] embrace these things as your earthly gods [. . . learning . . .] to reckon your years from *tishri* only at the end of your days, when it is too late.

[. . . Let . . .] the Jewish spirit [. . . .] teach you the spring-reckoning of your earthly years, [lest] the earth becomes for you a cemetery in which graves stare at you from all sides, in which lurking death casts the fear of extinction over everything, in which cheerfulness becomes for you a sin, pleasure a trespass and joy a folly, so that you cast yourself on the ground in despair, and [. . . .] only sigh, "All, all is vanity" [Ecclesiastes 1:2].

For mark this: in the Jewish spirit, in the Jewish holiness there is nothing without value. The Jewish sanctuary was not built over graves; death and the signs of death remained far from its precincts. Its halls were not to be trodden in sadness, it was built for joy. Within its circuit, time was reckoned from morning to morning.

The Jewish spirit reckons by springtimes. The spring paradise—not that of the other world—is placed by it at the very beginning of human history. It also pictures the spring paradise as the goal of history, in order to teach of a life upon earth in which there will be nothing transitory, in which everything will be eternal, infused with an everlasting, eternal and joyful godliness. It teaches thus of a way of life in which even toil and labor, mourning and pain are transformed into blessed cheerfulness, and the most short-lived germ, the most fleeting moment is comprehended by the divine spirit in man as an everlasting blossom in the garland of perfection. It teaches of a life in which already here on earth salvation flourishes and makes its home, and in the midst of storm and night enjoys a perpetual springtime and daytime rejuvenation. To teach men how to count and live from morning to morning and from springtime to springtime—that is the sum and substance of the Jewish message of salvation. [. . .]

The solemn, yet joyous month of festivals is past, and you now enter the placid and quiet month of *heshvan*; but your heart carries a wealth of reverberating echoes into this quietness, and this month is, therefore, a suitable period for surveying the splendor which lies in Jewish still-life. What a significant month *heshvan* can be if you have been fully imbued with the spirit of *tishri*! School and home, business and communal life now commence the tranquil half-year of their winter activity with all its strivings and enjoyments. With renewed zest boys and girls go off to school, youths and young women again take up the task of preparing for life; with fresh courage the man devotes himself to his occupation, while the woman tends the home; [. . .] and evening assembles them all together again, every cottage becomes a sanctuary, every table an altar, and every breath a hymn to God. A spirit of peace and love, of happiness and quiet confidence fills husband and wife, the young man and young woman, and overflows into the merry and innocent souls of the little ones. Oh, that we were truly Jews! That we would once and for all resolve to be Jews, in the full meaning of this glorious name, with all the determination and vigor that this path of salvation demands! That we might once and for all cease from carping and fault-finding; and that we might put to the test God's word and the sustaining power of His doctrine only in the sphere where it truly can be tested, namely in life, in real existence, in action. That we might at last have the courage to build our homes as Jews, to conduct our married life as Jews, to educate our children as Jews, to enlighten our minds and warm our hearts as Jews, to enliven our conversation and plan our actions as Jews, to consecrate our enjoyments as Jews; that we might have the courage to carry out all this in the Jewish spirit, in the complete Jewish spirit, so that we might confidently await all the blessings that would spring from such a way of life. How firmly should we stand in the midst of this unstable generation, how closely should we be knit together by bonds of holiness in this age of disintegration; what strength could unfold in us, even though all else succumbed to weakness, what truth would spring forth even though in all else deceit was rampant; what love would ensue, even though all else was slave to selfishness; what blessing, what joyous well-being would reside in our midst, even though all else fell prey to care and sadness. Has our weak sliding into the un-Jewish way of life brought us such great benefits that we cannot tear ourselves from the delusion that holds us in its throes? Have our hearts become lighter, our spirits more joyous, our marriages happier, our family relationships more sincere since we have forsaken the Jewish path of life; are our children better, our youth more pure, our men and women sturdier, than were our mothers and fathers? Have we exchanged our Jewish life of tranquility for conditions that give promise of a more satisfying lot? Is the ground so firm on which we have disembarked from our tiny Jewish skiff? Is it a sound environment into which we have stepped? Is it a goodly blossoming tree of life that has received us into its shade? [. . .]

[. . .] What a splendid thing Jewry would be today if all Jews were Jews; if the freedom and culture, material wealth and science and art that have fallen to the present generation in such rich measure had not estranged them from Judaism, and if Jews had not deserted those guardian spirits that protect, enlighten, guide and bless, and which ought to accompany the tranquil life of Jews in all walks of life and through all stages of its development, dedicating it to God.

Milah, tzitzit, tefillin, mezuzah, shabbat, berakhot[22] are the names of these spirits of tranquil life, to whose guidance you must commit yourself if you wish to train yourself to be a Jew [. . .] an ever-fresh, ever-new inspiration to continuance in such a life.

The *berakhot,* however, permeate all moments of your life with the spirit of acceptance and dedication; they cause you to look upon your life as a continual service to God and to complete it as such.

Whatever you see and hear, whatever you receive or lose, the benefits you enjoy and the activities in which you indulge, nothing will find you void of thought; everything rouses and admonishes you, and strengthens you in the resolve to be in everything and with everything not only blessed but yourself a blessing, to become a being that in blessing furthers the will of Him Who is all around you, blessing you in everything and with everything, and Who in turn is to become *barukh* through you, Himself awaiting a blessing through you. So will your whole life be spent as an object-lesson of that one word which He spoke to your ancestor, *heyeh berakhah,* become a blessing [Genesis 12:2].

HERMANN COHEN

Religious Postulates

Hermann Cohen (1842–1918) was the founder of the Marburg (Germany) School of neo-Kantianism. Like Kant, he examined the logical presuppositions of scientific knowledge, but unlike Kant, he posited that thought produces everything out of itself; thought "constructs" the world of objects. He wrote *Die Logik der reinen Erkenntnis* (Logic of Pure Thinking), 1902, *Die Ethik des reinen Willens* (Ethic of Pure Willing), 1904, and *Die Aesthetik des reinen Gefühls* (Aesthetic of Pure Feeling), 1912, "pure" meaning independent of sense experience. His ethic emphasizes the dignity of man. At this stage of Cohen's thinking, God is the guarantor of the realization of man's ethical aims within the natural order of being. This God was a concept, an idea, rather than the existent, personal being of traditional Judaism. And "man" is man in general, not the individual person. Morality is to be fully realized in the messianic age, as envisaged by the biblical prophets.

In 1912, Cohen terminated his Marburg professorship and moved to Berlin, where he taught Jewish philosophy at the liberal *Hochschule für die Wissenschaft des Judentums.* (Among his students was Franz Rosenzweig.) By then, Cohen's concept of religion had changed. He realized that not ethics but only religion has consideration for the individual person, that categories such as sin, repentance, and forgiveness are not found in the sphere of ethics but of religion, and that human reason is not the source and origin of reality; God is. The documentation of Cohen's changed attitude in his last work, *Die Religion der Vernunft aus den Quellen des Judentums* (Religion of Reason from the Sources of Judaism), 1918. The essay that follows is excerpted from an address Cohen gave in 1907.

It should be obvious to any educated person that only philosophy can devise—because it alone can substantiate—a *Weltanschauung*. And the recent claim by some spokesmen of religion that religion *as* religion can offer a world view is due precisely to that erroneous assumption which will be the main point of my discussion.

Religion considers itself to be, essentially, a teaching about God. And it also feels, and justifiably so, that there ought to be no positive *Weltanschauung* without a concept of God. But it makes a mistake when it assumes to be adequately equipped to substantiate and guarantee the idea of God. This popular misconception has, in fact, been refuted by the history of all religions. For in all of them, dogmatics—or the system of their religious tenets—emerges out of, and as, philosophy. Hence, there must be a natural connection between religion and philosophy. Religion, actually, can arrive at a reasoned theological position or, as it were, at the God of *Weltanschauung* only by virtue of such a connection.

Recently, however, the aversion against religion has become more pronounced among the educated, owing to their distrust of philosophy and lack of respect for it. Modern academicians view philosophy and religion with equal coolness, particularly with regard to the problem of God. This goes so far that a philosopher's scientific credentials are already suspect if he does not observe an official silence concerning theological questions.

This attitude, by now almost predominant in our circles, also constitutes the greatest threat and danger to our existence. For our existence is grounded in our religion, whose sole foundation is the idea of the One God.

Before going on, I must remind you that for decades we have neglected this fundamental idea in our religious discussions. We prefer to talk exclusively of our moral teachings because they seem to provide legitimate proof that we are decent people. But decent morals do not, by any means, constitute sufficient grounds on which to base a religion. A religion's right to exist is derived from its concept of God. And this concept must be constantly reaffirmed and perfected.

This is particularly true of Judaism which, as a matter of principle, makes no distinction between religion and ethics. For the God of Judaism is the God of morality. That means that His significance lies wholly in His disclosure as well as His guarantee of ethics. He is the author and the guarantor of the moral universe. This significance of God as the ground of the moral universe is the meaning of the fundamental principle of God's unity.

But what, actually, is the supreme distinction of this divine unity? The tasks posed by the moral universe are, after all, so manifold that one can understand why polytheism felt moved to distribute them among different gods. And how could one retain within Christianity the concept of one[23] God, even though in the form of a trinity?

The supreme distinction of God's unique Oneness does not consist in the difference between unity and plurality. Divine Oneness implies, instead, that difference between God's being and all being capable of being enumerated, which constitutes the true spirituality of our One God. Anything pertaining to the senses, and therefore also to anything human, is far removed from this God-concept, which, to us, implies the eternal, unshakeable, irreplaceable, primeval ground of the moral universe. Without this God-concept, morality might seem to us to be no more than the expression of a natural human inclination, and as such it could easily be a sweet delusion.

This, then, is my first postulate: in our scholarly as well as in our popular treatment of religious questions, we ought to make the idea of God a guiding principle whose inexhaustible meaning we must come to comprehend ever more clearly.

[In keeping with the spirit of our times, many Jews say:] Judaism, like any other religion, represents God's teachings; but we have no relationship to God. These Jews cling to the predominant notion that universal education and full participation in European culture preclude a positive relationship to Judaism. In the face of this idolization of universal education (and, unfortunately, also of specialized, scientific education) we assert: there can be no universal education, nor can there be any European culture or any ethics without the idea of the One God as the God of morality. For no culture has any ground or foundation without a scientifically reasoned ethics. But such an ethics, in turn, must be grounded in the idea of the One God. It can do without other gods but not without the One God. Consequently, there is neither a European culture nor an ethics in which Judaism does not have a fundamental share.

Nature and morality are not one and the same, yet both have their origin in, and are vouchsafed by, the unity of God. But though nature and morality are and must remain different, they interact and are conjoined at a certain point: in man. For when I live in accordance with moral concepts, I am no animal, no mere creature of nature, but a member of the moral universe. It is, however, only the idea of God which gives me the confidence that morality will become reality on earth. And because I cannot live without this confidence, I cannot live without God.

As my second postulate, I should like to discuss our relationship to the state. Like all questions pertaining to Judaism, this one too must be determined in the light of the concept of the One God. Because the One God is the God of morality, He exists primarily not for the individual, the family, tribe or nation, but for all mankind. Concern with the needs of the individual or the tribe is not lacking even in polytheism. Through its ancestral cult and graveside symbolism, mythical religion provides for the individual's and the tribe's continued existence in the beyond, and often also for atonement and absolution.

What is new and unique about the One God as the God of morality is the fact that He takes care not merely of the individual person or the individual people, nor even merely of the people among whom He first revealed Himself, but that He calls all nations to Himself; that He unites them all in the bond of one mankind, under the name of the One God who is the Father of all men; and that He holds out to them the promise of a time when a sense of ethics will be highly developed among all men. This in fact will be the infallible and only certain mark of their union under Him. Thus, and from the beginning, the One God implies a mankind united in the ideal of morality.

It seems we have gradually stopped talking of the national God of the Jews, or at least we do so only with a certain hesitation. But we are as yet far from drawing the right conclusions from the insight we have finally gained. I must limit myself here to a discussion of only those conclusions which have a bearing upon our relationship to the state.

Inasmuch as the One God is the God of all mankind, He cannot be the God of only one nation. No matter how limited one's notions of the Messiah—who represents an age, the so-called "days of the Messiah"—one cannot possibly deny that the Messiah for Israel must also be the Messiah for all nations. Along with the Jews, therefore, all nations, even those from the remotest isles, must draw near to Jerusalem. Nor must there remain any distinction between the children of Israel and the sons of strange lands. For the latter, too, will some day become priests and Levites. Ahead of us lies an era in which the "new covenant" will be made, an age of which it is said, "I will put my law in their inward parts, and in their heart will I write it" (Jeremiah 31:33). Ahead of us, that is, lies an era when all nations will say: "For Thou art our Father, though Abraham knoweth us not" (Isaiah 63:16). This is the way Jeremiah and Isaiah expressed their patriotism.

We should not, therefore, let anything keep us from adopting the profound political wisdom of the jeremiads as our guiding principle: "Weep ye not for the dead, neither bemoan him; but weep sore for him that goeth away, for he shall return no more, nor see his native country" (Jeremiah 22:10). This explains the tragedy of our wandering among the nations of the earth. The One God has taken our country from us so that He might give us the concept of mankind. The One God cannot be the God of any one country or state. He can be the God only of a mankind that is united in morality. It is therefore incumbent upon us to gain recognition in the world for this One God. This is our world-historical task.

Were it not or were it no longer for this mission of ours, the preservation of our community would have no specifically Jewish significance. Only this task of ours—the dissemination and deepening of the idea of the One God, and its elaboration throughout the millennia—only this mission on earth justifies and explains our continued existence as the creedal community of the One God.

Contemporary terminology should, therefore, no longer refer to a Jewish nation; for modern history and political science regard the nation merely as vehicle for the state. For this reason a distinction must be made between nation and nationality. The modern state requires a uniform nation but by no means a uniform nationality. Nationalistic movements are therefore wrong on theoretical as well as moral grounds not to take this distinction into consideration.

Our way has been clearly marked for us by our history. And our history is but a manifestation of the essence of our religion. Just as the banishment from Paradise constitutes man's entrance into civilization, so does our banishment from our country usher in our global pursuit of the idea of the One God. As it is said: "And the remnant of Jacob shall be in the midst of many peoples, As dew from the Lord" (Micah 5:6). The establishment of a state of our own is incompatible with the messianic concept and with Israel's mission.

Moreover, despite all the suffering and insults we have to endure as the destiny imposed upon us by our faith, or as the yoke of the kingdom of God, our dispersion has long ceased to mean exile to us. We do live in our native land, and we live in our state as well as for it. And it is this state of ours which makes available to us the blessings of general culture.

It is not true that we maintain, or even wish to maintain, a separate Jewish culture. The distinctiveness of Jewish culture is limited to its ethical concept of God, a concept it has contributed to general culture. But just as our great men have always derived their knowledge of mathematics, philosophy, and medicine, or the art of poetry from general culture, so do we ourselves participate fully in all these aspects of cultural life. It is in the domain of religion alone that we wish to preserve our distinctiveness. Here we are and intend to remain Jews.

The task of teaching and indeed of living the idea of the true—that is, the truly One—God among the nations of the earth must continue to fill us with a sense of elation. But it is inherent in this task that we become an integral part of these nations and their cultural pursuits. Let their people be our people, for their state is our state [as their country is our country]. Except for our idea of the One God, there is nothing that sets us apart. We certainly do not pursue science and art or economic and civic matters in any specific way. In all these areas, we work in conformity with the methods and toward the goals of general culture. And cherishing these goals, we extend the love our country has instilled in us to its intellectual and moral concerns as well.

Love of our country is a necessary corollary of the idea of the messianic God, as is our striving for a fatherland where we can be at home and where general culture and intellectual pursuits can flourish. For messianic mankind by no means implies a disintegration of all nations, but rather their unification in a spirit of morality. Even a league of nations would not mean the disappearance of different states but merely their alliance for the establishment of a genuinely international law. The messianic God does not represent merely a future image of world history, however. He demands—by virtue of the eternal ideas conjoined in Him—political action [in the present] and continuous, tireless participation in various concrete national tasks. It is the duty of any Jew to help bring about the messianic age by involving himself in the national life of his country.

Every nation and every state have their world-historic task with regard to the actualization of the messianic ideal. And in each state the Jew, too, must therefore selflessly and unreservedly pledge himself to the fulfillment of these national tasks, and bring to them all his energy and the full strength of his freely offered and pure love. Our state [that is, the country in which we live] is our fatherland. And it is our messianic religion which, by its very nature, not only commands but also enables us to acknowledge and love our state as our fatherland.

And as a third postulate, I am asking for a deepened concern with Jewish scholarship. That we have had to take a back seat in Bible scholarship is clearly due to the fact that our scholars depend, outwardly as well as inwardly, on their congregations. Yet we ought to regain prominence in this—our very own—field. Even though we owe much of our understanding of prophetism to

Protestant thought as taught at our universities, there too the influence of theology remains all too evident. Consequently, the Protestant concept of Messianism, circumscribed as it is by Christology, has not yet emerged with that profundity and clarity of the God-idea which we have developed naturally.

But we we wish to work once again effectively in the field of Bible scholarship, in a free scientific spirit as well as in accordance with the spirit of Judaism, we must gradually leave our literary ghetto—as [Leopold] Zunz has called it—and try to make our way to the university. For this is the forum where opposing views must be argued and reconciled. Of course, it will take some time before the walls of this intellectual ghetto of ours will fall. But it is beyond doubt that they will come down, as must all barriers to intellectual freedom among men, especially those among citizens of the same country. Until such time, though, we must remain and indeed become ever more intent upon deepening, broadening, and making more comprehensive the scope of our own teaching institutions so that their spirit will be commensurate with that of the university. Towards that end, we must vigorously and eagerly support the efforts which have recently been made regarding the promotion of higher learning among us. And this includes politics and science as much as religion.

In the last analysis, our political equality rests on whatever spiritual strength we can derive from our religious sources. Even from a purely political point of view we therefore urgently need an ever-increasing awareness that we as Jews derive sustenance and guidance not only from the modern culture that surrounds us but also from our specific Jewish culture.

But the duty to promote higher Jewish learning must also be seen as the most proper concern of religion. No religion can survive meaningfully in our contemporary culture if it persists in merely observing its customs, no matter how devoutly. All cultural life, including the religious, must involve the mind as well as the heart. It is not enough that our soul be satisfied with and exalted by our old customs and ancient spiritual treasures. These treasures must be acquired ever anew. They must be rediscovered by new efforts, and comparative studies must throw new light on them so as to give them creatively new forms. This holds true for rabbinic no less than biblical literature. And there is a rich, open field of which general scholarship is as yet totally unaware: the broad area of our religio-philosophical literature, which dates back to the ninth century.

Thus, this third task must be added to the first two. For only if we can demonstrate that throughout the history of our philosophy of religion—which is the history of our dogmatics—the inter-relatedness of the ideas of the One God and of moral mankind has been acknowledged and affirmed, can we be convinced of the truth of our religion, and continue to profess it in all its majesty.

HAYYIM NAHMAN BIALIK

Halakhah and *Aggadah*

The preeminent Hebrew poet Bialik (1873–1934) was born in Volhynia, Russia and grew up in the world of the rich and colorful Jewish tradition. But while still a student at the famous yeshivah of Volozhin he became acquainted with the ways of the West. He moved to Odessa, a center of Hebraic renaissance, and, simultaneously, receptive to Russian and German literature. Here his poetic gifts flourished and, before long, he became known as the most distinguished Hebrew poet of the time. In 1921 Bialik left Russia, lived a few years in Germany as a publisher of Hebrew books, and in 1924, settled in Tel Aviv. In the poetry of his early period Bialik extolled the traditional House of Study as the source of the pure Hebraic spirit; praised the ascetic, dedicated student of the Talmud; criticized spiritual apathy; and rose in anger against the Russian pogroms. His *Megillat ha-Esh* (The Scroll of Fire), 1905, deals symbolically with the destruction of the Temple and the struggle between faith and despair. The long poem *Mete Midbar* (The Dead of the Desert), 1902, refers both to the generation of the exodus from Egypt and to the central problems of modern man. With Y. H. Rawnitzki he compiled *Sefer ha-Aggadah*, a treasure of non-legal material from the Talmud and the *midrash*, as part of his attempt to popularize Hebrew classics.

Among his many essays is "Halakhah and Aggadah" (1917), here reprinted. Bialik used the two terms, meaning talmudic law and legend, respectively, to denote an attitude of strict duty versus an esthetic approach to life and stressed the need in modern life for the former.

The face of *Halakhah* is grim; that of *Aggadah* is gay. *Halakhah* is narrow and heavy, hard as steel—of the quality of justice; the latter is candid, buoyant—of the quality of mercy. The first commands and swerves not a hair's breadth; its yes means yes and its no means no. The second counsels and reckons with human capacities and insights; its yes and no are flexible. *Halakhah* is all husk, body, action; *Aggadah* is all content, soul, aspiration. The first is hardening inertia, compulsion and submission; the second, continuous renewal, freedom and spontaneity. These are the ways *Halakhah* and *Aggadah* are described in their relation to life; in relating them to literature it is customary to add that *Halakhah* is prose, a fixed, precise style and colorless, monotonous language— the supremacy, that is, of the intellect; while *Aggadah* is the freshness of poetry, a flowing and varied style, colorful language— the supremacy, that is, of emotion.

These antitheses can be extended indefinitely, and each in its own way may indeed contain a grain of truth. But does this imply, as so many claim, that *Halakhah* and *Aggadah* are irreconcilable opposites?

Those who say so mistake what is secondary for what is primary, form for content. It is as if a man were to regard the ice and the water in a river as two distinct elements. Like ice and water, *Halakhah* and *Aggadah* are really two things in one, two facets of a single entity. They are related to each other as words are related to thought and impulse, or as a deed and its material form are to expression. *Halakhah* is the concretization, the necessary end product of *Aggadah*; *Aggadah* is *Halakhah* become fluid again. [. . .] The vision moves forward to expression; the will becomes deed; the thought, word; the flower, fruit—and *Aggadah* becomes *Halakhah*. But concealed within the fruit lies the seed from which new fruit will grow. Out of *Halakhah*, raised to the status of a symbol (and there is such a symbol, as will be shown later) emerges in turn new *Aggadah*, either fashioned in its own image or of altogether different complexion. *Halakhah*, living and powerful, is *Aggadah* of the past and future—and vice versa. Beginning and end are interwoven.

And what are all the six hundred and thirteen commandments of the Torah but the end result, the synthesis upon synthesis of legendary words, of *Aggadah* and ancient custom, of a Torah of life, a Torah of the lips and heart which floated in space, as it were, for thousands of years since ages primeval, until the time came when it was concretized in the form of legal statutes chiseled in stone or inscribed on parchment? The regulations pertaining to sacrifices, to the clean and the unclean and to the forbidden foods are rooted in sacerdotal myth; the "Commandments of Remembrance" are linked with national and historical *Aggadah;* the ordinances governing the relations "between man and his neighbor" are bound up with the popular sense of justice and mercy as expounded by great men. But even when fixed in writing, these did not harden or petrify, for the Torah of the heart and lips did not in fact cease for so much as a moment. Out of its vibrant, pulsating vitality the written Torah continually took shape. It was this that informed and quickened the written code, now amplifying, now limiting, sometimes even annulling it—during brief periods or whole epochs—as circumstances and new views and ideas might dictate.

Halakhah as Art

The process by which *Halakhah* and *Aggadah* in turn solidify and dissolve is common knowledge and becomes particularly clear in times of revolution when new ordinances are established. The old, outmoded *Halakhah*, grown useless, descends into the crucible of the heart where it is converted into *Aggadah* which may or may not resemble it; the refined *Aggadah* emerges and enters into the forms of thought and action, where it again solidifies into *Halakhah* but in a new and revised version. *Halakhah*, therefore, is no less dynamically creative than *Aggadah*. Its art is the greatest in the world: the art of life and of the ways of life; its subject matter is the living human being in all the passions of his heart; its method is individual, social and national education; and its fruits are an unending chain of virtuous lives and fitting deeds, a way of life marked out between the irregular and tortuous path of the individual and that of the mass, an existence on earth worthy of human beings, a *defined attitude toward life*. The works of the *Halakhah* are not as those of the other arts—sculpture, painting, architecture, music, poetry—concentrated in space and time and uniform in material. They are composed gradually, piece by piece, out of collective human experience and activity, with *one* result, *one* form emerging in the end, whether perfect or weighed down with faults. The *Halakhah* is didactic art, the art of educating a whole people, and all that it engraves in the soul of the people, the coarse as well as the delicate lines, is shaped by inspiration and high provident wisdom. Day after day, hour by hour, from moment to moment, it is intent on the shaping of only a single form: the original form of all things created—the image of God. The cathedrals of Cologne and Milan, Notre Dame in Paris, complete in their majesty became what they did through the toil of immortal artists over the course of many, many centuries, each in his time dedicating his life and the best of his creative energy to this work. [. . .] But all of them made themselves servitors of a single, central idea, which to them represented the height of sublimity, and it was because of this that the "divine work" prospered in such measure at their hands. That idea—the building of a house to their God—hovered before their eyes—"Like unto the vision which thou wert shown" [Numbers 8:4], inspiring them, guiding the ruler and quadrant, chisel and brush in their hands, prompting every line and curve, every stone and beam. These at last, after centuries of work by people remote from each other in space and time, grew into a single great and glorious edifice.

The children of Israel have likewise a mighty masterpiece: the holy and august *day* that is "Princess Sabbath." In popular imagination she became a living being with corporeal form, the very essence of beauty and radiance. She it was that the Holy One, blessed be He, led into the world, as a man leads his newly-wed.

[. . .] According to another popular *Aggadah*, Sabbath sits like a princess, "like a bride among her playfellows, decked in many colors," hidden in a palace in paradise, in the innermost of seven chambers, and her six handmaids, the days of work, wait upon her. On her entrance into the city all turn their faces towards the gate and receive her with the greeting, "Welcome, O bride, thou Princess Sabbath!" The Hasidim even go out into the fields to meet her, as it were, halfway. [. . .] All the poets of Israel, from Judah ha-Levi to Heine, sang her their songs. Is she not then, in the fullest sense a product of *Aggadah*? Is she not in herself a wellspring of life and holiness for a whole nation and a never-failing source of inspiration to poets and singers? Yet who shall tell, who decide whose handiwork she is, through whom she became what she did—through *Halakhah* or *Aggadah*?

The talmudic tractate *Shabbat* numbers 157 pages, as against only 105 in the tractate *Erubin*, and the amount of *Aggadot* in them is pitifully small. For the most part, these pages consist of disquisitions and ritualistic details pertaining to the thirty-nine main kinds of forbidden labor and all their sub-divisions [. . .]. What materials may be used for the Sabbath light? What may be placed on an animal when it is let out? How may the bounds be joined? What mental lucubration is this! What a sorry expense of ingenuity over every jot and tittle! And yet when I leaf through these pages and visualize the hosts of Tannaim and Amoraim[24] at their work, I cannot but reflect that what I see before me are artists of life in their workshops, cunning workmen laboring to bring forth. So mighty a labor of the spirit, at once ant-like and giant-like, performed for its own sake, out of love and boundless faith, could not possibly have come about without inspiration. Each one of them did his part according to his own individual aim and natural propensities, yet all were subsumed beneath a higher and loftier will which controlled them all. Only one sublime idea, one original image of the Sabbath hovered before all these separate men; its spirit brought them together from over all the generations and made them comrades in project and performance. [. . .] And what is the fruit of this strenuous labor of *Halakhah*? A day that is wholly *Aggadah*.

There are more than a few of such examples. There is the Day of Atonement, Passover and the other holidays. Beauty in its highest sense lies unmistakably at their basis. All are beautiful works, filled with living and stirring content and high, exalted purpose; yet all are children of the strict *Halakhah* and are surrounded on all sides by its "fences." While the artists of other peoples sat in their studios and with delicate and subtle feeling sought in marble, say, for harmonious measures and forms to gratify the senses of men, the sages of Israel sat in their schools and by inspiration and purity of feeling sought, in the example, say, of charity, for harmonious measures and inner forms to gratify and embellish man himself and ennoble mankind. I do not pretend to decide which work deserves precedence over the other, but I am convinced that both are creative, both make ideas concrete, both make thought actual through the creative human spirit; in both the order of beauty finds its place and unveils its full radiance, both are necessarily instinct with inspiration and divine grace. Their difference is one only of material and methods, just as are the differences between the more commonly recognized arts—between music and painting, for instance.

But, to be sure, there also exists a more fundamental difference; the products of the other arts address themselves to man as an individual and, as has already been said, are uniform and concentrated in material, space and time. They are to be perceived at once, immediately and directly. This is not true of the products of the *Halakhah*. These are addressed not to men, but to mankind, and at the same time are composed of elements scattered over an immense area in material, space and time. Their shape, the sum of all their parts, reveals itself to the understanding only after long meditation and only from a great height. Were a great city to be built according to a mighty and fertile idea stemming from some architect-artist, that idea in all its purity of feature and total beauty could only be discerned from a ground plan or from the top of a high lookout—certainly not by strolling the streets between the houses where the whole would be impaired by its details. "Not to see the wood for the trees" is an old and wise adage, but does this make the form of an idea the less beautiful or perfect? Advise anyone who wants to enjoy it to climb the mountain![25]

Necessity of Interaction

So what does it all amount to? A return to the *Shulhan Arukh*?[26] Anyone who deduces this attitude from what I have said has not understood me at all. The actual terms *Halakhah* and *Aggadah* are talmudic, and their meanings are precise in their contexts; but as concepts they can be universalized as two forms complete in themselves, two antithetical styles which accompany each other through life and letters. And just as every generation has its *Aggadah*, so every *Aggadah* has its own *Halakhah*.

We are not interested here in this *Aggadah* or that *Halakhah*, but in the concept of *Halakhah*, in *Halakhah* as a great legal sanction, as a tangible shaping, complete in itself, of concrete life—a life not floating in the air or hovering in a mist of beautiful feelings and phrases, but with a beautiful body too and a beautiful substance. And I maintain that this *Halakhah* is the integral complement of *Aggadah*, the logical period at the end of the sentence. Indeed the greatness of *Aggadah* lies in the very fact that it leads to *Halakhah*. Any *Aggadah* which does not so issue is a mere sentimental bauble. In the end, it evaporates, but not before exhausting the energies of its authors.

When someone says, "All I know is *Aggadah*," his *Aggadah* should be looked at to see whether it is not just a sterile flower. And what is he like? Like a man who says, "I pluck flowers but discard the fruit." There will come a day when he will no longer be able to pluck flowers, for without fruit there is no seed, and without seed whence shall the flower come?

The shafts of the *Aggadah* dart hither and thither, wavering as though shot into the air from a slackened bow-string; those of the *Halakhah* fly straight and true, strongly and unswerving, as if sped from a taut bow. *Aggadah* gives you air in which to breathe; *Halakhah*, a place to stand on, solid bedrock. The one introduces something fluid and liquid; the other something fixed and rigid. A people that has not learned to combine *Halakhah* with *Aggadah* delivers itself to eternal confusion and runs the danger of forgetting the one direct way from the will to the deed, from the effort to the realization.

The union of *Halakhah* and *Aggadah* is evidence of a people's health and proof of its maturity. Whenever *Aggadah* exists alone, a widow unmated, the power and volition of a people are bound to be enfeebled and in need of rejuvenation. This ought to be taken to heart especially by those who put form above content as the attribute of national consciousness.

Many generations in Israel have sinned grievously against *Aggadah* by breaking their living contact with it. Countless simple minds interpreted its utterances literally and took them for articles of faith, and countless overclever minds, likewise interpreting them literally, took them for idle chatter. Both showed bad taste and bad sense. Small wonder, too, that their eyes were also blinded to the gleams of poetry in *Halakhah*, and that they could not discern the essential truth behind the parable. They had ceased to understand its language.

We are now blessed with a generation that is completely *Aggadah*, *Aggadah* in its literature and *Aggadah* in its life. The whole world is nothing but a great *Aggadah*. The *Halakhah* with all its nuances is no longer known. [. . .] No matter how violently the truth is denied by those who find it unpleasant, it cannot be changed. Like a tramp, the greatest part of our recent literature has chosen for its permanent abode what are culturally the basement steps in the edifice of thought and feeling. All "the fifty gates of insight" are closed to it and nothing is left but a little side door of doubtful "beauty"—the *Aggadah* of today. A few novels and a few poems are the total content of its beggar's sack. There are not other contributions from higher spiritual sources. *Halakhah* has ceased in Israel. And worst of all, this our contemporary literature shows no inclination whatsoever toward self-recognition, shows no desire to rise out of this, its public grave of poverty, and strive higher. On the contrary, the charm of the place is found superior to those who created it. And with the increase among them of commonplace and ignorant men, there has become apparent on their part something more or less of a conscious tendency to plant the notion in the minds of the masses that there is no other kind of literature or creative activity than the beautiful and artistic, and that everything else is worthless. [. . .]

And I repeat: I do not want to weigh *Halakhah* and *Aggadah* against each other, nor do I claim the one to be valuable and the other worthless. I am concerned with them as universal concepts, as twin forms of life and letters. And I ask: what will be the end of any *Aggadah* which has not its *Halakhah* close beside it? [. . .]

In the final analysis the right of literature to exist as an art consists solely in its capacity to provide a firm link between the individual who shapes and the multitude that is to be shaped. "Poetry for its own sake" and "singing as the birds do" are justifiable only as the relaxations of those who toil the rest of the time by the sweat of their brows to build a literature powerful enough to embrace all fields of human culture—a literature that will shape and ennoble life itself. Apart from this, there is no justification for what is, after all, a poetry of boredom and idleness.

Such is the state of affairs in literature. And in life? The growing generation is being reared in an atmosphere charged with nothing but poetry, song and other foibles, all of which are just so much prattle and wind. A kind of arbitrary Judaism is spreading; there are strident slogans: nationalism, renascence, literature, creation, Hebrew education, Hebrew thinking, Jewish labor—and all these things hang by the thin thread of some sort of love: love of country, love of language, love of literature. What price a love that's ethereal?

Love? —But where, is duty? Where is that to come from? Whence shall that draw its strength? From *Aggadah?* *Aggadah* is by nature arbitrariness itself: its yes and no are too uncertain.

A Judaism that is only *Aggadic* is like steel heated in fire but never chilled. The heart's aspirations, good will, an elevated mind, inward love—all these are fine and significant things if only they issue in *deeds*, deeds hard as iron, and in stern duty. [. . .]

The lofty visions of the Second Isaiah stirred the heart, but when the hour for building drew near, prophesying came to an end with Haggai and Zechariah, the two prophets among the builders, and *Halakhah* began; and those who came after, Ezra and his party, were men of *Halakhah* only.

"Set up ordinances for yourselves!" [Nehemiah 10:33]. Let molds be given us that our fluid, inchoate desires may be poured into fixed and definite shapes. We are hungry for deeds. Train us in life for action rather than talk, and in writing, for *Halakhah* rather than *Aggadah*.

We bend our necks: where is the iron yoke? Why do the strong hand and the outstretched arm delay?

JACOB FICHMAN, RACHEL, YITZHAK LAMDAN, ABRAHAM BROIDES, YEHUDA AMICHAI

Zion –Jerusalem

What Zion and Jerusalem mean is best expressed by poets not journalists or historians, secular or sacred, and rarely by writers of fiction. In antiquity there was the psalmist, in the Middle Ages Judah ha-Levi and the masters of liturgic poetry, in the modern period a host of men and women, some well-known, some not. All together they contribute toward a majestic, triumphant, and elegiac song of Zion.

Jacob Fichman (1881–1958) was born in Bessarabia and settled in the Land of Israel in 1912. He introduced individualistic impressionism into Hebrew literature. (Translation by Simon Halkin)

Rachel (1890–1931) came to the Land of Israel before World War I. Lyrical poet, she sings of the experience of taking root in the land of the Bible. (Translation by Maurice Samuel)

Yitzhak Lamdan (1899–1954), born in the Ukraine, settled in the Land of Israel in 1920. His epic poem *Masada* (1927), which became a classic of the Halutz (Pioneer) movement, treats that movement as the last stand of modern Jewry battling for survival. (Masada was the last fortress in Judea in the war against the Romans; it fell in 73 c.e.). (Translation by Simon Halkin)

Abraham Broides, born in Vilna in 1907, came to the Land of Israel in 1923. He is a poet of the poor and humble, and of the children. (Translation by Simon Halkin)

Yehuda Amichai, born in Germany in 1924, settled in the Land of Israel in 1936. His poetry makes use of the most modern idiom and phraseology, borrows terms from technology and law, and creates an atmosphere of freshness and "the now." (Translation by Warren Bargad)

JACOB FICHMAN

Upon These Fields of Night

Upon these fields of night, serenely pure,
My feet tread lightly and securely, as if upon
A soil most native, sacred from the day
When first my star began to guide me hither.
How friendly are the wings of night! My eye
Distinguishes each bush, each rock, each clod,
As if a good and loyal hand were leading me.
Few are the days I have been here;
Yet like a grain of seed, untouched by frost,
This land so strange absorbed me lovingly. . . .
As if all that I knew and loved, from days
Of childhood rich in mystery till now,
Had ever sought but this one land of peace
Where my soul would be revealed to me
And where God's face would whitely glimmer forth.

RACHEL

A Jug of Water in the Hand

A jug of water in the hand, and on
My shoulder—basket, spade and rake.
To distant fields, to toil, my path I make.

Upon my right the green hills fling
Protecting arms; before me—the wide fields!
And in my heart my twenty Aprils sing. . . .

Be this my lot, until I be undone;
Dust of the road, my land, and thy
Grain waving golden in the sun.

YITZHAK LAMDAN

O God, Save Masada!

Steady, O God, the footsteps of those who have slipped off the
    gallows
In strange lands, and have risen upon the walls of the fortress;
Steady them that they may not stumble and fall, for weary they
    are, and still stagger . . .
Soften the hard rocks of Masada under their heads when they do
    fatigue:
Do not let the cold hail of despair blast that which they have sown
    here, the seed of souls and of dreams.
Bid, O God, many rains of solace to fall upon it, and may the dew
    fructify it at night,
Till it be rewarded with the promise of harvest! . . .
For if this time again you will not be merciful, O God,
Nor accept our dream, nor heed the offerings of those who strive
    to make the dream come true. . . .
O God, save Masada!

ABRAHAM BROIDES

. . . And Bless My God

For good I find it to broil in the sun of my land in the East,
To press my lips to spouts of springs
And bless my God and Creator.

And good I find it to starve serenely with a dozen comrades,
Then feast upon a green tomato and burnt crust of bread,
And bless my God and Creator.

YEHUDA AMICHAI

I Have Nothing To Say (1973)

I have nothing to say on the war
I have nothing to add, I'm ashamed.

I forgo all knowledge I've absorbed
in my life, like a desert that forgoes water.
I'm forgetting names that I never thought
I would forget.

And because of the war I say once again
for the final, simple sweetness of it all:
The sun revolves around the earth, yes it does,
the earth is flat as a piece of lost lumber that flowers, yes it is,
there is a God in heaven, yes there is.

ABRAHAM ISAAC KOOK

On Prayer

Abraham Isaac Kook (1865–1935), Lativian-born rabbinic authority, emigrated to the Land of Israel in 1904, and in 1921 became Ashkenazic Chief Rabbi of the land. He was both a mystic and a man interested in human affairs. He strongly advocated the upbuilding of the Land of Israel and worked toward improvement of traditional Jewish education. To him, Zionism manifested both national and religious aspects. He viewed the chief rabbinate as the first step toward the re-establishment of the Sanhedrin of old. And he appreciated as well the modern secular, non-religious settlers and Kibbutzniks, for they too contributed to the cultivation of the holy land. Nationalism was to him not an end in itself, but a movement leading to universalism. His love for humanity was truly universal. Kook recognized no contradistinction between the holy and the profane; whatever was of value to human life was potentially sacred. For him there was only one basic sin: forgetfulness. Man forgets God as the source of reality and concomitantly forgets also his own roots. Among Kook's works are *Orot ha-Kodesh* (The Lights of Holiness), *Iggerot ha-Raya* (Letters), and a *Commentary on the Prayer Book*. The selection that follows is from the last work.

The Necessity and the Pleasure of Prayer

Prayer is, both for us and for the world itself, an absolute necessity, and the purest of pleasures. The waves of our soul continually flow, and we desire of ourselves and of the world such perfection

69

as finite existence cannot give us; and thus we find ourselves in great distress, the pain of which can lead us astray from our own and our Maker's laws. But [. . .] in prayer we pour forth the words in us and rise to a world of perfect existence and then our own inner world too becomes perfect, our mind is filled with ease. [. . .]

The Form of Prayer

Before praying the soul must be depressed through the feeling of its imperfection and its distance from the everlasting King. It must feel that it can cast this burden off only by pouring itself out to its Creator and Father in heaven. This will give the soul strength and fill it with joy and a new spirit of happiness. [. . .]

Even if one has the inner urge to pray, it alone can still not form the basis for prayer, which must be the will to worship God. One must therefore be aware of the fact, that though feeling is a prerequisite for the right kind of prayer, its main feature is far above human sensation. Therefore it should be recited in the form of supplication. However, adding the recognition of God's glory to the feelings of the human soul is yet not enough. Intellect is even more important than sensation. If the natural feelings are accompanied by an intelligent original thought, then only can one pray with holy feelings.

All of these three requirements—the right feeling, supplication, and original thought—are mentioned in the Talmud: "Rabbi Eliezer said: If one gives his prayer a fixed form, it is not a plea for mercy. What is a fixed form? Rabbi Jacob bar Iddi said: If his prayer is a burden to him. The sages say: If he does not recite it in the form of supplication. Both Rabbi and Rab Joseph say: If he does not add an original thought."[27]

Torah as a Mode of Prayer

Craftsmanship is a product of intelligence and experience. But there may be a man whose power of imagination is so great, and his tools so excellent, that they can produce a work of art without previous experience. Now study of the Torah should lead to practice, and since prayer gives form to religious feelings, it is closer to practice than is abstract intelligence. Through the power of prayer man's heart is softened, and he is more eager to practice the principles he derived from his studies. But some of our talmudic sages were influenced by the holy spirit of the Torah to such a degree that in order to elevate their feelings they did not have to depend on the power of prayer, but their Torah impressed itself on their tools, comparable to the ideal artist and to Bezalel (*see* Exodus 32:2–3), who was filled with the divine spirit in such measure as to be able to do without experience. Therefore those rabbis were exempt from the obligation to pray, because their studies had the function of prayer itself.

The Need for Prayer

[. . .] All beings long for the very source of their origin. Every plant, every grain of sand, every lump of earth, small creatures and big ones, the heavens above and the angels, every substance together with its particles—all of them are longing, yearning, panting to attain the state of holy perfection. Man suffers all the time from this homesickness of the soul and it is in prayer that he cures it. When praying, man feels at one with the whole creation, and he raises it to the very source of blessing and life.

The Direction of Prayer

Before praying, one must feel the need for prayer and the pleasure of prayer. Prayer does not desire to change anything in the divine, which is the source of eternity and hence without alteration, but to be exalted together with all the changes to which the world and the soul are subject—insofar as the soul is bound to the world. All this is to be exalted into the divine sublimity. In speaking of divinity, the soul yearns unto it according to its qualities with great freedom, and in this freedom it has revelation of the divine light and truth. Prayer speaks to God as to a sovereign whose will may change, as to a father ready to change, as to a just and generous God whose justice and generosity may increase through stimulation by another spirit, for in its very will to be exalted unto the divine, its will is already exalted, and its will is the very essence of its being.

AHAD HAAM

After the Balfour Declaration

Ahad Haam (Asher Ginzberg, 1856–1927) is best known as advocate of "cultural Zionism." Born in Skvira, Russia, he was attracted by both Jewish traditional literature and Western, mainly English and German, writings. In 1884 he settled in Odessa, center of modern Hebrew literature. His first articles, "Lo zeh ha-Derekh" (This Is Not the Way), 1889, and "Emet me-Eretz Yisrael" (Truth from the Land of Israel), 1891, criticized political, economic Herzlian Zionism as premature and established Ahad Haam as a champion of the primacy of educational, spiritual, scholary work. "The Jewish people will be saved by prophets, not by diplomats," he wrote. As editor of *Hashiloah*, important Hebrew monthly, from 1896 to 1903, his voice became widely heard. His literary medium was the essay; his style clear, concise, free of artifice. He set an example for Hebrew essayists who came after him. After a sojourn in London he settled in the Land of Israel in 1922.

The essay here reprinted was written in Hebrew in 1920; it appeared in English in *Nationalism and the Jewish Ethic: Basic Writings of Ahad Haam*, published in New York in 1962. Ahad Haam's collected essays appeared in four volumes under the title *Al Parashat Derakhim* (At the Crossroads) in Odessa in 1895. His letters *(Iggerot Ahad Haam)* appeared in six volumes in Jerusalem from 1923 to 1925.

The details of the diplomatic conversations in London which led to the Declaration have not yet been made public; but the time has come to reveal one "secret," because knowledge of it will make it easier to understand the true meaning of the Declaration.

"To facilitate the establishment in Palestine of a National Home for the Jewish people"—that is the text of the promise given to us by the British Government. But that is not the text suggested to the Government by the Zionist spokesmen. They wished it to read: "the reconstitution of Palestine as the National Home of the Jewish people"; but when the happy day arrived on which the Declaration was signed and sealed by the Government, it was found to contain the first formula and not the second. That is to say, the allusion to the fact that we are about to *re*build our *old* national home was dropped, and at the same time the words "constitution of Palestine as the national home" were replaced by "establishment of a national home in Palestine."[. . .]

It can scarcely be necessary to explain at length the difference between the two versions. Had the British Government accepted the version suggested to it—that Palestine should be reconstituted as the national home of the Jewish people—its promise might have been interpreted as meaning that Palestine, inhabited as it now is, was restored to the Jewish people on the ground of its historic right; that the Jewish people was to rebuild its waste places and was destined to rule over it and to manage all its affairs in its own way, without regard to the consent or non-consent of its present inhabitants. For this rebuilding (it might have been understood) is only a renewal of the ancient right of the Jews, which overrides the right of the present inhabitants, who have wrongly estabished their national home on a land not their own. But the British Government, as it stated expressly in the Declaration itself, was not willing to promise anything which would harm the present inhabitants of Palestine, and therefore it changed the Zionist formula, and gave it a more restricted form. The Government thinks, it would seem, that when a people has only the moral force of its claim to build its national home in a land at present inhabited by others, and has not behind it a powerful army or fleet to prove the justice of its claim, that people can have only what its right allows it in truth and justice, and not what conquering peoples take for themselves by armed force, under the cover of various "rights" invented for the occasion. Now the historic right of a people in relation to a country inhabited by others can mean only the right to settle once more in its ancestral land, to work the land and to develop its resources without hindrance. And if the inhabitants complain that strangers have come to exploit the land and its population, the historic right has a complete answer to them: these newcomers are not strangers, but the descendants of the old masters of the country, and as soon as they settle in it again, they are as good as natives. And not only the settlers as individuals, but the collective body as a people, when it has once more put into this country a part of its national wealth—men, capital, cultural institutions and so forth—has again in the country its national home, and has the right to extend and to complete its home up to the limit of its capacity. But this historic right does not override the right of the other inhabitants, which is a tangible right based on generation after generation of life and work in the country. The country is at present their national home too, and they too have the right to develop their national potentialities so far as they are able. This position, then, makes Palestine common ground for different peoples, each of which tries to establish its national home there; and in this position it is impossible for the national home of either of them to be complete and to embrace all that is involved in the conception of a "national home." If you build your house not on untenanted ground, but in a place where there are other inhabited houses, you are sole master only as far as your front gate. Within you may arrange your effects as you please, but beyond the gate all the inhabitants are partners, and the general administration must be ordered in conformity with the good of all of them. Similarly, national homes of different peoples in the same country can demand only national freedom for each one in its internal affairs, and the affairs of the country which are common to all of them are administered by all the "householders" jointly if the relations between them and their degree of development qualify them for the task, or, if that condition is not yet fulfilled, by a guardian from outside, who takes care that the rights of none shall be infringed.

When, then, the British Government promised to facilitate the establishment *in Palestine of a national home* for the Jewish people—and not, as was suggested to it, the reconstitution of Palestine as the national home of the Jewish people—that promise meant two things. It meant in the first place recognition of the historic right of the Jewish people to build its national home in Palestine, with a promise of assistance from the British Government; and it meant in the second place a negation of the power of that right to override the right of the present inhabitants and to make the Jewish people sole ruler in the country. The national home of the Jewish people must be built out of the free material which can still be found in the country itself, and out of that which the Jews will bring in from outside or will create by their work, without overthrowing the national home of the other inhabitants. And as the two homes are contiguous, and friction and conflicts of interest are inevitable, especially in the early period of the building of the Jewish national home, of which not even the foundations have yet been properly laid, the promise necessarily demands, though it is not expressly so stated, that a guardian shall be appointed over the two homes—that is, over the whole country— to see to it that the owner of the historic right, while he does not injure the inhabitants in their internal affairs, shall not on his side have obstacles put in his way by his neighbor, who at present is stronger than he. And in course of time, when the new national home is fully built, and its tenant is able to rely, no less than his neighbor, on the right which belongs to a large population living and working in the country, it will be possible to raise the question whether the time has not come to hand over the control of the country to the "householders" themselves, so that they may together administer their joint affairs, fairly and justly, in accordance with the needs of each of them and the value of his work for the revival and development of the country.

This and no more, it seems to me, is what we can find in the Balfour Declaration; and this and no more is what our leaders and writers ought to have told the people, so that it should not imagine more than what is actually there, and afterwards relapse into despair and absolute skepticism.

But we all know how the Declaration was interpreted at the

time of its publication, and how much exaggeration many of our workers and writers have tried to introduce into it from that day to this. The Jewish people listened, and believed that the end of the *galut* had indeed come, and that in a short time Palestine would be a "Jewish State." The Arab people too, which we have always ignored from the very beginning of the colonization movement, listened, and believed that the Jews were coming to expropriate its land and to do with it what they liked. All this inevitably led to friction and bitterness on both sides, and contributed much to the state of things which was revealed in all its ugliness in the events at Jerusalem last April.[28] Those events, in conjunction with others which preceded them, might have taught us how long is the way from a written promise to its practical realization, and how many are the obstacles, not easily to be removed, which beset our path. But apparently we learned nothing; and only a short time after the events at Jerusalem, when the British promise was confirmed at San Remo, we began once more to blow the messianic trumpet, to announce the "redemption," and so forth. The confirmation of the promise, as I said above, raised it to the level of an international obligation, and from that point of view it is undoubtedly of great value. But essentially it added nothing, and the text of the earlier promise remains absolutely unaltered. What the real meaning of that text is, we have seen above; but its brevity and vagueness allow those who so wish—as experience in Palestine has shown—to restrict its meaning much more—indeed, almost to nothing. Everything, therefore, depends on the good will of the "guardian," on whom was placed at San Remo the duty of giving the promise practical effect. Had we paid attention to realities, we should have restrained our feelings, and have waited a little to see how the written word would be interpreted in practice.

I have dwelt perhaps at undue length on this point, because it is the fundamental one. But in truth we are now confronted with other questions, *internal* questions, which demand a solution without delay; and the solutions which we hear from time to time are as far from realities as are the poles asunder. It will not be long, however, before these visionary proposals, which are so attractive, have to make way for actual *work*, and we have to show *in practice* how far we have the material and moral strength to establish the national home which we have been given permission to establish in Palestine.

And at this great and difficult moment I appear before my readers and repeat once more my old warning: Do not press on too quickly to the goal, so long as the actual conditions without which it cannot be reached have not been created; and do not disparage the work which is possible at any given time, having regard to actual conditions, even if it will not bring the Messiah today or tomorrow.

JUDAH L. MAGNES

A Letter to Gandhi

The American-born liberal rabbi Judah L. Magnes (1877–1948)
settled in the Land of Israel in 1921 and became, in 1925, the first
chancellor of the Hebrew University in Jerusalem. In 1935 he
became its president. Magnes was a pacifist and a prophetic
humanist. This idealistic outlook prompted him to advocate Arab–
Jewish understanding and a binational commonwealth where both
nations would live in harmony together. His efforts were unsuccess-
ful. He founded *ha-Ol* (The Yoke), a religious society that taught
"acceptance of the Yoke even unto death of martyrdom; public
sanctification of the divine name; to be a servant of God." *In the
Perplexity of the Times* (1946) is one of the collections of his articles
and addresses. The opening line in "A Letter to Ghandi," the text
that follows, refers to an article by Gandhi in *Harijan*, November 26,
1938. There was no reply.

What you have said recently about the Jews is the one statement I
have yet seen which needs to be grappled with fundamentally.
Your statement is a challenge, particularly to those of us who had
imagined ourselves your disciples.

79

I am sure you must be right in asserting that the Jews of Germany can offer Satyagraha to the "godless fury of their dehumanized oppressors."

But how and when? You do not give the answer. You may say that you are not sufficiently acquainted with the German persecution to outline the practical technique of Satyagraha for use by the German Jews. But one of the great things about you and your doctrine has been that you have always emphasized the chance of practical success, if Satyagraha be offered. Yet to the German Jews you have not given the practical advice which only your unique experience could provide, and I wonder if it is helpful merely in general terms to call upon the Jews of Germany to offer Satyagraha. I have heard that many a Jew of Germany has asked himself how and when Satyagraha must be offered without finding the answer. Conditions in Germany are radically different from those that have prevailed in South Africa and in India. Those of us who are outside Germany must, I submit, think through most carefully the advice we proffer the unfortunates who are caught in the claws of the Hitler beast.

If you take the sentences of your statement as to what you would do were you a German Jew, you will find, I believe, that not just one German Jew, as you require, has had "courage and vision," but many whose names are known and many more who have borne witness to their faith without names being known.

"I would claim Germany as my home." There has never been a community more passionately attached to its home than the German Jews to Germany. The thousands of exiles now to be found everywhere are so thoroughly German mentally, psychologically, in their speech, manners, prejudices, their outlook, that we wonder how many generations it may take before this is uprooted. The history of the Jews in Germany goes back to at least Roman times, and though the Jews throughout their history there have been massacred and driven out on diverse occasions, one thing or the other has always brought them back.

"I would challenge him to shoot me or to cast me into the dungeon." Many Jews—hundreds, thousands—have been shot. Hundreds, thousands have been cast into the dungeon. What more can Satyagraha give them? I ask this question in humility, for I am confident that you can give a constructive answer.

"I would not wait for fellow Jews to join me in civil resistance, but would have confidence that in the end the rest are bound to follow my example." But the question is, how can Jews in Germany offer civil resistance? The slightest sign of resistance means killing or concentration camps or being done away with otherwise. It is usually in the dead of night that they are spirited away. No one, except their terrified families, is the wiser. It makes not even a ripple on the surface of German life. The streets are the same, business goes on as usual, the casual visitor sees nothing. Contrast this with a single hunger strike in an American or English prison, and the public commotion that this arouses. Contrast this with one of your fasts, or with your salt march to the sea, or a visit to the Viceroy, when the whole world is permitted to hang upon your words and be witness to your acts. Has not this been possible largely because, despite all the excesses of its imperialism, England is after all a democracy with a Parliament and a considerable measure of free speech? I wonder if even you would find the way to public opinion in totalitarian Germany, where life is snuffed out like a candle, and no one sees or knows that the light is out.

"If one Jew or all the Jews were to accept the prescriptions here offered, he or they cannot be worse off than now." Surely you do not mean that those Jews who are able to get out of Germany are as badly off as those who must remain? You call attention to the unbelievable ferocity visited upon all the Jews because of the crime of "one obviously mad but intrepid youth." But the attempt at civil resistance on the part of even one Jew in Germany, let alone the community, would be regarded as an infinitely greater crime and would probably be followed by a repetition of this unbelievable ferocity, or worse.

"And suffering voluntarily undergone will bring them an inner strength and joy." I wonder that no one has drawn your attention to the fact that those German Jews who are faithful to Judaism— and they are the majority—have in large measure the inner strength and joy that comes from suffering for their ideals. It is those unfortunate "non-Aryans" who have a trace of Jewish blood

but who have been brought up as German Christians who are most
to be pitied. They are made to suffer, and they do not know why.
Many of them have been raised to despise Jews and Judaism, and
now this despised people, this scorned religion is, in their eyes,
the cause of their suffering. What a tragedy for them!

But as to the Jews—I do not know if there is a deeper and
more widespread history of martyrdom. You can read the story of
it in any Jewish history book, or, if you wish a convenient account,
in the *Jewish Encyclopedia* published in New York a generation
ago. To take Germany alone, you may be interested in one
document that has come down to us from the Middle Ages. It is
called the *Memorbuch* of Nürnberg—Nürnberg of the Nürnberg
laws, whose synagogue has just been torn down, and a 15th-
century covering of a Scroll of the Law stolen and presented
recently to the city's arch-fiend.

The *Memorbuch* gives a list of the places where massacres took
place in Germany during the Crusades from 1096 to 1298. There
are some fifty of these massacres entered chronologically. There is
a further entry of some 65 large pages containing dates and places
with the names of those martyred from 1096 to 1349. Take what
happened in this very Nürnberg on Friday, the 22nd of Ab, 5058
of the Jewish calendar, the 1st of August, 1298 of the Christian
calendar. We find the names of 628 men, women and children,
whole families, old and young, strong and sick, rabbis and scholars, rich and poor, slaughtered on that day—burned, drowned, put
to the sword, strangled, broken on the wheel and on the rack. In
some places the Jewish elders killed the young and then put an
end to their own lives to keep them from the hands of the torturer.

In Spain and Portugal in the thirteenth, fourteenth, and fif-
teenth centuries where Jews were given the chance of conversion
to Christianity, what usually happened in a stricken town was that
about a third converted, and a third succeeded in escaping, and
always at least a third accepted their agony with the praise of God
and His unity on their lips. Hebrew literature is in many ways a
literature of martyrdom. The Talmud, which covers a period of
about 1,000 years, is a literature that grew up in large measure
under oppression, exile and martyrdom, and it contains discus-

sions, traditions and rules bearing upon our duty to accept martyrdom rather than yield to "idolatry, immorality, or the spilling of
blood." The Hebrew liturgy throbs with elegies in which poets and
teachers commemorate the martyrs of one generation after
another.

If ever a people was a people of non-violence through century
after century, it was the Jews. I think they need learn but little
from anyone in faithfulness to their God and in their readiness to
suffer while they sanctify His Name.

What is new and great about you has seemed to me this, that
you have exalted non-violence into the dominant principle of all of
life, both religious, social and political; and that you have made it
into a practical technique both of communing with the divine and
of battling for a newer world, which would respect the human
personality of even the most insignificant outcast. You exhort the
German Jew to add "the surpassing contribution of non-violent
action" to the precious contribution he has already made to
mankind. But you could be of much greater help by showing how
the technique of Satyagraha could be of practical use to the
German Jews.

You would have the right to say that some Jew should point
this technique out. But we have no one comparable to you as
religious and political leader.

There are, as I am aware, other elements besides non-violence
in Satyagraha. There is non-cooperation, and the renunciation of
property, and the disdain of death.

The Jews are a people who exalt life, and they can hardly be
said to disdain death. Leviticus 18:5 reads: "My judgments, which
if a man do he shall live in them," and the interpretation adds, as a
principle of Jewish life, "and not die through them." For this
reason I have often wondered if we Jews are fit subjects for
Satyagraha. As to property, it is but natural that Jews should want
to take along with them a minimum of their property from
Germany or elsewhere, so as not to fall a burden upon others. It
would, I am sure, give you satisfaction to see how large numbers of
refugees, who in Germany were used to wealth, comfort, culture,
have, without too much complaint and very often cheerfully,

buckled down to a new life in Palestine, many of them in the fields or in menial employment in the cities.

It is in the matter of non-cooperation that I have a question of importance to put to you.

A plan is being worked out between the Evian Refugee Committee and the German Government which appears to me to be nothing short of devilish. The details are not yet known. But it seems to amount to this: The German Government is to confiscate all German Jewish property, and in exchange for increased foreign trade and foreign currency which Jews are to bring them, they will permit a limited number of Jews to leave Germany annually for the next several years. The scheme involves the sale of millions of pounds of debentures to be issued by a Refugee or Emigration Bank to be created. Whether Governments are to subscribe to these debentures, I do not know. But certainly the whole Jewish world will be called upon to do so.

Here is the dilemma: If one does not subscribe, no Jews will be able to escape from this prison of torture called Germany. If one does subscribe, one will be cooperating with that Government, and be dealing in Jewish flesh and blood in a most modern and up-to-date slave market. I see before me here in Jerusalem a child who is happy, now that he is away from the torment there; and his brother, or parent, or grandparent. One of the oldest of Jewish sayings is: "Who saves a single soul in Israel is as if he had saved a whole world."[29] Not to save a living soul? And yet to cooperate with the powers of evil and darkness? Have you an answer?

You touch upon a vital phase of the whole subject when you say that, "if there ever could be a justifiable war in the name of and for humanity, a war against Germany, to prevent the wanton persecution of a whole race, would be completely justified. But I do not believe in any war. A discussion of the pros and cons of such a war is therefore outside my horizon and province."

But it is on "the pros and cons of such a war," that I would ask your guidance. The question gives me no rest, and I am sure there are many like myself. Like you, I do not believe in any war. I have pledged myself never to take part in a war. I spoke up for pacifism in America during the World War, alongside of many whose names are known to you. That war brought the "peace" of Versailles and the Hitlerism of today. But my pacifism, as I imagine the pacifism of many others, is passing through a pitiless crisis. I ask myself: Suppose America, England, France are dragged into a war with the Hitler bestiality, what am I to do and what am I to teach? This war may destroy the life of a large part of the youth of the world, and force those who remain alive to lead the lives of savages. Yet I know I would pray with all my heart for the defeat of the Hitler inhumanity; and am I then to stand aside and let others do the fighting? During the last war I prayed for a peace without defeat or victory.

The answer given by Romain Rolland in his little book, *Par la révolution la paix* (1935), seems to be that while he himself as an individual continues to refuse to bear arms, he will do everything he can to help his side (at that time, Russia) to win the war. That is hardly a satisfying answer.

I ask myself how I might feel if I were not a Jew. Is the Hitler iniquity really as profound as I imagine? I recall that during the last war the arguments against Germany were much the same as those of today. I took no stock in those arguments then. Perhaps it is the torture of my own people that enrages me unduly? Yet it is my conviction that, being a Jew, my sense of outrage at injustice may, perhaps, be a bit more alive than the average, and therefore more aware of the evils which the Hitler frenzy is bringing upon all mankind. The Jew, scattered as he is, is an outpost, bearing the brunt earlier of an action against mankind, and bearing it longest. For a dozen reasons, he is a convenient scapegoat. I say this in order to make the point that if the Jew is thoroughly aroused about an evil such as the Hitler madness, his excitement and indignation are apt to be based not only on personal hurt, but on a more or less authentic appraisal of the evil that must be met.

If you will take the trouble of looking at the little pamphlet I am sending, "Fellowship in War" (1936), you will see that I have an ineradicable belief that no war whatsoever can be a righteous war. The war tomorrow for the "democracies" or for some other noble slogan will be just as unrighteous or as fatuous as was the "war to save democracy" yesterday. Moreover, to carry on the war, the democracies will perforce become totalitarian. Not even a war against the ghastly Hitler savagery can be called righteous, for we all of us have sinned, conquerors and conquered alike, and it is because of our sins, because of our lack of generosity and of the spirit of conciliation and renunciation, that the Hitler beast has been enabled to raise its head. Even on the pages of the Nürnberg *Memorbuch* we find the words, "Because of our many sins," this and that massacre took place. There can be no war for something good. That is a contradiction in terms. The good is to be achieved through totally different means.

But a war against something evil? If the Hitler cruelty launches a war against you, what would you do, what will you do? Can you refrain from making a choice? It is a choice of evils—a choice between the capitalisms, the imperialisms, the militarisms of the western democracies, and between the Hitler religion. Can one hesitate as to which is the lesser of these two evils? Is not a choice therefore imperative? I am all too painfully conscious that I am beginning to admit that if Hitler hurls his war upon us, we must resist. For us it would thus become not a righteous war, nor, to use your term, a justifiable war, but a necessary war, not for something good, but, because no other choice is left us, against the greater evil. Or do you know of some other choice?

I have already written you an inordinately long letter, but I must abuse your patience further and refer to Palestine, I hope in not too lengthy a way.

I am burdening you with a further pamphlet of mine called "Like all the Nations?" May I refer you to pages 14 and 15, and then to pages 29–32? You will see that on page 31 I say that we must overcome all obstacles in Palestine "through all the weapons of civilization except bayonets . . . brotherly, friendly weapons"; and on p. 32, the Jew "should not either will or believe in or want a Jewish Home that can be maintained in the long run only against the violent opposition of the Arab and Moslem peoples." There are other Jews who hold the same views and who regard the Mandate as suspect because, as you say, "the Mandate has no sanction but that of the last war." In an address in New York in May, 1919, I said: "Palestine is, so they say, to be 'given' to the Jewish people.

To my mind, no peace conference has the right to give any land to any people, even though it be the Land of Israel to the People Israel. If self-determination be a true principle for other peoples, it is just as true for the Jewish people. . . . If we are to be true democrats, we must be true democrats in Jewish life as well. Our new beginnings in Palestine are burdened by this gift" (p. 60 of the above pamphlet).

But the attachment of Israel to Palestine is as old as the Bible, and there has been no period of history in which this attachment has not expressed itself, and, as we know more and more clearly from archaeological excavations and the recovery of lost documents, there has never been a time when Jewish settlements were utterly absent from the Holy Land.

Jewish life will always be lacking in an essential constituent if Judaism and the Jewish people have no spiritual and intellectual center in Palestine. It is true they can exist without it, as history shows. But they have never ceased experiencing the deep need for such a center and of trying to establish it in Palestine on innumerable occasions. Such a spiritual and religious center must, for the Jewish people, take on the qualities of a National Home. The Jewish people are not like the Catholic Church, for whom the ecclesia is the supreme authority. Judaism is peculiar in this, that it derives its final authority out of life, out of the sufferings, the aspirations, the accumulated traditions, the God-consciousness of a people, composed of ordinary, everyday, hard-working human beings. It is for this reason that the Jewish center cannot be composed only of priests and scholars. The Jewish center to fulfil its true functions, should be endowed with all the problems and possibilities that life itself imposes, and, as no one knows better than yourself, life expresses itself in many forms, political and social, as well as religious and spiritual.

It is, I think, in recognition of all of this that 52 nations accepted the doctrine that the Jews are in Palestine as of "right" and not just on sufferance. Do you not think that all of this, added to the barbarous treatment meted out to Jews in all too many places, constitutes a kind of "right" at least as valid as the other varieties of "rights"?

But essential as the center, or National Home, seems to be, in the opinion of many, for the Jews and Judaism, I think you would find great numbers of Jews agreeing with you that "it would be a crime against humanity to reduce the proud Arabs."

The question is, what is meant by reduce, and are the Arabs being reduced?

You say that "Palestine belongs to the Arabs in the same sense that England belongs to the English."

"Mine is the land" (Leviticus 25:23), saith the Lord.

May I point out at least two ways in which Palestine does not "belong" to the Arabs as England does to the English?

Usually a land "belongs" to that people which has conquered it. That is an ugly fact. The Jews conquered the land long ago. They lost it to conquerors who themselves lost it, and eventually the Arabs conquered it. But the Arabs lost it to the Crusaders, and they again to the Arabs, and they to the Mongols and to the Mamelukes, and they to the Turks, from whom it was conquered by the Allied Powers, primarily by England. The Arabs do not therefore possess political sovereignty from conquest, and the land does not "belong" to them in this sense.

Palestine does "belong" to the Arabs in the sense that they have been in the land in large numbers since the Moslem conquest, that most (by no means all) of those working the land are Arabs, and most (by no means all) of those owning the land are a comparatively small number of Arab landholders, and Arabic is the chief spoken language.

But Palestine is different from England also in this, that it is a sacred land for three monotheistic religions; and in this, that a people, the Jews, who became a people in Palestine and whose great classic, the basis of their life, the Bible, was produced there, have never throughout all the centuries forgotten the land or ceased to yearn for it.

That is a unique fact of no mean importance.

The basic problem is, as you put it, the need for the Jews of settling in Palestine "with the goodwill of the Arabs," and not "under the shadow of the British gun."

I would not be honest if I conveyed the impression to you that in my opinion my people have always gone at this in the right way. They have done wonderful things in building up the land. They have planned intelligently and with high social ideals. They have borne sufferings and hardships willingly. They love the land, and they have been rescuing it from further decay. They have revived the Hebrew tongue. In this sense the land also "belongs" to them. But I am sure that it has been the tragic pressure of Jewish life in Central and Eastern Europe which has made my people impatient and often intolerant. The tragedy of the Jewish wanderer and refugee did not begin with Germany. We have had this problem with us always, and it was one of the chief reasons for the rise of modern Zionism. And now with the German barbarities and what is impending in Poland and elsewhere, the pressure for space and a home has grown to be almost unbearable.

During the past three years, when the Jewish community here has been under continual attack by Arabs, it is a fact that the Jewish community has been non-violent. Our young men and women are hot-blooded, as are others. But there are very few of ascertained reprisals on their part. This self-restraint, this *havlagah*, as it is called, can be ascribed to many factors. But, as the never-ceasing discussion of *havlagah* shows, a deep ethical passion has been the predominant factor in this non-violence.

I wonder, therefore, if the question of the Jews offering "Satyagraha in front of the Arabs" arises in Palestine. The Jewish youth has had organized self-defense units which are now, for the most part, merged with the constituted forces of the country. As far as I am aware, you do not advocate the abolition of police or military forces anywhere. The record shows that in no single instance have the legalized Jewish forces in Palestine committed an act of aggression. I should like to know if you think that the Jewish settlements should have remained, or should now be unarmed, and that when bands come into a town like Tiberias and murder and mutilate babes in their mothers' arms, they should offer "themselves to be shot or thrown into the Dead Sea without raising a little finger against them"? As I have understood Satyagraha, it must, in order to be effective, be offered in front of constituted authority and not in front of merciless assassins.

Will you not speak to the Arabs in terms of Satyagraha? That would also have a profound influence upon the Jews.

Great as is the need for finding a refuge in Palestine for persecuted Jews, and great as are the possibilities of spiritual and intellectual, social and political achievements in the Jewish National Home, there are many who agree with you that we must not "reduce" the Arabs. If I understand what you mean by the word "reduce," I would give it as my opinion after many years of residence in Palestine that the Arabs have not been reduced. But that does not at all absolve the Jews from the primary duty and the vital necessity of "seeking to convert the Arab heart." Perhaps you could help us in this through suggestions?

SIMON DUBNOW

The Sociological View
of Jewish History

The Belorussian Simon Dubnow (1860–1941) tended early toward a
thorough study of Jewish history. After a number of preliminary
researches, including an adaptation of Marcus Brann's *An Outline of
Jewish History,* and after a *History of the Jews in Russia and Poland*
(3 volumes, 1916–1920), he published a ten-volume *Die Weltge-
schichte des jüdischen Volkes* (World History of the Jewish People)
from 1925 to 1929, which was a translation of the original Russian
manuscript. Between 1930 and 1932 his *History of Hasidism* appeared (in Hebrew). History taught him to understand the past.

When still a young man, Dubnow already rejected Jewish
observance and "religion," Zionism, and Hebraism. He advocated
secularism, a universalist outlook and, practically speaking, internal
autonomy of Jewish communities within existing political structures,
with Yiddish as the language of these communities. His *World
History of the Jewish People* is sociologically oriented in contradistinction to Graetz's "suffering and learning" motif. He viewed
Jewish history after the destruction of the Temple as a succession of
partly autonomous "centers," holding that the Jewish communal
system replaced what would normally have been a people's natural
life. His historiography and outlook on life are influenced by Com-
te's positivism, J. S. Mill's individualism, and the beliefs of Ernest
Renan and Leo Tolstoy.

In 1922, Dubnow left his native land for Germany. In 1933 he
took refuge in Riga, Latvia. In 1941, when the Germans occupied

Riga, the old historian was placed in a ghetto and after a short interval put to death.

The piece here reproduced is from Dubnow's introduction to his *World History of the Jewish People*.

World History of the Jewish People is perhaps an unusual title, but it corresponds fully to the content and scope of this unusual segment of the history of mankind. It is customary to speak of world history in conjunction with the general history of highly developed nations, as distinguished from the history of single countries and peoples. The destiny of the Jewish people, however, has unfolded in such a way that it possesses a world history of its own in the literal sense of the word. It embraces in a physical sense almost the entire civilized world (except India and China) and it coincides chronologically with the whole course of the historical microcosm, and thus there is excellent justification for speaking of a world history of the Jewish people.

The dominant method for the world history of Jewry, as for the world history of mankind, must be that of synthesis. The major task of the historian is to clarify the general goals and paths of historical life in varying times and places, and to uncover the organic connection among the individual fragments of time and space, distributed over three thousand years of national development. The historian who follows the synthetic method, and deals with materials already collected and more or less analyzed, must not shirk the labors of independent analysis, of critical examination of the sources and of a re-examination of the facts. On their long historical way, these sources were bound to diminish considerably in reliability and completeness, and without strict re-examination they are bound to cause distorted generalizations. Still, the chief task consists in bringing to the fore the main outlines of the historical process that lie behind the great mass of facts, to draw up a carefully worked-out plan of procedure and then to erect the towering structure of history in keeping with the plan. The first condition for such a work of synthesis, however, is a clear general conception of Jewish history, a clear idea of its bearer or subject, the Jewish people, a conception that is not marred by dogmatic and scholastic concepts; and this in turn will determine in advance the pertinent methods of scientific research.

Until quite recently there were great obstacles in the way of such a scientific conception of the history of the "most historical" of peoples. With regard to the most ancient part of Jewish history, the part which occupies the exceptional position of "sacred history," the theological conception still dominates the minds not only of the orthodox, who accept the religious pragmatism of the historical books of the Bible without reservations, but also of the advocates of free biblical criticism, who substitute their own, no less theological pragmatism, for that of the Bible. In the treatment of the medieval and modern history of the Jews, we likewise find the dominance of a one-sided spiritualistic conception that is based on the axiom that a people deprived of state and territory can play an active role in history only in the field of intellectual life, while elsewhere, in its social life, it is condemned to being a passive object of the history of the peoples among whom it lives. Jewish historiography initiated by Leopold Zunz and Heinrich Graetz thus paid attention mainly to two basic factors in presenting the history of the diaspora: it dealt mostly with intellectual activities and with heroic martyrdom (Geistes- und Leidensgeschichte).

The main content of the entire life of the people was thus usually reduced to a history of literature, on the one hand, and to a martyrology on the other. The horizon of history was confined within these limits. The division into epochs, too, was adapted to this one-sided view of "post-biblical" history. The periods set up were the talmudic, gaonic, rabbinic, mystical and enlightenment periods—a periodization valid for the history of a literature, but not for the history of a nation.

Only recently have we arrived at a more comprehensive and more strictly scientific conception of Jewish history that may be termed "sociological." Basic to this conception is the idea derived from the totality of our history, that the Jewish people has at all times and in all countries, always and everywhere, been the subject, the creator of its own history, not only in the intellectual sphere but also in the general sphere of social life. During the period of its political independence as well as in its stateless period, the Jews appear among the other nations, not merely as a religious community, but with the distinctive characteristics of a nation. This nation, endowed with perennial vitality, fought always and everywhere for its autonomous existence in the sphere of social life as well as in all other fields of cultural activity. Even at the time of the existence of the Judean state, the diaspora had already attained high development and had its autonomous communities everywhere. Later on, it also had central organs of self-administration, its own legislative institutions (corresponding to the Sanhedrin, the Academies and patriarchs in Roman-Byzantine Palestine; exilarchs, geonim, and legislative academies in Babylonia; the *aljamas* and congresses of communal delegates in Spain; *kahals* and *vaads,* or congresses of *kahals,* in Poland and Lithuania, etc.). The latest national movement among the Jews, linked as it is with this historical process and combining the older heritage of autonomism with the modern principle of national minority rights, testifies to the immortality of this eternal driving force of Jewish history. Even during the epoch of assimilation and of revolutionary change in the life of the people, it has been able to assert itself.

The causes of the one-sided conception of Jewish history, which was still widespread in the recent past, are obvious. Scientific Jewish historiography originated in western Europe in the middle of the nineteenth century, when the dogma of assimilation held complete sway there. This dogma asserted that Jewry is not a nation, but a religious community. Jewish historiography was also carried away by the general current and therefore concerned itself more with the religion of Judaism than with its living creator, the Jewish people. Even an opponent of this universally accepted dogma, like Graetz, was not able to go counter to this current. The profound revolution of national consciousness which characterizes our age inevitably wrought a transformation in our conception of the historical process. The secularization of the Jewish national idea was bound to effect the secularization of historical writing, liberating it from the shackles of theology and, subsequently, of spiritualism or scholasticism. A new conception of Jewish history came into being, a conception much more appropriate for the content as well as the scope of this history. Slowly the awareness grew that the Jewish people had not been entirely absorbed all these centuries by its "thought and suffering," but that it had concerned itself with constructing its life as a separate social unit, under the most varied conditions of existence, and that, therefore, it was the foremost task of historiography to try to understand this process of building the life of the Jewish people.

The subject of scientific historiography is the people, the national individuality, its origin, its growth, and its struggle for existence. In the course of a succession of centuries, the initially amorphous national cell became differentiated from the surrounding milieu of the peoples of the ancient Orient, took on a firmly outlined national form, established its own state and then lost it again, integrated in its own way the elements of universal culture which it had absorbed and, while so doing, lifted its spiritual creativity to the heights of the prophetic movement. The movement toward the final formation of the national type coincided with that of the first political catastrophe (the Babylonian Exile), and the succeeding Persian, Greek, Hasmonaean and Roman epochs were marked by the rivalry between theocracy and the secular state. The second political catastrophe, brought on by the irresistible onslaught of Rome, gave rise to new forms of struggle by the dispersed people for its national unity. The indomitable urge to autonomous life and to the preservation of the greatest measure of social and cultural individuality while amidst alien peoples found expression, not in political, but in other social forms. The entire spiritual vitality of the nation came to be directed to this goal. The religion of Judaism was fashioned in accordance with the image of social conditions of the nation's existence, and not the reverse.

From the realistic and sociological conception of Jewish history there follows of necessity a new evaluation of many of the important individual historical events, which have previously been interpreted from the theological or scholastic point of view. We shall cite a few especially appropriate examples to illustrate the difference between the new and the older conception of interpreting the outstanding problems of Jewish history.

The older historiography was in hopeless confusion regarding the problem of the Pharisees and Sadducees, whose mutual relations were so decisive for the national life during the Hasmonaean and Roman periods. Even the historians who were not influenced by theology attributed the origin of these parties to religious-ritualistic and dogmatic controversies. These historians, basing their interpretation on the Hellenistic and philosophically colored history of Flavius Josephus, and also on the later talmudic traditions in which the political element had already become disintegrated, converted the most significant national controversy—the controversy over the very character of the national type itself, that is, whether the Jewish people should be a worldly or a spiritual nation, a nation like the average member of the international family or a unique type of people—into a struggle between "sects" or "schools." The controversy between the two parties, however, also had a social background. The Sadduceean aristocracy, which clung to political power, fought against the Phariseean democracy, which was chiefly interested in its spiritual influence upon the masses of the people. This sociological view of the origin and activity of these parties, which is elaborated in the second volume of this history, follows necessarily from everything we know about the political and spiritual conflict between the Pharisees and the Sadducees and from their entire record of activity from the Hasmonaean epoch down to the collapse of the state of Judea. The religious and ritualistic differences were merely incidental to the profound national and social antagonisms of both parties. Their conflicting attitude toward the Oral Law was only a consequence of their difference of opinion on the vital question of the propriety of Judea's creating a fence around itself and isolating itself from the surrounding culture and way of life of the Graeco-Roman world.

Another instance of distortion of true historical perspective in the older viewpoint is the generally accepted evaluation of the significance of the Sanhedrin at Jamnia [Jabne]. At the moment of the greatest upheaval in Jewish history, after the destruction of the Jewish state by the Romans, a center of self-administration was formed in a town close to devastated Jerusalem. Historians accepting the naive though beautiful legend, according to which Rabbi

Yohanan ben Zakkai escaped with the permission of the Romans from beleaguered Jerusalem and founded an academy for the study of the Torah in Jamnia, estimate in various ways the significance of this new establishment for the subsequent destiny of the Jews. While some glorify the heroic raising of the banner of scholarship upon the ruins of statehood, others see in it the beginning of national decay and of the ossification of Judaism in the letter of the Law. In reality both are wrong, since the idea that the center established in Jamnia was primarily a scholarly academy is wholly erroneous. What really happened there was one of the most significant acts of national and social reorganization. Not an academy was established in Jamnia, but a center of nomocracy, a center of administration by means of the authority of the Law. The academy for talmudic law was identical with the legislative body or the Sanhedrin which, after the destruction of the state, was called upon to weld together and unite the scattered fragments of the Jewish people by the ties of homogeneous laws regulating the entire internal life on an autonomous basis. From here resounded the call to reorganize the defeated national army and to substitute a new social order for the shattered forms of political life. This is, above all, a chapter in the history of national reconstruction and only secondarily of the history of religion, learning and literature.

Other complex historical problems can likewise be brought closer to solution by means of the sociological approach. Thus the antinomy between nationalism and universalism and the conflict between political and spiritual forces in the activity of the prophets become intelligible. This conflict between two principles, which was caused by Israel's position among the states of the ancient Orient, is resolved in the great synthesis of the prophetic movement. The nation is the core and the state is merely the shell, and if the shell is broken the core remains nonetheless intact. If the core is sound the nation will succeed in maintaining its autonomy against the heteronomy of its surrounding environment, and it will stand as a model of spiritual steadfastness. The exact opposite of this doctrine was later preached by the prophet and apostles of Christianity. They held that only the individual religious personality has worth and not the collective historical individuality in the form of the nation. These new prophets wanted to plunge the Jewish nation into the abyss of non-existence at the very moment it was locked in a life and death struggle with insatiable, all-devouring Rome, and, in consequence, the prophets of national suicide were particularly unpalatable to the healthy national instincts of self-preservation. This also clarifies the deep meaning of talmudism, and its iron national discipline of religious sanctions, for all subsequent Jewish history. The Talmud is above all the literary monument of the national hegemony of the Jewish autonomous centers in Roman Palestine and Persian Babylonia, the perpetual expression of centuries-long efforts made by national leaders who made it their most important goal to clothe the softening national core with the firm cover of the Law.

I am fully persuaded that the general conception presented here is the only possible presupposition for a scientifically objective methodology of Jewish historiography. This conception provides a way out for our historiography from the labyrinth of theological and metaphysical theories and places it upon a firm bio-sociological foundation. The subject of investigation is not an abstraction but a living organism which has developed out of an original biological germ, the "tribe," into a complex cultural historical whole, the nation. The method of investigation is strictly evolutionary. The period of the formation of the national individuality is to be examined first; then, after this individuality has assumed a more fixed form, the period of its struggle for separate existence, for the preservation and unfolding of its characteristic national traits and of the cultural treasures it accumulated in the course of centuries. In presenting this dual process of individuation and struggle for the emerging individuality, we start from the basic assumption that a strong and clearly molded national collective personality as the product of historical evolution is, not only a natural phenomenon, but also represents a high cultural value. This, however, by no means implies that the historian must consider as valuable all those direct or winding paths that led to the preservation of the collective personality. If, for example, he is forced to recognize normal separation as an indispensable condition of national existence, he must not fail, on the other hand, to point out those periods during which cultural isolation—even though it was often necessary for the purpose of self-preservation—led to deplorable excesses, culminating in the complete alienation of the Jewish people from the valuable achievements of universal culture. It is incumbent upon him to present a vivid description of the struggle between centripetal and centrifugal forces that no national organism can escape, as well as the tragic conflicts in the life of the people induced thereby. The historian, however, who starts with the firm acceptance of national individuality as a cultural value, will evaluate the end results of the centripetal and constructive efforts differently from the centrifugal and destructive tensions.

Another obvious postulate of the sociological method is that due consideration be given in historiography, not only to the social and national, but also to the socio-economic factors which were so badly neglected by the old school. This is not to be interpreted as a concession to the materialist interpretation of history, which seeks to reduce all historical facts to the evolution of the economic conditions of life. We do not reject the antiquated, spiritualistic conception of history only to become captives of the opposite doctrine, the no less one-sided materialistic view of history which equally obscures all historical perspective. The economic order, like the cultural order, is but one element of the natural and social conditions of the nation's life. Commanding sovereignty over the life of the nation is exercised by the totality of all social and spiritual factors it creates. Consideration of the reciprocal relations between the individual factors shows that there is interdependence as well as conflict among them. We find nowhere, however, that all these varied functions of life are subordinate to any one single factor.

The full value of this new conception of Jewish history is especially apparent to those who, like the author of this work, had themselves previously strayed along the crooked path of the old Jewish historiography. I myself at one time acclaimed the generally accepted principles without reservation. I myself passed through all the above-mentioned phases of historical thinking, in my search for a comprehensive synthesis of Jewish history, a synthesis which I pursued unceasingly from the first day of my scientific research. [. . .] The deficiencies of the old method became increasingly clear to me only after I had spent many years in detailed examination of the sources of general Jewish history, and after I had to write a history of the Jewish nation and not only of its literature. At the same time, the frame of investigation and generalization was visibly broadened and the historical horizon opened up until what was once hidden behind the veil of scholastic mystification finally came to the fore. Then I undertook to check the results I had arrived at inductively by the opposite, the deductive method, and I found that my conclusions, which had thus turned into assumptions, were fully confirmed when applied to the historical materials.

YEHEZKEL KAUFMANN

On the Fate and
Survival of the Jews

The biblical scholar and intellectual historian of Judaism, Yehezkel
Kaufmann (1889–1963) was born in the Ukraine, studied Judaica in
Odessa and Petrograd and philosophy in Berne, Switzerland. After
World War I he lived in Berlin and in 1928 settled in the Land of
Israel. In 1949 he became professor of Bible at the Hebrew University. In *Golah ve-Nekhar* (Diaspora and Alien Lands), 1929–30, he
examined the reason for the Jewish people's survival in the diaspora;
he found in religion the force that overcame all elements of dissolution. This major work is *Toledot ha-Emunah ha-Yisraelit*, eight
volumes, 1937–57, abridged in an English version by Moshe
Greenberg under the title *The Religion of Israel* (1960). In this
work, the records of biblical faith from its beginnings to the Babylonian exile are investigated in detail and with great acumen. Contrary to the opinion of modern Old Testament scholarship that sees
biblical religion as developing from pagan origins, Kaufmann main-
tains the primacy of monotheism in Israel; the Bible, he asserts,
shows no evidence of polytheistic mythology. The one God is God
of all humanity. The first chapters of Genesis depict humanity
rather than a particular people, and the messianic vision of the
prophets pertains to a united world that has accepted pure
monotheism. Christianity and Islam continued the Judaic opposition
to idolatry. Nothing but moral goodness will bring redemption; the
prophetic imperative still stands. Our selection is from *Golah
ve-Nekhar*.

The singular history of the people of Israel consists of a unique
combination of two basic factors: the *national* and the *religious*.
Operative in this history were the qualities of its ethnic existence,
a certain action of political forces, the laws of demography and of
the extension of settlement, the laws of national assimilation, the
influence of the religious basis upon the life of Israel and of the
peoples in whose midst it lived and functioned. Although out of
the operation of these factors there emerged a history which bears
a unique and anomalous character, we can understand and explain
this history empirically only by a study of the nature of these
factors, by a study of their foundation which operates in human
history in general. The exile of Israel is a unique sociological
phenomenon in the history of the world, but its roots are planted
in the nature of the ethnic and the religious factors, and in the
manner of their causal operation in the life of every people.

From such an empirical historical examination the question of
Israel's fate takes on a new form which is totally different from that
which was given it by the earlier religious outlook, whether Jewish
or Christian. The religious outlook struggled with the question of
the destruction of ancient Israel, the subjugation, the dispersion,
the exile. Why did idolatrous nations destroy the kingdom of Israel
and why were they allowed to subjugate Israel and to exile it from
its land? The question was basically one of *reason* and *purpose*,
and the religious outlook in its own way sought an answer. From
the viewpoint of an empirical historical study the problem ceases
to be a problem. The destruction and the dispersion in themselves
are phenomena such as we find in the history of many nations.
Assyria, Babylonia, and Rome did not destroy only the state of
Israel or subjugate only the people of Israel. Therefore this destruction and this subjugation do not require a special explanation:
the determining factor was the relation between the political forces
of Israel and those of its conquerors. But, on the other hand, there
arises the difficult problem of a singular phenomenon which we
find in the history of Israel and of no other people: *the existence of
the people of Israel in its dispersion and exile*. For the religious, or
teleological, conception, the explanation of this phenomenon is not
very difficult. The existence of the people of Israel, the sole bearer
of God's true teaching, has a clear purpose; this existence fits

nicely into the divine scheme embodied in history, into the view of history as a "Divine Comedy." Yet for the causal study of history it presents a difficult problem.

The basic question does not concern the war which the people of Israel waged for its physical existence during the generations of the exile, the war for a loaf of bread or a place of rest. With all of its anomalous and unique conditions, this war is nevertheless not in itself a singular phenomenon. It is the war which every ethnic group wages with its surroundings. This struggle for existence, despite its exilic form, is essentially the same as the war of the people of Israel with its enemies in ancient times. Formerly, Israel fought its battle for life by the sword like every other people. During the generations of the exile it gradually learned other modes of warfare. Not with a mighty hand, not with their sword and bow, did the Jews come to distant lands to seek a livelihood, but with their staff and their pack. When their neighbors made trouble in one country, they wandered to another. Their God dealt charitably with them in that he scattered them among the nations and taught them to wander from land to land. A people of one-time shepherds and farmers eventually became merchants in some places, and moneylenders in others. They possessed no noblemen or proud aristocrats living by the sword. But many of them succeeded valiantly with their money, and others turned to intellectual disciplines, thereby gaining both sustenance and honor. In place of ministers of state and heroes of war, there arose among them *shtadlanim*[30] and *parnasim;*[31] in place of political organization there emerged inner unity and extensive solidarity. This entire war, together with its implements, is the natural and common war for existence which teaches living creatures to use all their abilities and to adapt as much as possible to the conditions of life. Although this struggle for existence is of major importance, it is not the basic problem in the history of Israel. Since the people of Israel did not cease being a special ethnic group even after it went into exile, it was obviously required to wage the struggle for existence of every ethnic group, though under special conditions and in special ways, as demanded by the circumstances of life in the exile.

The basic problem for historical inquiry is the phenomenon

itself, which previously was not a problem at all—the very nature of Israel's national particularity in the diaspora: Why did it not cease being an ethnic group? What is the reason for the fact that the people of Israel persisted in being a nation although faced with conditions of life such as always entail, without exception, national assimilation? It is a law that every nation and tribe defends itself against enemies which rise against it to destroy or to dispossess it. But it is also a law that every nation and tribe which is scattered or intermingled among other nations becomes swallowed up and absorbed by them. What, therefore, brought it about that the people of Israël should be a single people despite its being scattered and dispersed among the nations?

In order to be able to understand this problem fully, we must emphasize the *singular character* of Israel's existence in the diaspora. When the people of Israel was scattered among the nations, it, too, went the way which was laid out for every scattered and dispersed people—the way of assimilation. The Jews were influenced by the culture of their neighbors, became attached and clung to the lands of their habitation, learned the ways of their neighbors, adopted their manners and customs, their clothing, food and drink, etc. That is, the nature of social reality drew Israel toward national absorption. The change of language, which the Jewish people underwent, is particularly important in this connection—language is a people's primary expression of ethnicity, and forgetting its language means the extinction of the ethnic group. Not the dispersion in and of itself is unique to exilic Jewry: many nations have a "dispersion," i.e., they are divided into smaller units which dwell in different parts of the world. But there is no people in the world which was scattered among other nations, adopted their languages, and nevertheless continued to exist. On the one hand, dispersion and linguistic assimilation, and on the other, national distinctiveness for numerous generations— this is the special quality of the people of Israel which makes its existence a singular and special problem in the history of the nations. . . .

[. . .] If we examine the culture of Israel from its *general aspect,* its universal and secular content, we see that in this regard it deserves no special consideration nor does it possess any particular power which might be able to motivate men to struggle for many generations against the nature of reality for the sake of their national distinctiveness. Idolatry produced richer and deeper cultures than the culture of Israel. Babylonia, Egypt, Persia, Greece, and Rome produced grand and sublime works in philosophy, science, poetry, art, morality, law, and politics. In many respects these nations outdid Israel immeasurably in their creative powers; and in numerous other respects they at least approximated it. But what was the fate of those cultures and the fate of the nations which created them? Whatever was good and beautiful in these cultures became the legacy of all peoples. But as for the nations which produced the cultures, when their time came, they were either dispersed and perished or, due to the circumstances of the time, the special connection between them and their culture was broken. From this we learn that the spiritual wealth of a culture, its universal value and greatness, cannot save a group from extinction. Roman civilization, Latin language and literature, Roman law—even the Roman Empire—continued to exist for a long time after the Roman *people* disintegrated and perished. The peculiar force which united the scattered people of Israel and preserved its distinctiveness in foreign lands is therefore not to be found in its culture—however great—to the extent that the culture is a secular and universal creation.

It is even less possible to find this force in the national foundations of Israel's civilization, in its historical *forms*. To the degree that they served as bases for secular existence, there was no singular quality to Israel's land, language, customs, historical memories, or way of life. All the power of these foundations of life, in every instance, lies in their being forms of life which possess a natural existence, in their serving as a garment for the nature of reality. They influence the lives of men and nations and they arouse them to fight for them as long as they exist and *because* they exist. But a land *of the fathers*, a *dead* language, an *artificial* mode of life—all these no longer possess secular, natural, and normal force. Why should we suppose that the love of the Jews for their land, their language, their songs, their customs, their food and drink, their clothing—to the extent that each of these was the product of secular human life, ways of fulfilling physiological or spiritual needs—was singular and different from the normal love of every man for his ethnic mode of life? In any case, history proves that there is no basis whatsoever for this supposition. More than once the Jews clung to the lands of their exile with a faithful love. They learned the foreign languages, spoke them, thought and wrote poetry in them. As a living language, Hebrew was forgotten, and in more than one land the Jews' mode of life in every respect resembled that of their neighbors. Not here, therefore, should we seek the secret of the distinctiveness.

Entirely different from the secular cultural dimension is the dimension of religion. On the one hand, religion differs in its general character from the other components of culture. It is in the nature of religion to subjugate a person to its fixed values and to compel him to guard them well in all the circumstances of life. On the other hand, we find that religious creativity was embodied in Israel in a *singular form* like none other in the world. Therefore, it is in the operation of this unique factor, no doubt, that one must seek the secret of the special course of Israel's history.

Indeed, when we examine the people of Israel's national consciousness in the diaspora, we see that all of the values to which it clung and by which it lived were *religious* values. The land, the language, the memories, the past with all of its heroes, its destiny, race, customs—all of these were not taken as secular matters; they were sublimated and became religious values. Of course, there were in its life secular national forces as well; vital biological forces were also operative. The wars of Israel with its enemies in the Hellenistic period and in the Roman period, as well as the struggle for existence in the Christian and Muslim worlds, are a people's secular conflicts. But the ultimate source of all such manifestations of life is religious. "Israel" itself is a religious concept. The highest ideal inscribed on the soul of the nation, the ideal for which it waged a desperate struggle—the existence of Israel—is a religious ideal. This is not Israel as a collection of the descendants of a single ancestor which at one time inhabited a single land and constituted a single state, but rather Israel as the bearer of the word of God, which lives by the commandment of God. Israel's genealogical consciousness is religious, not aristocratic and secular. "Abraham," the progenitor of the nation, is first of all a religious figure, and the feeling of attachment which binds the individual to the nation is a religious sentiment. Of course this love contains, as well, an element of fraternal love which is racial and secular. But the particular thrill which accompanies this sentiment and augments it with a special force is religious: Israel is a *holy* nation. The fundamental aspiration which aroused the nation to struggle with its total environment, which aroused its conscious and instinctive forces and armed them for war, was the aspiration to establish Israel as the bearer of religious sanctity and religious goals. The idea, therefore, which operated in the depths of the nation's soul, which compelled it to walk on its special path and impressed its seal upon all the manifestations of its life, was a religious idea.

A *religious idea*—not religion as a regimen of laws and commandments, as one is accustomed to think. The religious idea began to play its special unifying role in the life of Israel as early as the Babylonian Exile, during the period when the religion had not yet crystallized into a fixed regimen of laws. It singled Israel out from the nations still before the Torah had become the people's book. Even before Ezra, even before the canonization of the Torah, it brought about the remarkable phenomenon of the return to Zion. Those scholars who consider Ezra the father of Jewish particularity and his commandments the beginning of the later Judaism ignore the fact that Ezra began his activity after about 150 years of particularity. The late laws and commandments did not create the attachment of the people to the religious idea; they were its natural result. The religion and its laws were not *means* which someone invented to preserve the people from extinction or the race from mixture, as one is accustomed to think; *their action was that of a primary cause.* Isolated commandments and ordinances were indeed established as a fence and shield against foreign influence. But here, too, the internal force which created these was the power of faith: the power of the fundamental idea of the existence of Israel, the bearer of the religion of God. Moreover, one must not think that religion was only *one* of the forces which sustained the nation, along with other factors. Of course, various forces operated in the life of Israel and in different periods left their mark upon it. The political lot of the people was of decisive importance in its life and it ultimately determined the lot of its religion. But all of these factors were joined to the religious factor. The one and only primary cause for Israel's individuality in the diaspora was its religion alone. It constituted the cultural foundation to which the nation clung even after it lost its national treasures; it was an attachment which caused it to distinguish itself from its neighbors and to create for itself a particular kind of life. Thus religion was the sole source of its national will. In the workshop of its religion, that life was created for which the people struggled against the nature of reality. Its religion created the idea of Israel together with all its ramifications. Were it not for the operation of this primary force which fashioned and sustained the goal and purpose of Israel's struggle for its distinctiveness, there would certainly have been no place for this battle and for all of the auxiliary forces it embraced.

However, if at first religion functioned in the life of Israel as a positive faith, in the course of time it became a social force independent of faith in the narrow sense. The fact that the breakdown of faith in modern times has not reduced the stature of Judaism, nor put an end to the struggle of Israel with its surroundings, has provided historical scholarship with the possibility of ascribing the existence of Judaism to an objective factor aside from the religious one. But the truth is that the religion itself is the objective factor which operates even where there is no longer faith—religion in its broad sense, the religious factor in the full scope of its social function.

WALTHER RATHENAU

Of Faith: A Polemic

Walther Rathenau (1867–1922), born in Berlin, succeeded his father Emil Rathenau as president of Allgemeine Elektrizitäts-Gesellschaft (General Electrical Company), one of the three leading enterprises in Germany. At the beginning of World War I he directed the distribution of raw materials for the war in the Prussian war ministry, took part in the preparations for the Peace Conference at Versailles (1919) and for the London Conference (1921); he became German minister of reconstruction (1921), represented Germany at the Cannes Conference, was foreign minister (1922), and signed the Rapallo Treaty with Soviet Russia (1922).

As a thinker, Rathenau was a moralist who envisioned a new humane society; he opposed mechanization of life. His collected works, in five volumes, include *Von kommenden Dingen* (In Days to Come), 1917, and *Die neue Gesellschaft* (The New Society), 1919. As for his attitude toward Judaism: in a pseudonymous essay, "Hoere, Israel" (Hear, O Israel), published in 1897, he called for radical assimilation and complete adaptation to German thought and way of life. Later this view changed. He became conscious of the elements of freedom and choice in Judaism, and of the absence of dogma in it. In response to an appeal by a Prussian nobleman, Curt von Trützschler-Falkenstein, that Jews convert to Christianity, he replied that such a step would mean leaving a free community of believers and entering an organized church, a mechanized form of faith, with priests, dogmas, sacraments, images, liturgies. This defense he proffers in "Of Faith: A Polemic," issued in 1917. It is interesting to compare this response to Moses Mendelssohn's answer to Lavater.

Rathenau, a victim of lifelong hostility engendered by his Judaism, was assassinated by nationalist terrorists on June 24, 1922.

You ask for a comment on your treatise, *The Solution of the Jewish Problem in Germany;* and you do that by appealing, as you put it, to my humanism. If I understand you rightly, you invoke my sense of the fellowship of humanity and my consciousness of the unity of the human spirit.

Your treatise is inspired by pure faith and humane convictions. This is why I am moved by your appeal. And the leisurely calm of this wartime Good Friday, so grim and un-springlike, will be devoted to you and to your reflections.

You ask that the German Jews embrace Christianity. In the last two thousand years the same demand has been often put forth, in loving kindness, and in hate and wrath. This in itself does not make your demand unjustified. For questions and answers change their aspect according to the times they mirror. Your arguments are not those of Lavater, and my reply will not be Mendelssohn's.[32]

Judaism an Undogmatic Faith

Let me say first a few words about the Mosaic creed, the features of which have likewise changed in the course of centuries. First it was a tribal faith, then a church religion, and then it was subjected to dogmatic speculation and the influence of enlightened deism; finally it was exposed to the disintegrating effects of scientific investigation. To many, the innermost essence of this creed has proved a riddle difficult to solve. There are Jews who cling to primeval rites and scholastic minutiae—just as there are Christians in certain regions of Germany whose effigies of the Holy Virgin exchange visits with one another or whose consecrated symbols are driven about in carriages. There are Jews who dissolve their concept of God into sheer pantheism—just as there are Christians who read communistic ethics into the salvation doctrine of the Gospels.

Nevertheless, Judaism, like Christianity, can be apprehended as a pure concept in a timeless sense, under the aspect of eternity, to which the disturbing inflections of place, period, and culture are of no more moment than the streaks in the crystal lenses of a refractor.

In contrast to post-Pauline Christianity, the Mosaic religion forms no church. The law of the land may organize Jews into religious communities; but this is a state measure, not a religious one. There is no Temple; the one that stood on Zion hill while Judaism was still embodied in a state religion and church is destroyed, and no law commands that it be rebuilt. The houses of prayer called synagogues are simply schools or places of worship where the rites of the cult may be performed at the discretion of the particular community. No law requires their attendance. Those who perform the religious rites are not priests but officers of the cult or, as their name implies, teachers of the congregation. They are appointed and they are dismissed. They have no authority to interpret the faith in any binding sense, let along prescribe doctrine. Even as a body they lack the authority and power to do this. They cannot join, they cannot separate; they can neither grant nor withhold eternal grace. The authority to supervise religious belief, enforce ecclesiastical discipline, or excommunicate rests neither with them nor with their congregations—nor with anyone else on earth. Ceremonial practices are voluntary: no one has to join in them, and it is up to the congregation concerned to determine their forms. To abstain from them does not involve the forfeiture of any right. There are a great many cultivated Jews who lead a religious life, yet never participate in ceremonial observances or ever visit a house of prayer. They are not subject to reprimand or reproach from anyone.

What then is the factor unifying this church-less religion? Only the profession of belief in the oneness of God. The Hebrew original form of this profession of belief has four words; in our language they go as follows: "The Lord our God, the Lord is One."[33]

For a long time the books of the Pentateuch, with all their ritual, social, juridical, and hygienic prescriptions, were regarded as canonical. And there still may be numerous congregations, especially in Eastern Europe, that remain under the spell of this canon. But many of its regulations can no longer be complied with, as, for example, all those that relate to the priestly caste and the Ark of the Covenant. Thus, as in the days of Ezra and Nehemiah the Pentateuch was compiled, emended, and canonized in the course of one human generation, so any single individual could and can strip it, in part or in whole, of its binding power. No religious authority exists which can restore it to that status of state-ecclesiastical law to which it was raised by men at the time of the great Persian empire.

There have never been any other canonical writings. The prophetical, historical, and poetical books of the Old Testament, the enormous literature of the commentators, and the decisions and codifications of later times have in the course of centuries given edification and joy, hope and sorrow, fear and despair. Regarded at moments as infallible, at other times completely rejected, they have been treated with every conceivable degree of esteem and lack of esteem. Yet, whether they were made responsible for truth or for error, they have always remained the handiwork of men.

No educated man at present can be expected to remain faithful to the teachings of a philosopher of the past; just as little can a believing Jew be bound by the teachings and decisions of any religious authority no matter how ancient its prestige. Neither messianic faith nor the creation of the world, neither the Seven Heavens nor the divine Throne-Chariot, neither the sanctity of the Sabbath nor the separation of clean from unclean—none of these is an inalienable element of religious salvation or religious wisdom. The Jew can reject them all, invoking the old formula of spiritual freedom which declares: "My soul too was present at Sinai."[34] The Mosaic religion is not only without a church, it is also without a dogma.

You will believe, I trust, that I do not bring all this up in order to glorify Judaism. The time is past when religions were praised or vilified in disputes and controversies. Today we feel that form and action, language and poetry, thought and belief are organic expressions of the soul, which cannot be transformed or exchanged at will. Therefore I can understand that one raised within the fixed and unambiguous forms and disciplines of a church might find a shapelessness, if not a lack of control, in the flexibility and the freedom of impulse granted by an undogmatic faith. It seems significant to me, however, that this flexibility, inherent in all the great Oriental religions, has withstood the test of centuries. It was able to survive and assimilate the intellectual content of antiquity, of the Christian Middle Ages, and of modern philosophy and science. And it could accomplish all this without struggle or bitterness and without surrendering its own essence.[35]

The Jewish Problem

Let me return to your demand. Anyone wishing to join an ecclesiastical community must not only examine his attitude toward dogmas and symbols the interpretations of which have been laid down once and for all and can hardly be affected by the course of events; he must also take a political position. He has to acknowledge and reconcile himself to the power concept of the state church, and to approve of it by the very nature of his decision. Without this concept no denominational divisions would be visible; your whole problem of inter-denominational reconciliation would disappear, and with it the solution you proposed for that problem.

My letter has grown into a dissertation, and Easter Sunday—a bright and cool one—is already past. I am reluctant to close this dissertation with a flat "no." I have circled away from your problem and then back to it, first by way of the church and then by way of the state church. Let me point out the prospects which met my eyes along the way.

You conceive of the Jewish problem as a religious one. I have not contradicted you as to that; for, apart from its social aspect dealt with repeatedly in my writings, the problem also has a religious side, which used to be regarded as its chief aspect, but which for a long time now has not received due consideration.

The religious problem too requires solution, and I share your hopeful expectation that it will be achieved by reconciliation alone. And I mean by that a real reconciliation, not an amalgamation. The variegated wealth of all things created and begotten on earth, found in all realms and epochs, in all elements and minds, is so magnificent and so inviolable that no truly creative idea has the right to demand that anything organic and deeply rooted be sacrificed once and for all for the sake of some other organic entity. All reconciliation is synthesis.

Let me make myself clearer.

I want the supreme life of the religious consciousness and I believe in an absolute truth which is reflected in the finite human mind. But I do not hold religions and churches to be identical in general. I regard churches to be the mundane forms—mechanizing forms, I called them—which enclose pure faith, protecting it from the onslaught of time and adapting it to the masses according to their kind and capacity. I believe in the survival, the sacred mission, and the growing spiritualization of churches, and I praise those most of all which organically sustain their living existence through self-renewal and development. But I also believe in the possibility of a faith without a church, the free congregation and personal credo. I consider the degree of intensity with which religion penetrates life to be the measure of the strength of earthly faith, not the number of adherents of any particular religious form. I believe in the inner necessity of variety in the forms of belief, and would sooner see that variety increased than lessened. For, just as the energy of life realizes itself in thousandfold forms, divine energy realizes itself in the thousandfold variousness of its radiance.

I am in favor of the Christian state, for we together with the whole western world of thought and feeling have grown up on its soil. But I do not think that state power or a state church is necessary to keep the Christian spirit alive in countries with numberless millions of Christian subjects. Were they needed, it would follow that the present forms of Christian belief had lost their vitality and stood in need of transformation. But this is not the case; in our own time Christianity has gained new strength in just those states which are alienated from and even hostile to churches. The state owes aid and support to every form of faith, provided its following is large enough and its teachings are not contrary to reason and morality. But to draw a political conclusion from the fact of membership in one of the recognized religious denominations is not in accord with political justice.

I am in favor of religious education. But I am in favor neither of religious schools nor of ecclesiastical control of schools. The state may supervise education through civil agencies to see that nothing is taught which might conflict with morality or the tenets of a particular faith. The state may also require and supervise the exercise and acceptance of religious instruction, and test its results. But any attempt to force the propagation of specific and one-sided forms of faith would not be consistent with the dignity of a mature and educated people.

We live and breathe in anticipation of liberty. But the German people will never demand license or anarchy. If there actually is a realm where freedom is tangible, and if that realm can be called the kingdom of souls and the Kingdom of God, then its earthly image, the kingdom of faith, must also be one of freedom.

ALBERT EINSTEIN

Jewish Ideals

The German-born Albert Einstein (1879–1955), who was to become one of the most famous scientists in the world, was trained in physics and mathematics at Zurich University and published his first important papers in 1905. A professor in Zurich and Prague, he became director of the Kaiser Wilhelm Academy of Science in Berlin in 1914. He found a single mathematical formula that included the laws of electromagnetism and gravitation, and won the 1921 Nobel Prize for Physics. In 1933 he resigned from the Academy, renounced his German citizenship, and accepted a professorship of theoretical physics at Princeton's Institute of Advanced Study. As a Jew he spoke up for justice, peace, the upbuilding of the Land of Israel, and a cosmic religious feeling. The two sections that follow are from his *Ideas and Opinions* (1954), a record of earlier essays and speeches.

The pursuit of knowledge for its own sake, an almost fanatical love of justice and the desire for personal independence—these are the features of the Jewish tradition which make me thank my stars that I belong to it.

Those who are raging today against the ideals of reason and individual liberty and are trying to establish a spiritless state-slavery by brute force rightly see in us their irreconcilable foes. History has given us a difficult row to hoe; but so long as we remain devoted servants of truth, justice and liberty, we shall continue not merely to survive as the oldest of living peoples, but

by creative work to bring forth fruits which contribute to the
ennoblement of the human race, as heretofore. [. . .]

In the philosophical sense there is, in my opinion, no specifically Jewish point of view. Judaism seems to me to be concerned
almost exclusively with the moral attitude in life and to life. I look
upon it as the essence of an attitude to life which is incarnate in
the Jewish people rather than the essence of the laws laid down in
the Torah and interpreted in the Talmud. To me, the Torah and
the Talmud are merely the most important evidence of the manner
in which the Jewish conception of life held sway in earlier times.

The essence of that conception seems to me to lie in an
affirmative attitude to the life of all creation. The life of the
individual only has meaning in so far as it aids in making the life of
every living thing nobler and more beautiful. Life is sacred, that is
to say, it is the supreme value, to which all other values are
subordinate. The hallowing of the supra-individual life brings in its
train a reverence for everything spiritual—a particularly characteristic feature of the Jewish tradition.

Judaism is not a creed: the Jewish God is simply a negation of
superstition, an imaginary result of its elimination. It is also an
attempt to base the moral law on fear, a regrettable and discredit-
able attempt. Yet it seems to me that the strong moral tradition of
the Jewish nation has to a large extent shaken itself free from this
fear. It is clear also that "serving God" was equated with "serving
the living." The best of the Jewish people, especially the prophets
and Jesus, contended tirelessly for this.

Judaism is thus no transcendental religion; it is concerned with
life as we live it and as we can, to a certain extent, grasp it, and
nothing else. It seems to me therefore doubtful whether it can be
called a religion in the accepted sense of the word, particularly as
no "faith" but the sanctification of life in a supra-personal sense is
demanded of the Jew.

But the Jewish tradition also contains something else, something which finds splendid expression in many of the Psalms,
namely, a sort of intoxicated joy and amazement at the beauty and
grandeur of this world, of which man can form just a faint notion.

This joy is the feeling from which true scientific research draws its spiritual sustenance, but which also seems to find expression in the song of birds. To tack this feeling to the idea of God seems mere childish absurdity.

Is what I have described a distinguishing mark of Judaism? Is it to be found anywhere else under another name? In its pure form, it is nowhere to be found, not even in Judaism, where the pure doctrine is obscured by much worship of the letter. Yet Judaism seems to me one of its purest and most vigorous manifestations. This applies particularly to the fundamental principle of the sanctification of life.

It is characteristic that the animals were expressly included in the command to keep holy the Sabbath day, so strong was the feeling of the ideal solidarity of all living things. The insistence on the solidarity of all human beings finds still stronger expression, and it is no mere chance that the demands of socialism were for the most part first raised by Jews.

How strongly developed this sense of the sanctity of life is in the Jewish people is admirably illustrated by a little remark which Walther Rathenau[1] once made to me in conversation: "When a Jew says that he's going hunting to amuse himself, he lies." The Jewish sense of the sanctity of life could not be more simply expressed.

LEO BAECK

The Tension of Jewish History

Religious thinker, rabbi, scholar, Leo Baeck (1873–1956), born in Lissa, Posen, Germany (now Poland), studied rabbinics at the seminaries in Breslau and Berlin and philosophy under Wilhelm Dilthey. From 1912 on he served as rabbi in Berlin and taught *midrash* and homiletics at the *Hochschule*. His importance as a scholarly writer became evident when, in 1905, he published *Das Wesen des Judentums* (The Essence of Judaism), an apologetic and polemical work against *Das Wesen des Christentums* (The Essence of Christianity), 1900, by the Protestant theologian Adolf von Harnack. Under the influence of Kant and Hermann Cohen, Baeck defined Judaism as ethical monotheism. Later, he modified his definition by supplementing the idea of commandment with the element of mystery. The Jew lives and acts in the tension between the two.

In the Nazi period, Baeck was a fearless, heroic leader, teacher, and guide of his people. He continued this activity when he was deported to the concentration camp in Theresienstadt (1943). In the camp he completed on scraps of paper his work *Dieses Volk: Jüdische Existenz*, which was published under the English title *This People Israel* in Philadelphia in 1965. After liberation from the concentration camp at the end of the war, Baeck lectured in London, New York, and Cincinnati, and continued writing. We reprint here a passage from *This People Israel*.

The history of this people is also a history of boundaries, of eras that divided it deeply, of domains and areas that created manners, of spheres of history within the one history. At times there existed a tension between the parts, but the parts never broke apart. In the end, the tension had the strength to create strength. The unity always endured.

It will endure, and blessing will stream from the whole to the parts and from the parts to the whole, as long as there are beings here who exist, and constantly arise again, who "live by their faith" [Habakkuk 2:4], so that the faith lives through them. Rabbi Simlai, who hearkened to both East and West, has said that the summation of all the commandments is that "the righteous shall live by his faith."[36]

Everything declares itself in faith which, as certainty and experience, from the very beginning, had its earthly place within this people: the certainty of the covenant of God, of human freedom, of the revelation, of the reconciliation, of the soil and the community, of the readiness and the renunciation, of the will to Torah, to the message, to the contemporary and the coming, to work, and to the Sabbath, and the certainty of the gift of prayer and expectation. Faith appears as something manifold, but is one. In this totality, in this unity, and through this unity and totality, this people lived generation after generation, for the sake of the generations—"from Egypt even until now" (Numbers 14:19). Thus, thus alone, will it continue to live.

"From Egypt even until now." Until this time, in which mankind is once more changing, its parts striving to separate, this people, participating in or drawn into everything, is yet to remain within its individuality in order to recognize and fulfill new tasks. Until this time, when once again focal points shifted or were displaced, when this people came to experience all the displacement in itself, it held fast to its own enduring focal point. Until this time, when the New World, which had become great, became the land of most of this people, and when in the Old World, nations were awakening, a new life had grown for this people upon the soil of the Promised Land. Until this time, when there arises, among peoples and religions, an almost undreamed of understanding for this people and its religion, and also a previously unknown adversary, this people is to be prepared and work willingly that "righteousness and peace may come together" [Psalm 85:11]. Until this time, when mankind searches for itself and yet cannot find itself, this people is to cling fast to the fact that it has its existence in humanity and for the sake of humanity. "From Egypt even until now."

Moses once pleaded with God for his people that had gone astray: "Pardon, I pray Thee, the iniquity of this people according unto the greatness of Thy lovingkindness, and according as Thou hast forgiven this people, from Egypt even until now" (Numbers 14:19). When this people prays for forgiveness year after year on the Day of Atonement, it utters these words. He who considers the future of this people finds these words forcing themselves to his lips and into his heart.

What will a later generation see when it looks about? What must it recognize, what may it recognize when it looks at itself? These are questions which the generation that lives today must address to itself, just as they were addressed to every previous generation, whether it heard them or not. Every generation by choosing its way, its present way, at the same time chooses an essential part of the future, the way of its children. Perhaps the children will turn from the eternal way, but in this, too, they will be determined by the direction of their parents. The responsibility to those who follow after us is included in the responsibility to ourselves. The way of the children, whether accepting or rejecting the direction, emanates from our way. Ways bind, wind, and wander.

Nevertheless, ever again a child is born; an individual, a promise of the likeness of the image of God; the great miracle within humanity is reborn. With the birth of a human being the whole problem of humanity is raised anew. The great possibility, the message to humanity, the annunciation of the confidence that must never end, is brought anew into life through the child. It always re-enters humanity in the sequence of the generations, and in history.

When people or peoples assume that they can fit history into a personally fixed pattern, they delude themselves. They want to make things easy for themselves. Responsibility in which freedom turns to freedom is so much harder. But all strivings and endeavors to bind history are in vain. An inheritance cannot be fabricated, let alone forced; it can only be assumed by a freedom that has the ability to build on it. The work of the clever and the mighty, who think they have established a lasting inheritance, breaks down so much easier, generally, than the work of the simple and the insignificant. The shrewd think they are securing the future; and one day, often very near, they or those who follow them stand before ruins. The question is raised, and many questions join in it: Is an inheritance possible, that can endure from generation to generation, not in its forms, but in its power (for the nature of form is change), that remains in its blessing, in order to endure any fate? When this people raises this question, it raises the question of its existence.

In all of the declines of history in which humanity apparently destroys itself or seems to refute itself, one thing surely endured and experienced renewal. That which was searched out and formed by the spirit arose out of ruins and beyond ruins; it wandered from land to land. It could speak to men everywhere; it could engage them in dialogue. This history of these rebirths encounters the works of the spirit—and in the spirit, in its best and ultimate forms, lies an essential part of the actual history of humanity. What would humanity be without it? Would it exist without it? The many things the tool built, the tool then destroyed in many ways. That which spirit has fashioned is indestructible. It endures, even when it is rejected. In the Bible, the word "spirit" has the sound of holiness. The spirit comes from God, and in it, too, man can sanctify himself.

MARTIN BUBER

Judaism and Civilization and Thoughts on Jewish Existence

Martin Buber (1878–1965) is universally known as the author of *I and Thou*, a behest to overcome the I-It relationship to world and man and to maintain an I-Thou attitude toward all existence; as interpreter of Hasidism, the eighteenth-century pietist movement with its stress on inwardness, simplicity of faith, and dedication to divine service; as translator with Franz Rosenzweig of the Hebrew Bible into German, while remaining true to the stylistic characteristics of the original; and as a moving force in the modern Judaic renaissance. What connects and interrelates all (or most) of his activities is a deep, believing humanism based on biblical and Judaic sources. For the sake of this humanism he addressed himself to Jew, Christian, and agnostic; some called him "the Jewish apostle to the Christians."

Buber was born in Vienna, grew up in the home of his grandparents in Lemberg, Galicia, attended universities at Vienna, Leipzig, Zurich, and Berlin (where he was a student of Wilhelm Dilthey and Georg Simmel), joined the Zionist movement in 1898, and edited the Zionist organ, *Die Welt*. From 1906 on, he published a series of works introducing the lore and legend of Hasidism to the West (e.g., *The Tales of the Hasidim*, 2 volumes, New York, 1947 and 1948). In 1923 he published *Ich und Du* (I and Thou) and from 1925 on taught Jewish religion and ethics at the University of Frankfurt am Main. In 1925, too, he embarked on the translation of the Bible, which he completed alone in 1961. In 1938, prohibited from continuing his educational activity in Germany, he settled in Jerusalem and became professor of social philosophy at the Hebrew University. Among his other works are *Das Königtum Gottes* (The Kingship of God), 1932 (English edition published in 1967); *Torat ha-Neviim* (The Prophetic Faith), 1942 (English edition, 1949); *Moses* (1946); *Two Types of Faith* (1951); *Israel and Palestine* (1952); *The Knowledge of Man* (1965). A bibliography of his writings from 1897 to 1957 enumerates 857 titles.

The first piece that follows is taken from an address, "Judaism and Civilization," delivered in 1951 in New York. Buber was conscious of the fact that he was speaking "in the center of the diaspora, in the hour when the deciding crisis of Judaism begins to become manifest." The second selection is culled from *The Way of Response: Martin Buber* (New York, 1966) and offers in the form of aphorisms some of Buber's thoughts on Jewish existence.

I

Among the great civilizations of the ancient world there was one in which the action of the religious and normative principle upon all spheres of public life manifested itself with peculiar, unique pregnancy. All others shared, though in varying degrees of development, the basic doctrine of a heavenly-cosmic society to which the earthly, human one corresponds or rather ought to correspond—to which it corresponded once, say in the Golden Age, or will correspond some day, say after the complete victory of light over darkness. In ancient Israel the place of this doctrine was taken by that of the Lord of all being and all coming to be, who, just as He has set the sun in the sky, has set the commandment of truth and justice above the heads of the human race. True, in the other civilizations as well, the normative principle was carried and guaranteed by divine beings who ruled that upper society; but only Israel knew a God who had chosen a human people—just that people—to prepare the created earth as a kingdom for Him by the realization of justice. For Israel, the principle is the norm and the law; for Israel's God, it is the mobile foundation, symbolized by the Ark with the Tablets, on which He wishes to place His earthly throne. This is why the principle here binds the deity and mankind together in the unparalleled concreteness of the Covenant. And this is also why here, and only here, civilization is mysteriously both affirmed and negated: God wants man's entire civilization—but not as left to itself but as hallowed to Him.

Now we generally observe that man's resistance to the spiritual demand, a resistance which, as we said, manifests itself already in the genetic phase of a civilization, increases decisively as the civilization approaches its height. In proportion to the development of its specific forms, every civilization strives increasingly to render itself independent of its principle. In the great Western civilizations, this manifests itself partly by their individual spheres isolating themselves and each of them establishing its own basis and order, and partly by the principle itself losing its absolute character and validity, so that the holy norm degenerates into a human convention, or by the attachment to the absolute being reduced, avowedly or unavowedly, to a mere symbolic-ritual requirement, which may be adequately satisfied in the cultic sphere. A civilization may now, in its isolated individual spheres, produce works more splendid than it has ever produced before; its spiritual unity is lost. Periclean Athens and the Italian High Renaissance may serve as examples.

The development of the Eastern civilizations was different. Here, the individual spheres never fully emancipated themselves from the unifying bond, but even here the principle became more and more an object of doctrine rather than of life-relationship, and its service, originally embracing real existence, both private and historical, became more and more a merely symbolic and formal one. And here as well, the civilization, by converting the principle by whose action it had first arisen from an active reality into a revered fiction, undermined its own foundations.

Everywhere there were men who recognized this movement toward the abyss for what it was and tried to halt it; but there was only one civilization in which an elemental protest, concentrating all the spiritual passion of the people, was raised against the invalidation of the principle. It was, naturally enough, that civilization in which, as in no other, the absolute had made a covenant

with the entire domain of human existence and refused to abandon
any part of that domain to relativity. At no other time or place has
the spirit been served in the human world with such militancy,
generation after generation, as it was by the prophets of Israel.
Here, the men of spirit took it upon themselves to actualize that
affirmation and negation of civilization in the reality of the historical hour. Their fight was directed against all those who evaded the
great duty, the duty of realizing the divine truth in the fullness of
everyday life, by side-stepping into the merely formal, the merely
ritual, that is to say, the noncommittal—all those who taught and
practiced such evasion and thereby degraded the divine name
which they invoked to the status of a carefully guarded fiction. This
fight was waged for the wholeness and unity of civilization, which
can be whole and united only if it is hallowed to God. The men
who demanded from those in power the abolition of social injustice
for God's sake did not know the concept of civilization, but they
staked their lives to save civilization. Thereby, the protest against
the false emancipation of civilization was registered in such a way
that it was bound to act, and did in fact act, as a reminder and
warning upon the whole future of mankind and quite especially
upon the problematics of the last following civilization, that of the
Christian West.

To appreciate fully the significance of prophetic religion for
mankind and its civilization, we must ask ourselves why it was
precisely in Israel that the normative principle voiced its protest
against any such development of civilization as tended to deprive
it, the normative principle, of its absolute validity. In answer, we
must point to that religious realism peculiar to Israel which has no
room for a truth remaining abstract, hovering self-sufficiently
above reality, but for which every truth is bound up with a
demand which man, the people, Israel, are called upon to fulfill
integrally on earth. Now integral fulfillment means two things: it
must, in the first place, comprise the whole life, the whole
civilization of a people, economy, society, and state; and secondly,
it must incorporate the whole of the individual, his emotions and
his will, his actions and abstentions, his life at home and in the
market place, in the temple and in the popular assembly. That is

to say, it means the wholeness and unity—not otherwise possible—of the civilization. Men, especially the possessors of power and property, naturally resist the demand for the integral fulfillment of divine truth and justice; they therefore try to limit the service of God to the sacral sphere, and in all other spheres recognize his authority merely by words and symbols. This is where the prophetic protest sets in.

A characteristic example may illustrate our point. In the ancient East, the king was generally regarded as a son of the supreme god; he was considered either as adopted or as actually procreated by the god. This conception, in the first-mentioned form, of course, was not strange to Israel, either: the Psalmist makes God say to the king at his anointment on the Holy Mount, "Thou art my son; this day have I begotten thee" [Psalm 2:7]. His anointment in the name of God made the incumbent of the throne responsible to God, not only as a viceroy is responsible to his sovereign but as a son is responsible to his father. Other peoples of the ancient East also knew this relationship of the king to the god. In Babylonia it expressed itself merely by the fact that on the New Year holiday, as the day on which the world begins anew, the priest struck the king a symbolic blow on the cheek, which settled the matter for the rest of the year; in Egypt there were only intimate conversations between the king and his divine father without any visible result. Not so in Israel. Here, the prophet again and again appeared before the king and actually called him to account. This prophetic realism crystallized in the divine message transmitted to David by the prophet Nathan: God proposes to adopt David's son as His, God's, son, but if he sins, He will chastise him, as a father chastises his son, and He will do it by the hand of man [II Samuel 7:14], by the hand of the enemies of Israel, to whom an Israel not upholding justice must succumb.

But the example of the attitude of the prophets to the unfaithful kings is calculated still further to elucidate the nature of the relationship between Judaism and civilization. The conflict appearing here is not to be understood as one between civilization and religion: it proceeded within a civilization (in the widest sense of the term), namely between its guiding principle, whose action had first produced it, and the spheres of life, which more and more repudiated the sovereignty of that principle. Often enough, therefore, the line of battle cut across religion itself, namely, when established religious authority, personified by the priesthood, sided with and sanctioned power. In this case, religion, in order to maintain itself, by virtue of its pact with power, in possession of the particular sphere which the latter had assigned to it, dissociated itself from the claim of the religious principle to be the mover of the whole. That coalition of established power and established authority was faced by the prophet as the man who had neither power nor authority. It is only in the early days of Israel, before the emergence of the situation that called forth the protest, that we find personalities such as Moses and Samuel, endowed at once with prophetic qualities and with history-making power and authority. Later, the powerlessness of the prophet was a typical feature of the age.

But the example chosen here can lead us yet deeper into the nature of our subject. For the experience of the divine demand remaining unfulfilled engendered the messianic promise; and just as the experience centered around the nonfulfilling king, the promise centers around the king who will bring the fulfillment. He is called Messiah, "the anointed," because he will at last carry out the mandate that the kings received upon their anointment. In him, man will at last go to meet God. Around him, first Israel and then the city of mankind will be built up as the fulfilled kingdom of God. But the latter is not conceived of as conquering and superseding a defective human civilization, but as hallowing, that is to say, purifying and perfecting it. When the life of man, with all its various spheres fully developed, becomes a united whole, hallowed to the divine, then, just as Abraham at the altar once called out the name of God over Canaan [Genesis 12:7f.], the name of God will be called out over the whole earth as the domain over which He assumed government.

According to the ancient Persian doctrine, a world-smelting fire will transform the human substance; a new, divine work will replace the dilapidated work of man. Christianity, and also the apocalyptics of Hellenistic peripheral Judaism, developed this basic conception. Central Judaism rejected it. It took with it into its long exile the prophetic doctrine that, in answer to man's return to God, the dislocated human substance will experience His redeeming force, which will perfect the creation of man with man's cooperation. Civilization, despairing of itself, will offer itself up to God and be saved by Him.

This realistic faith in the future of the divine image—in whose loss Judaism has never believed—cannot be dismissed with the cheap slogan "civilization optimism." It is the belief that just as every sinner can find forgiveness by "turning" to God, so can a sinful civilization. Just as man can hallow himself and gain admission to the holy without curtailing his existence, without "primitivizing" his way of life, thus human civilization, too, can without curtailment hallow itself and gain admission.

Here as everywhere else, Israel's religious-normative principle manifests itself as an essentially historical one. Just as its revelation, in distinction to the revelations of all other religions, presents itself as an incident of national history, so its highest goal, too, is historical in character. Here, the suprahistorical molds the historical but does not replace it.

With this historical faith—at once realistic and messianic—inscribed both in its book and in its soul, the Jewish people went forth into its worldwide exile and thus, in its majority, into a civilization whose religious-normative principle was the Christian. This situation was decisively determined by the fact that Christianity had its origin in a deformative late phase of Jewish Messianism, in which it strove no longer to conquer history but to escape from it to purer spheres, while, on the other hand, the group of peoples among which Christianity established itself had just started out to conquer history. Into their existence with its contradiction, the Jewish people was inserted with its existence and the contradiction thereof, enjoined to dwell among them, history-less, with its unfulfilled historical faith—among them who controlled history and whose faith commanded them to overcome history. We know what developed from this basic situation in the course of time.

The principle of our faith, the truth and justice of God, which strives to fulfill itself in the domain of human life and human history and which paints the messianic picture of fulfillment on the firmament of that domain, continued to radiate from our Book; and some protagonists of the Christian faith were hit by its rays, so that one or the other of them conceived the idea that his people, like Israel of old, was enjoined to become a holy people and to hallow its civilization in all its departments. We ourselves were denied actualization of our principle in the world. In the era of dispersion, great things have happened within the Jewish community, in relation to God and to the brethren; but the development of a national personality expressing the divine intent was now made impossible to us by the fact that we were no longer a free and independent community. The messianic idea, cut off from its natural area of realization, lost itself in late-Gnostic speculation and collective ecstasy. And yet, in every hour of genuine self-rediscovery we knew: What matters is the test of history.

When at last we stepped out of the ghetto into the world, worse befell us from within than had ever befallen us from without: the foundation, the unique unity of people and religion, developed a deep rift, which has since become deeper and deeper. Even the event of our days, the re-entry of the Jews into the history of the nations by the rebuilding of a Jewish state, is most intimately affected and characterized by that rift. A home and the freedom to realize the principle of our being have been granted us anew, but Israel and the principle of its being have come apart. It is said that we are now assured of the renewal of a great Jewish civilization. But has a great civilization ever arisen otherwise than by the unfolding of such a basic principle? People try to conceal the rift by applying basic religious terms, such as God of Israel, and Messiah, to purely political processes; and the words, ready to hand, offer no resistance—but the reality which was once meant by them escapes any speech which does not mean just it, that is, the fulfillment of God's truth and justice on earth. True, it is a difficult, a tremendously difficult undertaking to drive the plowshare of the normative principle into the hard sod of political fact; but the right to lift a historical moment into the light of what is above history can be bought no cheaper.

So much for the new Jewish community. But how about the

diaspora—still vigorously alive despite the immense destruction and devastation? Nowhere in it, as far as one can see, is there a powerful striving to heal the rift and to hallow our communal life. And if in our own country the question of the existence of Judaism, that is, of the survival of the principle of Jewish being, may still be veiled by political controversy and danger, in the diaspora at this hour it confronts us in its nakedness. Are we still truly Jews? Jews in our lives? Is Judaism still alive? And in mankind, meanwhile, the great crisis of its civilizations and its civilization, which is a crisis of man, has broken out more and more manifestly. Every original tie seems to be dissevering, every original substance disintegrating. Man tastes nothingness and lets even it dissolve on his tongue; or he fills the space of an existence emptied of its meaning with the mass of his programs.

Where does the world stand? Is the ax laid to the roots of the trees—as a Jew on the Jordan once said,[37] rightly and yet wrongly, that it was in his day—today, at another turn of the ages? And if it is, what is the condition of the roots themselves? Are they still healthy enough to send fresh sap into the remaining stump and to produce a fresh shoot from it? Can the roots be saved? How can they be saved? Who can save them? In whose charge are they?

Let us recognize ourselves: we are the keepers of the roots.

How can we become what we are?

II

The great deed of Israel is not that it taught the one real God, who is the origin and goal of all being, but that it pointed out that this God can be addressed by man in reality, that man can say Thou to Him, that he can stand face to face with Him, that he can have intercourse with Him. Wherever there is man, to be sure, there is also prayer, and so it has probably always been. But only Israel has understood, or rather actually lives, life as being addressed and answering, addressing and receiving answer.

God in all concreteness as speaker, the creation as speech: God's call into nothing and the response of things through their coming into existence, the speech of creation enduring in the life of all creation, the life of each creature as dialogue, the world as word—to proclaim this Israel existed. It taught, it showed, that the real God is the God who can be addressed because He is the God who addresses.

Among all the peoples in the world, Israel is probably the only one in which wisdom that does not lead directly to the unity of knowledge and deed is meaningless. This becomes most evident when we compare the biblical concept of *hokhmah* with the Greek concept of *sophia*. The latter specifies a closed realm of thought, knowledge for its own sake. It is totally alien to the *hokhmah*, which regards such a delimitation of an independent spiritual sphere, governed by its own laws, as the misconstruction of meaning, the violation of continuity, the severance of thought from reality.

The supreme command of *hokhmah* is the unity of teaching and life, for only through this unity can we recognize and avow the all-embracing unity of God.

True human life is conceived to be a life lived in the presence of God. For Judaism, God is not a Kantian idea but an elementally present spiritual reality—neither something conceived by pure reason nor something postulated by practical reason but emanating from the immediacy of existence as such, the mystery of immediacy which religious man steadfastly faces and nonreligious man evades. God is the sun of mankind. However, it is not the man who turns his back on the world of things, staring into the sun in self-oblivion, who will remain steadfast and live in the presence of God, but only that man who breathes, walks, and bathes his self and all things in the sun's light. He who turns his back on the world comprehends God solely as idea, and not as reality. . . .

[In Judaism] God is wholly raised above man. He is beyond the grasp of man, and yet He is present in an immediate relationship with these human beings who are absolutely incommensurable with Him and He faces them. To know both these things at the same time, so that they cannot be separated, constitutes the living core of every believing Jewish soul; to know both, "God in heaven," that is, in complete hiddenness, and man "on earth," that is, in the fragmentation of the world of his senses and his understanding; God in the perfection and incomprehensibility of His being, and man in the abysmal contradiction of this strange existence from birth to death—and between both, immediacy!

We Jews are a community based on memory. A common memory has kept us together and enabled us to survive. This does not mean that we based our life on any one particular past, even on the loftiest of pasts; it simply means that one generation passed on to the next a memory which gained in scope—for new destiny and new emotional life were constantly accruing to it—and which realized itself in a way we can call organic. This expanding memory was more than a spiritual motif; it was a power which sustained, fed, and quickened Jewish existence itself. I might even say that these memories realized themselves biologically, for in their strength the Jewish substance was renewed.

If we were only one nation among others, we should long ago have perished from the earth. Paradoxically we exist only because we dared to be serious about the unity of God and His undivided, absolute sovereignty. If we give up God, He will give us up. And we do give Him up when we profess Him in synagogue and deny Him when we come together for discussion, when we do His commands in our personal life, and set up other norms for the life of the group we belong to. What is wrong for the individual cannot be right for the community; for if it were, then God, the God of Sinai, would no longer be the Lord of peoples, but only of individuals. If we really are Jews, we believe that God gives His commands to men to observe throughout their whole life, and that whether or not life has a meaning depends on the fulfilment of those commands.

A people which seriously calls God Himself its king must become a true people, a community where all members are ruled by honesty without compulsion, kindness without hypocrisy, and the brotherliness of those who are passionately devoted to their divine leader. When social inequality, distinction between the free and the unfree, splits the community and creates chasms between its members, there can be no true people, there can be no "God's people." So [prophetic] criticism and demand are directed toward every individual whom other individuals depend upon, toward everyone who has a hand in shaping the destinies of others; that means directed toward every one of us. When Isaiah speaks of justice, he is not thinking of institutions but of you and me, because without you and me the most glorious institution becomes a lie.

Israel is a people like no other, for it is the only one in the world which, from its earliest beginnings, has been both a nation and a religious community. In the historical hour in which its tribes grew together to form a people, it became the carrier of a revelation. The covenant which the tribes made with one another and through which they became "Israel" takes the form of a common covenant with the God of Israel.

The biblical question of leadership is concerned with something greater than moral perfection. The biblical leaders are the foreshadowings of the dialogical man, of the man who commits his whole being to God's dialogue with the world, and who stands firm throughout this dialogue. . . . Whatever the way, man enters into the dialogue again and again; imperfect entry, but yet one which is not refused, an entry which is determined to persevere in the dialogical world. All that happens is here experienced as dialogue, what befalls man is taken as a sign, what man tries to do and what miscarries is taken as an attempt and a failure to respond, as a stammering attempt to carry out responsibility as well as one can.

The prophetic faith involves the faith in the factual character of human existence, as existence that factually meets transcendence.

Prophecy has in its way declared that the unique being, man, is created to be a center of surprise in creation. Because and so long as man exists, factual change of direction can take place towards salvation as well as towards disaster, starting from the world in each hour, no matter how late. This message has been proclaimed by the prophets to all future generations, to each generation in its own language.

[This] view preserves the mystery of the dialogical intercourse between God and man from all desire for dogmatic encystment. The mystery is that of man's creation as a being with the power of actually choosing between the ways, who ever again and even now has the power to choose between them. Only such a being is suited to be God's partner in the dialogue of history. The future is not fixed, for God wants man to come to Him with full freedom, to return to Him even out of a plight of extreme hopelessness and then to be really with Him. This is the prophetic *theologem*, never expressed as such but firmly embedded in the foundations of Hebrew prophecy.

The prophets knew and predicted that in spite of all its veering and compromising Israel must perish if it intends to exist only as a political structure. It can persist—and this is the paradox in their warning and the paradox of the reality of Jewish history—if it insists on its vocation of uniqueness, if it translates into reality the divine words spoken during the making of the covenant. When the prophets say that there is no security for Israel save that in God, they are not referring to something unearthly, to something "religious" in the common sense of the word; they are referring to the realization of the true communal living to which Israel was summoned by the covenant with God, and which it is called upon to sustain in history, in the way it alone is capable of. The prophets call upon a people which represents the first real attempt at "community" to enter world history as a prototype of that attempt. Israel's function is to encourage the nations to change their inner structure and their relations to one another. By maintaining such relations with the nations and being involved in the development of humanity, Israel may attain its unimperiled existence, its true security.

We make peace, we help bring about world peace, if we make peace wherever we are destined and summoned to do so: in the active life of one's own community and in that aspect of it which can actively help determine its relationship to another community. The prophecy of peace addressed to Israel is not valid only for the days of the coming of the Messiah. . . . Fulfillment in a "then" is inextricably bound up with fulfilment in the "now."

Israel's faith in the redemption of the world does not mean that this world is to be redeemed by another one; it is, rather, a faith in a new world on this earth. The words "trans-mundane" and "mundane" do not exist in the Hebrew language. This hope, which encompasses the whole world, means that we cannot talk with God if we leave the world to its own devices. We can talk with God only by embracing the world, to the best of our ability; that is, by infusing everything with God's truth and justice.

There is no re-establishing of Israel, there is no security for it save one: it must assume the burden of its own uniqueness; it must assume the yoke of the kingdom of God.

SIMON RAWIDOWICZ

Israel the Ever-Dying People

Simon Rawidowicz (1897–1957) was born near Bialistok, Poland, and was educated in the classical Jewish tradition before becoming a student of philosophy at the University of Berlin in 1919. In 1933 he moved to London and in 1941 was appointed professor of Jewish philosophy at Leeds University. In 1947 he accepted a call to the College of Jewish Studies in Chicago and in 1951 to Brandeis University, where he taught Jewish philosophy and headed the department of Near Eastern and Judaic Studies. Over the years, he founded the publishing institute *Ayanot* in Berlin and the *Ararat* Publishing Society of London, and edited seven volumes of the Hebrew miscellany *Metzudah.* He wrote on Ludwig Feuerbach's philosophy (1931), on various aspects of medieval Jewish philosophy, on Moses Mendelssohn, and, in masterful Hebrew, on a philosophy of Jewish history; and he edited Nahman Krochmal's *Writings* with an extensive, authoritative introduction (*Kitve Ranak,* 1924). He combined solid, philological scholarship with a leader's heed for the Jewish community. In his vision, concern for the Land of Israel was united with concern for the diaspora; to him, the term Israel denoted both, not only the Jewish state. A collection of his essays appeared in English in 1974 under the title *Studies in Jewish Thought,* which includes a memoir by his son Benjamin C. I. Ravid. The essay "Israel: The Every-Dying People" treats the recurrent motif of impending doom in Hebraic literature; "with the death of so-and-so (*mi-she-met*) . . . died this or that virtue." A portion of this essay follows.

From the Patriarch Abraham, who lamented that "I go hence childless, and he that shall be possessor of my house is Eliezer of Damascus" [Genesis 15:2], through the compilers of the *Mishnah* and the *Gemara*, and from Maimonides in the 12th century to [Joseph Hayyim] Brenner in the 20th, we encounter the same theme of *mi-she-met*, the last Jews! Rabbi Akiba was the last representative of Torah; Brenner and [Micah Joseph] Berdichevski, the last Jews.

When Brenner wrote about being the last, there were several million Jews in his country of origin, Russia, and another three millions or so in the other European lands. Now, after our great European tragedy—"tragedy" is too weak a word for this third great disaster in our history—the traditional dread of being the last naturally assumes dimensions of great magnitude in the minds of our European brethren—but not only with them. Every effort to revitalize Jewish life and learning is stamped—and handicapped—by the fear of being the last. Every Jewish teacher, community worker who toils for the sake of Israel, "for the sake of heaven in truthfulness," every Jewish scholar and thinker who dares to continue the great tradition of Jewish scholarship in the face of growing assimilation and adjustment to the outside world—each considers himself the last of his kind, and is so considered by those around him. They know he is the last—for they feel it in their very bones that they, too, are the last. How often do we feel—not only in the present-day diaspora—seeing a great creative Jew, watching a gathering of "good Jews" to preserve their identity by all means and whatever cost, that they are the last, that we all are the last; and how often are we full of doubt as to whether the future will give rise to further teachers, scholars and even plain ordinary Jews. Often it seems as if the overwhelming majority of our people go about driven by the panic of being the last. It hardly needs emphasizing that this sense of fear is naturally bound to exercise a most paralyzing effect on our conscious and subconscious life, on our emotions and thoughts.

When we analyze somewhat more deeply this constant dread of the end, we discover that one of its decisive psychological elements is the general, not particularly Jewish, sense of fear of losing ground, of being deprived of possessions and acquisitions—or, still deeper, the sense of fear which came over man when he first saw the sunset in the west, not knowing that every sunset is followed by a sunrise, as the *midrash* so beautifully described Adam's first great shock.

Is Israel alone a dying nation? Numerous civilizations have disappeared before there emerged the one in which we live so happily and unhappily at the same time. Each dying civilization was confident that earth and heaven would disappear with it. How often did man feel he was finished forever! When ancient Rome began to crumble, Romans and others felt sure that the end of the universe was at hand. St. Augustine thought that the "anti-Christ" would appear after the destruction of Rome and man would be called to his last day of judgment. In various aspects, this fear of being the last was also manifest in Christianity and Islam. In addition, the lamentation of *mi-she-met* has its psychological origin in man's great admiration for his living masters, in his fear lest the miracle will not occur again, lest there will be no second set of masters—as if genius rises only once, never again to re-appear.

Yet, making all allowances for the general motives in this dread of the end, it has nowhere been at home so incessantly, with such an acuteness and intensity, as in the House of Israel. The world may be constantly dying, but no nation was ever so incessantly dying as Israel.

Going deeper into the problem—and here I have to confine myself to a hint—I am often tempted to think that this fear of cessation in Israel was fundamentally a kind of protective individual and collective emotion. Israel has indulged so much in the fear of its end, that its constant vision of the end helped it to overcome every crisis, to emerge from every threatening end as a living unit, though much wounded and reduced. In anticipating the end, it became its master. Thus no catastrophe could ever take this end-fearing people by surprise, so as to put it off its balance, still less to obliterate it—as if Israel's incessant preparation for the end made this very end absolutely impossible.

Philosophers like Hegel and Schopenhauer have spoken of the guile of nature, of the guile of history. Is not this peculiar sense of the end also the guile of a nation *sui generis*, a nation that would use every device for its survival, even that of incessant anticipation of its disappearance, in order to rule it out forever? This aspect of national psychology deserves special attention.

As far as historical reality is concerned, we are confronted here with a phenomenon which has almost no parallel in mankind's story: a nation that has been disappearing constantly for the last two thousand years, exterminated in dozens of lands all over the globe, reduced to half or third of its population by tyrants ancient and modern—and yet it still exists, falls and rises, loses all its possessions and re-equips itself for a new start, a second, a third chance—always fearing the end, never afraid to make a new beginning, to snatch triumph from the jaws of defeat, whenever and wherever possible. There is no nation more dying than Israel, yet none better equipped to resist disaster, to fight alone, always alone.

As far as our foreign relations, if I may so call them, are concerned, there is much comfort in our thorny path in the world. The first ancient non-Jewish document which mentions Israel by name is, symbolically apt, a message of total annihilation. It is the monument—in possession of the British Museum—on which Merneptah, the thirteenth century B.C.E. Egyptian forerunner of Nasser, boasts of his great deeds and triumphs over nations, and, among other things, states succinctly: "Israel is desolated; its seed is no more." Since 1215 B.C.E. how often did prophets at home and abroad prophesy Israel's desolation! How often did nations try to translate this prophecy into practice, and in the most cruel ways! About 3,150 years after that boastful Egyptian conqueror, there arose Satan in the heart of Europe and began to predict Israel's total annihilation—and to prepare the most modern technical devices to make his prophecy come true. And after it was given to him—to our greatest sorrow and the world's greatest shame—to reduce Israel by one-third, Israel is still alive—weakened, to be sure, robbed of its best resources for recuperation, of its reservoir, its fountains of life and learning, yet still standing on its feet, numbering four times as many souls as in the days of the French Revolution, rebuilding its national life in the State of Israel, in the face of so many obstacles! Though not perfect, its spiritual creativity continues. Filled with fear of its end, it seeks to make a new beginning in the diaspora and in the State of Israel.

If so, many will say, what is all the lamenting about? Many nations have suffered, and, if we suffered a little more, we should not exaggerate or carry on hysterically. No need to worry, no need of superhuman efforts—wait and see—nothing will happen; and if it should happen—surely it has happened before. [. . .]

Such easy comfort, such exaggerated optimism is no less dangerous than the pessimism of Israel's end. Neither is justified, neither is helpful.

In the beginning, Israel's message was that of a universal optimism—salvation, happiness and perfection for all peoples. "The mountain of the Lord's house will be established in the top of the mountains" [Isaiah 2:2] means: the peoples of the world will also share alike, with Israel, in the blessing of the messianic age. Many well-known and understandable factors compelled post-exilic and medieval Messianism to become more one-sided and directed exclusively toward the redemption of Israel; optimistic toward Israel, pessimistic toward the world. In more recent times, most Jewish ideologies and political movements were dualistic inasmuch as they saw a world divided, Israel and world torn apart—nay, still more: Israel itself was to them no more. Thus, to give one illustration, Jewish Reform on both sides of the Rhine, 19th-century liberalism, was optimistic as far as the world's future was concerned, pessimistic for the survival of Israel as a nation with all national attributes. This same dualistic attitude was taken up by all kinds of assimilated Jewish revolutionaries in Eastern and Western Europe. Later, two Jewish ideologies fought each other in Europe: one was most optimistic for the remnant of Israel in Zion and pessimistic as far as the Jewish people in the diaspora was concerned, while the other reversed this dichotomy, maintaining that only diaspora Jewry had a future in some liberal or socialistic order.

Both made the fundamental mistake of dividing Israel into two parts. Israel must always be considered one and indivisible—yisrael ehad. As long as one part of Israel lives in a hell, the other cannot live in paradise.

I therefore say: we may not split up Israel into two spheres of reality. Israel is one. Neither may we approach the Jewish problem from an optimistic or pessimistic angle. Optimism and pessimism are only expressions or indications of our fears, doubts, hopes and desires. Hopes and desires we must have; fears and doubts we cannot escape. Yet, what we need most at present is a dynamic Jewish realism which will see our reality, the reality of the world, our problem, the problem of the world, in its entirety, without any dualism—hell-paradise or whatever.

Such a Jewish realism will also show us the real meaning of that fear of the end which is so inherent in us. A nation dying for thousands of years means a living nation. Our incessant dying means uninterrupted living, rising, standing up, beginning anew. We, the last Jews! Yes, in many respects it seems to us as if we are the last links in a particular chain of tradition and development. But if we are the last—let us be the last as our fathers and forefathers were. Let us prepare the ground for the last Jews who will come after us, and for the last Jews who will rise after them, and so on until the end of days.

If it has been decreed for Israel that it go on being a dying nation—let it be a nation that is constantly dying, which is to say: incessantly living and creating—one nation from Dan to Beersheba, from the sunny heights of Judea to the shadowy valleys of Europe and America.

To prepare the ground for this great oneness, for a Jewish realism built on it, is a task which requires the effort of Jewish scholarship and statesmanship alike. One nation, one in beginning and end, one in survival and extinction! May it be survival rather than extinction, a beginning rather than an ignominious end—one Israel, *yisrael ehad.*

FRANZ ROSENZWEIG

Two Theological Considerations

Franz Rosenzweig (1886–1929), born in Cassel, Germany, was trained in modern history and philosophy at the universities of Berlin and Freiburg and specialized in the political philosophy of Hegel. Member of an assimilated family, he discovered late the validity of faith, and, ultimately, of Judaism (1913). His *Der Stern der Erlösung* (The Star of Redemption), which he began while a soldier on the Balkan front during the First World War, proffers his religious philosophy. Opposing Hegel and German idealism, with its construction of reality out of concepts independent of experience, Rosenzweig restores the importance of the individual—the suffering, erring, despairing, loving human being whom idealism, stressing the "pure Ego," let disappear in the "whole." *The Star* goes back to the original three elements of reality: Man-World-God. These elements are not known to us "as such" but in the relationships that lead them to a state of reality. "Creation" (Rosenzweig uses biblical terminology) is the process that establishes the relation between God and world. In "Revelation" God in his love turns to man, a process which awakens in man the consciousness of an "I" and in which a person assumes reality. Man translates God's love into love for his neighbor—and initiates Redemption. In prayer and in the rhythm of the liturgical year, man experiences redemption in its fullness, eternity. Judaism and Christianity are two views of the world under the aspect of Creation-Revelation-Redemption. Both are equally "true" and valid views of reality. Man is given a part in truth; only God *is* truth.

In 1920 Rosenzweig assumed the leadership of the *Freies*

jüdisches Lehrhaus in Frankfurt am Main, a unique institute of Jewish study and free inquiry into the classical sources of Judaism. In 1922 Rosenzweig became ill with progressive paralysis, but succeeded in adjusting to the most adverse physical conditions. He spent his remaining years (until 1929) translating and commenting on poems by Judah ha-Levi, starting with Martin Buber a translation of the Bible, writing essays and thousands of letters to friends, colleagues, and disciples. Of the pieces that follow, the first deals with the difference between the people of Israel and the Christians, and is taken from *The Star of Redemption* (Part III, pp. 87–92); the second is a note on a poem by Judah ha-Levi and deals with the remoteness and nearness of God.

I. The Nations and Their States

And so the eternal people must forget the world's growth, must cease to think thereon. It must look upon the world, its own world, as complete, though the soul may yet be on the way: the soul can indeed overtake the final goal in one single leap. And if not, it must needs wait and wander on—to quote the wise Spanish proverb, "Patience, and a new shuffle of the cards." Waiting and wandering is the business of the soul, growth that of the world. It is this very growth that the eternal people denies itself. As nationality, it has reached the point to which the nations of the world still aspire. Its world has reached the goal. The Jew finds in his people the perfect fusion with a world of his own, and to achieve this fusion himself, he need not sacrifice a jot of his peculiar existence. The nations have been in a state of inner conflict ever since Christianity with its supernational power came upon them. Ever since then, and everywhere, a Siegfried is at strife with that stranger, the man of the cross, in his very appearance so antagonizing a character. A Siegfried who, depending on the nation he comes from, may be blond and blue-eyed, or dark and small-boned, or brown and dark-eyed, wrestles again and again with this stranger who resists the continued attempts to assimilate him to that nation's own longing and vision. The Jew alone suffers no conflict between the supreme vision which is placed before his soul and the people among whom his life has placed him. He alone possesses the unity of myth which the nations lost through the influx of Christianity, which they were bound to lose, for their own myth was pagan, and, by leading them into this myth, led them away from God and their neighbor. The Jew's myth, leading him into his people, brings him face to face with God who is also the God of all nations. The Jewish people feels no conflict between what is its very own and what is supreme; the love it has for itself inevitably becomes love for its neighbor.

Because the Jewish people is beyond the contradiction that constitutes the vital drive in the life of the nations—the contradiction between national characteristics and world history, home and faith, earth and heaven—it knows nothing of war. For the peoples of antiquity, war was after all only one among other natural expressions of life: it held no fundamental contradiction. To the nations war means staking life in order to live. A nation that fares forth to war accepts the possibility of dying. This is not significant so long as nations regard themselves as mortal. While this conviction lasts, it is of no importance that of the two legitimate reasons for waging war as given by the great Roman orator[38]—that of *salus* and that of *fides*, self-preservation and the keeping of the pledged word—the second may sometimes be in contradiction to the first. There is, after all, no good reason why Saguntum and its people shall not perish from the earth. But what it means becomes clear when Augustine, who is responsible for the clever refutation of Cicero, declares: the church cannot fall into such conflict between its own welfare and the faith pledged to a higher being; for the church, *salus* and *fides* are one and the same thing. What Augustine here says of the church holds in a narrower sense also for worldly communities, for nations and states which have begun to regard their own existence from the highest point of view. . . .

As against the life of the nations of the world, constantly involved in a war of faith, the Jewish people has left its war of faith far behind in its mythical antiquity. Hence, whatever wars it experiences are purely political wars. But since the concept of a war of faith is ingrained in it, it cannot take these wars as seriously as the peoples of antiquity to whom such a concept was alien. In the whole Christian world, the Jew is practically the only human being who cannot take war seriously, and this makes him the only genuine pacifist. For that reason, and because he experiences perfect community in his spiritual year, he remains remote from the chronology of the rest of the world, even though this has long ceased to be a chronology peculiar to individual peoples and, as Christian chronology, is accepted as a principle common to the world at large. He does not have to wait for world history to unroll its long course to let him gain what he feels he already possesses in the circuit of every year: the experience of the immediacy of each single individual to God, realized in the perfect community of all with God.

The Jewish people has already reached the goal toward which the nations are still moving. It has that inner unity of faith and life which, while Augustine may ascribe it to the church in the form of the unity between *fides* and *salus*, is still no more than a dream to the nations within the church. But just because it has that unity, the Jewish people is bound to be outside the world that does not yet have it. Through living in a state of eternal peace it is outside of time agitated by wars. Insofar as it has reached the goal which it anticipates in hope, it cannot belong to the procession of those who approach this goal through the work of centuries. Its soul, replete with the vistas afforded by hope, grows numb to the concerns, the doing and the struggling of the world. The consecration poured over it as over a priestly people renders its life "unproductive." Its holiness hinders it from devoting its soul to a still unhallowed world, no matter how much the body may be bound up with it. This people must deny itself active and full participation in the life of this world with its daily, apparently conclusive, solving of all contradictions. It is not permitted to recognize this daily solving of contradictions, for that would render it disloyal to the hope of a final solution. In order to keep unharmed the vision of the ultimate community it must deny itself the satisfaction the peoples of the world constantly enjoy in the functioning of their state. For the state is the ever changing guise under which time moves step by step toward eternity. So far as God's people is concerned, eternity has already come—even in the midst of time! For the nations of the world there is only the current era. But the state symbolizes the attempt to give nations eternity within the confines of time, an attempt which must of necessity be repeated again and again. The very fact that the state does try it, and *must* try it, makes it the imitator and rival of the people which is in itself eternal, a people which would cease to have a claim to its own eternity if the state were able to attain what it is striving for.

II. Remote and Near

A single thought animates this hymn—but it is the ultimate thought the mind of man can grasp and it is the first that Jewish thinking seizes on: that the remote God is none other than the near, the unknown God none other than the revealed, the Creator none other than the Redeemer. The short opening stanza[39] contains it in epigrammatic brevity, and the four following stanzas sound it in hymnic ecstasies streaming from the throne of heaven to the heart of man and soaring back again and again, in giant arcs. This is the thought which was discovered over and over in the sphere of revelation, which inside and outside that sphere was forgotten over and over throughout the centuries, from Paul and Marcion[40] to Harnack[41] and Barth.[42]

Discovered over and over and forgotten over and over! For theologians forget what men discover, and they forget the more readily the better theologians they are. Theology is most dangerous when it is most accurate. Today, after a long period of drought, we have a theology—largely Protestant—that leaves nothing to be desired with regard to accuracy. Now we know it! We understand that God is "wholly Other"; that to talk of him is to talk him away, that all we can tell is what his effect is on us. The result of this stupendous accuracy is that, just because we are accurate, we now stand in a circle like children: one says something quite accurate; his neighbor snubs him with the still more accurate statement that his utterance was false because it was accurate, and so we make the rounds until we get back to the first. The whole procedure is called theology.

The point is that we theologians cannot stop converting our

knowledge into rules and regulations for the conduct of God. We know that God can be perceived only through his presence, and instantly make this into the rule that he must not let himself be perceived in his absence. As a matter of fact, it would be quite safe to leave it to him just when and how and to what extent he wishes to be perceived. All we need do is simply to say what we know, and to say it calmly or vehemently (but whether calmly or vehemently is not up to us either), and as accurately as possible, and this accuracy *is* up to us!

When God comes near to us we do, indeed, perceive only the unutterable. But that is not our duty and—as we call it in our heart of hearts—our merit, because we are such very excellent modern theologians. We just cannot do otherwise, for he is so very close to us. We have no reason whatsoever to snub one another for uttering the unutterable. So long as it is and wants to be unutterable, it will see to it that we cannot utter it. So when we do begin to utter it, this probably happens because it itself makes possible our utterance, inadequate though that be, by its—or rather his, God's—withdrawal from us. In making himself remote he lets us perceive him as one who is remote, and when he is very remote, that is, when he has withdrawn from us completely, we can even—inquisitors of the new theology, hand me over to temporal justice!—we can even *prove* him!

The possibility of proving the existence of God is the very natural result of the fact that certain theologians never weary of repeating that God is the "wholly Other." Or not even the result. This otherness is, in itself, the modern proof of God's existence, for it is the residue of all other proofs rarefied to the utmost remoteness of abstraction. But before this extreme point of remoteness is reached, each earlier proof has its proper place—governed by the degree of man's remoteness—and constitutes the precise expression of what is still visible from there. And so it is not at all a sign of being hopelessly lost to know that God is perfect being, or the primordial cause, or even that he is the ideal of ethics. When such statements are proffered as honest knowledge, it is only a sign that at the moment such knowledge was gained God was really very far away from the one gaining it. But what do we mean by the phrase "honest knowledge"? Nothing but what it actually means, to wit, nothing that does not concern us and that we do not concern. Without such concern, even an investigation of agriculture in fifteenth-century Germany is worthless, while with it, dicta such as "God is holy," or even just "God is," are as true as our modern approximations.

For nearness and remoteness in themselves do not reveal whether this mutual concern, whether this sole condition that renders knowledge true, really prevails, whether here man concerns God, and God man. Even when God is terribly near, man can turn away his eyes, and then he has not the smallest glimpse of what has happened to him. And even at a very great distance, the burning gaze of God and man can fuse in such a way that the coldest abstractions grow warm in the mouth of Maimonides or Hermann Cohen—warmer than all our agonized drivel. It is not nearness or remoteness that matters. What matters is that, near or remote, whatever is uttered, is uttered before God with the "Thou" of the refrain of our poem, a "Thou" that never turns away.

MORDECAI M. KAPLAN

The Principles of Reconstructionism and Some Questions Jews Ask

Mordecai Kaplan, born in 1881 in Lithuania and brought to the U.S.A. at the age of nine, is best known as the founder of the Reconstructionist movement and of the Society for the Advancement of Judaism. His *Judaism as a Civilization* (1934) is Reconstructionism's chief statement. He thinks that the maturest expression of a civilization is its religion, which concerns itself with the highest good and life's meaning. Its concept of God is not anthropomorphic but "the Power that makes for self-fulfilment." "Life and love are manifestations of God." Classical Judaism's supernatural revelation is replaced by reason, intuition, and experience. Torah is central, but it permits change and revision. Kaplan rejects the notion of a chosen people if restricted to the people of Israel; Zion remains central. He has been imbued by two traditions: Rabbinic culture and discipline on the one hand, American pragmatism, naturalism, and democratic idealism on the other.

Among Kaplan's other works are *The Meaning of God in Modern Jewish Religion* (1936), *The Future of the American Jew* (1948), *The Greater Judaism in the Making* (1960), and *The Religion of Ethical Nationhood* (1970). His scholarly works include an edition of M. H. Luzatto's *Mesillat Yesharim* (1937) and *The Meaning and Purpose of Jewish Existence* (1964). He was for many years a professor of philosophies of religion at the Jewish Theological Seminary and exerted a profound influence on his students. In 1973 he settled in Jerusalem.

The piece that follows is the introductory chapter to his *Questions Jews Ask* (1956) with samples from this work.

1. Judaism, or that which has united the successive generations of Jews into one people, is not only a religion; it is a dynamic religious civilization.
2. Judaism has passed through three distinct stages in its evolution, and is now on the threshold of a fourth stage. It was primarily *national* in character during the First Commonwealth era, *ecclesiastical* during the Second Commonwealth era, and *rabbinical* from then until the end of the eighteenth century. It is now developing into a *democratic* civilization.
3. The emergence of the next stage calls for the reconstitution of the Jewish people and its enhancement, the revitalization of Jewish religion, and the replenishment of Jewish culture.
4. The reconstitution of the Jewish people is predicated upon the following:
   a) The reclamation of the Land of Israel as the home of the historic Jewish civilization;
   b) The renewal of the covenant binding all Jews throughout the world into one united people, with the Jewish community in Israel as the core;
   c) The formation of organic Jewish communities in all countries of the Jewish diaspora.
5. An organic community is one in which all activities and institutions conducted by Jews for Jews are interactive, and in which the fostering of Jewish peoplehood, religion and culture is given primacy.
6. The revitalization of Jewish religion can be best achieved through the study of it in the spirit of free inquiry and through the separation of its organized institutions from all political authority.
7. The revitalization of the Jewish religion requires that the belief in God be interpreted in terms of universally human, and specifically Jewish, experience.
8. By reason of the prevailing diversity in world outlook, there has to be room in Jewish religion for different versions of it.
9. The continuity of a religion through different stages, and its identity amid diversity of belief and practice, are sustained by its *sancta:* these are the heroes, events, texts, places, and

seasons that the religion signalizes as furthering the fulfillment
of human destiny.

10. The traditional conception of Torah should be expanded to
include:
    a) ethical culture, the fostering of love and justice in all human
    relations;
    b) ritual culture, the fostering of the religious *sancta* with all
    of their symbolic significance;
    c) esthetic culture, the fostering of the arts as a means of
    expressing the emotional values of Jewish life.

11. Every people, Jewish and non-Jewish, is nowadays confronted
with the problem of living in two civilizations. It has to blend
its *historic* civilization with the modern national civilization
of the country in which it lives.

12. Loyalty to Judaism should be measured by active participation
in Jewish life, in keeping with the foregoing principles.

*How would you answer the question of a child who asked: "Why
did God make polio?"*

To answer any difficult question raised by a child, two requirements are necessary: (1) the ability to answer the question to the
satisfaction of an adult, and (2) the ability to adapt that answer to
the child's mind in accordance with his age. The main difficulty in
answering this question is that we have not yet arrived at an
answer that is fully satisfactory to the modern adult mind.

It is evident that, from an adult viewpoint, the question is part
of the general problem of how to reconcile the existence of evil in
the world with faith in God. This question is the one on which
religious faith is most frequently wrecked. In the past, the belief in
a hereafter in which all evils suffered in this life would be
recompensed served, in large measure, as a solution of the problem. That is why the belief in reward and punishment as taking
place within a life that was assumed to extend beyond the grave
was considered an integral part of belief in God. To deny belief in
the hereafter was held to be as grievous a sin as to deny the
existence of God.

Today, however, thinking persons, even if they maintain a belief in immortality, hardly resort to it as a means of solving the problem of evil. Modern men cannot see why we must suffer *here* in order to be compensated *hereafter*. The atrocities perpetrated against six million Jewish victims by the Nazis, and the similar suffering imposed on many other human beings by Nazi, Fascist, and Communist persecution, and by the armies of both sides in recent wars, constitute a tragedy of such dimensions that no posthumous reward can compensate for it, or explain it away. Nor can we blame human sinfulness for the misery caused by earthquakes, floods, pestilences, and other natural catastrophes.

Tradition, therefore, offers no solution to the problem of evil, which can satisfy the spirit of our generation. It is not surprising that Samson Raphael Hirsch, the founder of the neo-Orthodox movement, has no satisfactory answer to offer to this question. But neither have such non-Orthodox Jewish theologians as Solomon Schechter and Kaufmann Kohler, or Leo Baeck and Martin Buber. Yet this question is at the very heart of the religious crisis of our day. We are sorely in need of a conception of God which is compatible with a satisfactory orientation to the problem of evil.

It is, therefore, most regrettable that the institutions which train spiritual leaders are apparently afraid to grapple with this problem. I have long been wrestling with the problem myself and have arrived at a solution which is satisfactory to me. But no matter how my idea of a solution may satisfy me, it can have little value, unless it is made part of a general context of live discussion, carried on in a spirit of dedication, tolerance, and search after the highest satisfaction of the human spirit. That kind of a context can be provided only by institutions and groups that concern themselves not merely with objective or historical research, but primarily with the discovery of those human values that can make for a more worthwhile life than we are enjoying at present.

Could you simplify the answer you gave to the question, "How would you answer the question of a child who asked, 'Why did God make polio?'" After reading your answer, I still don't know how to answer the child.

Children often ask questions which philosophers have asked from time immemorial, and to which they give answers in accordance with their general outlook on life. With every change in the intellectual climate, the answers change, but the questions remain. In my answer to the question, I did not so much endeavor to reply directly to the child, as to point out the need for more earnest intellectual consideration of the problem, which is too often evaded.

Nevertheless, since it must be a painful and shocking experience to a child to be told that the God whom he is expected to love and worship is responsible for his tragic affliction, I shall endeavor to answer the question in a way that might mitigate the evil effects of his suffering on his faith in God's goodness and help. Such an answer would be the following:

God did *not* make polio. God is always helping us humans to make this a better world, but the world cannot at once become the kind of world He would like it to be. When men make use of the intelligence God gave them, they learn more and more of the laws of health, by which all kinds of illness can be prevented or cured. When the doctor relieves your pain, when he helps you to get back more strength and better control over your muscles, it is with the intelligence that God gives him. When you use braces and other devices that help you get around and do some of the things you want to do, their manufacture is due to the intelligence and the concern for your welfare, that God puts into the minds of those who make these devices. Do not feel that God does not care for you. He is helping you now in many ways, and He will continue to help you. Maybe some day you will be restored by His help to perfect health. But if that does not happen, it is not because God does not love you. If He does not grant you all that you pray for, He will find other ways of enabling you to enjoy life. Be thankful to God for all the love and care that people show toward you, since all of that is part of God's love, and do not hesitate to ask God for further help. If the people around you are intelligent and loving, that help will come to you.

Since you maintain that the belief in God is essentially the belief

that the universe is favorable or congenial to man's salvation,
would you regard that belief as demonstrable, or as requiring to be
taken on faith?

The answer to this question becomes apparent when we bear in
mind the reason for our defining God as the Power that makes for
salvation. That definition identifies God with a phase of genuine
human experience. By so defining the God idea, we avoid the
pitfalls into which all those who have ever tried to offer a logical
demonstration of God's existence have stumbled.

We cannot infer the existence and nature of God from our
sensory experience of the outer world. Our belief in God is
implicit in our will to achieve salvation, or the maximum life.
There is no denying the reality of the will to live. In human
beings, who are aware of the power to choose alternate ways of
life, the will to live becomes the will to live life at its maximum.
The will to live that is characteristic of all living beings unquestionably finds fulfillment. Not so the conscious will to maximum
life, which is characteristic of human beings only. The fulfillment
of that will is questionable. However, the will to maximum life
would die of inanition, were it not for the faith that the possibilities
of its attainment are certainly present, and that the chances of
attaining the maximum life keep increasing with time.

Both our conception of what constitutes salvation, and our
conception of God as the Power or Process that enables us to
achieve it vary with our changing experiences. What remains
constant is our need for faith in the possibility of achieving
salvation, or the worthwhile life. That is why we assume that the
universe is congenial or favorable to such fulfillment. Though the
correctness of that assumption is not demonstrable, we hold to it,
because it is indispensable to mental health and the sense of moral
responsibility.

Can we ascribe to God conscious concern with man's salvation?

This is a problem that engaged the minds of Maimonides and other
Jewish theologians. Their response to the problem was to affirm
that the human mind cannot possibly grasp the true nature of God.

Any positive statement we may make about God can, at best, point to some analogy which is only partially valid. To think of God as a person, with mental processes similar to our own, is obviously unsatisfactory. Yet, if we do not think of God in such terms, we tend to think of him as analogous with some material object or mechanical force, which is even less satisfactory. Such an analogy would utterly distort our conception of God as a source of salvation.

So far Maimonides and the theologians—but we may go further. *Insofar as consciousness and purpose are indispensable to man's salvation, they are veritable manifestations of God as the Power that makes for salvation.* While, therefore, we can not say anything demonstrable about the nature of God, we can say something about how God manifests Himself in human life. To ascribe *consciousness* or *purpose* to God, in the same sense as when we apply them to human beings, is absurd. It is like ascribing to a multi-millionaire the fact that he can afford to buy a newspaper.

In the past the survival of Jewish life has been due fundamentally to segregation. Since, in America, such segregation is unthinkable and undesirable, how can we expect Judaism to have a future in this country?

There is no doubt that, in the past, segregation was an important factor in preserving Jewish identity. The segregation of Jewry was partly self-imposed and partly imposed by non-Jewish society. It is hard to determine whether voluntary or enforced segregation was the principal factor. But, be that as it may, there is no returning to segregation in our day in America.

Nevertheless, we still experience a sufficient momentum from the past to be worried about what to make of whatever Jewish consciousness we still retain. The question is: Can living as Jews in an environment of freedom and opportunity make sense? The answer rests with us and with no one else. It is entirely up to us to carry on our Jewish interests and activities in such a way as to help us to be better and happier men and women, and better Americans for being good Jews.

The only alternative, the one to which many Jews resort, is to try to destroy whatever roots they have in the past. But the mentally disintegrating and spiritually demoralizing effects of cultural and religious rootlessness are too well known to merit discussion. Hence the normal procedure is to cultivate our historical roots, as Jews. Specifically, that means fostering Jewish fellowship, replenishing Jewish culture, and so cultivating Jewish religious values as to have them answer our personal needs.

All these aims are embraced in the Reconstructionist program. It would have us foster Jewish fellowship by emphasizing the peoplehood of Israel and rendering Jewish communal life inherently worthwhile. It would have us replenish Jewish culture by encouraging the artistic expression of Jewish experience, creative writing on Jewish subjects, the development of new rituals, and a Jewish education for child, adolescent and adult, that is oriented to life in America. And it urges the cultivation of religious values by reinterpreting the religious tradition and revising the religious ritual for those Jews whom the existing versions of Jewish religion do not satisfy.

HORACE M. KALLEN

A Jewish View of Life

Horace M. Kallen (1882–1974) was born in Silesia, Germany, and was brought to the United States in 1887. He taught at various American universities and was a founder of the New School for Social Research. He was active in the Presidential Commission on Higher Education, the International League for the Rights of Man, and the Society for the Scientific Study of Religion. An exponent of cultural pluralism, pragmatism, freedom, humanism, cooperative individualism, and civil liberties, he termed his world view "Hebraism." "To believe in life in the face of death, to believe in goodness in the face of evil, to hope for better times to come, to work at bringing them about, that is Hebraism," he stated. His works include *Zionism and World Politics* (1921), *Judaism at Bay* (1932), *The Education of Free Men* (1949), and *Of Them Which Say They Are Jews* (1954). The essay that follows is taken from the latter collection of essays.

Is there a Jewish view of life?

Albert Einstein says that there isn't, "in the philosophic sense." He may be right. But also, he may be wrong. The question does not admit of a single, unambiguous answer.

For the Jews are an ancient people, and their history is long and varied. Their religion, Judaism, is not so old nor so varied as the history of its creators and adherents, yet its own life-history is marked with at least as many crises and alterations as the life-story of the Jewish people. And it could not be otherwise. For Judaism, like Hebraism, is an indefinite manifold. Its existence consists of the coming together and the moving apart of great numbers of diverse and contradictory items of thought, feeling and conduct. Each and every one of these items has a claim upon the consideration of any person endeavoring to establish what Judaism is or what Judaism is not.

But this claim is hardly ever honored. The definition which any citizen gives Judaism depends on his loves and hates, on his wishes and frustrations. Those cause him to react selectively to the entire shifting aggregate of which living Judaism is composed. They will lead him to affirm qualities which others deny, and deny qualities which others affirm.

To this rule, Einstein is no exception. In science, a specialist in astronomical mathematics; in human relations, a democrat, an internationalist and a pacifist, the loyalties and rebellions these terms imply determine in advance what items from the manifold of Judaism he will choose in order to make up an exclusive definition of "the Jewish view of life."

With Dr. Einstein's selection I have no quarrel. On the contrary, it is quite in harmony with the type of selection I myself make, as those well know who have read my works on this subject, especially my *Judaism at Bay*, where I have endeavored to show why some such view of Judaism may be held as peculiarly representative of the high place in the rise and fall of the Jewish tradition.

But demonstrating and establishing this definition call for the simultaneous recognition that there exist other opinions, other views of Jewish life, other and quite contrary definitions, each one of them an alternative demanding to be refuted and cast aside. Refuting them and casting them aside meant acknowledging that they had a place in the aggregate which is Judaism. Some of them include Maimonides and shut out Spinoza. Others include the Bible and exclude the *Siddur*.[43] Some include the *Shulhan Arukh*, but exclude Maimonides, Spinoza, the *Siddur* and the Bible. Others combine them all with the *Shulhan Arukh*.[44] Still others exclude the *Shulhan Arukh*, mutilate the *Siddur* and include a "mission of Israel" an "ethical monotheism" and at the same time glorify Maimonides and patronize Spinoza.

Who is right? Who is wrong? The answer does not depend on the intrinsic character of the definition nor on its historical correctness nor its religious sanctions. The answer depends entirely on its *consequences* to the strength, the enrichment of Jewish life.

Now in life, quite otherwise than in mathematics, consequences belong to an unpredictable future. They can not be established in advance. They are not foregone conclusions.

History, which can be written only by survivors in the struggle for life, is the judgment which the survivors pass upon both their struggle and their opponents'. Thus, Jewish history as written by Jews embodies the judgment of the victorious Elohist upon the defeated Yahwist,[45] the victorious priest upon the defeated prophet, the victorious Pharisee upon the lost Sadducee, the persisting rabbi upon the transient dissenter, the effortful nationalist upon the sentimental religionist, and so on. Contemporary parties in Israel employ or reverse these judgments in order to rationalize their own ends and to justify their own struggles. For example, the very reverend Dr. Cyrus Adler, President of the Jewish Theological Seminary, President of Dropsie College, President of the American Jewish Committee, etc., etc., will put together and invoke one set of historic judgments to justify his mortuary policy and attitude in Jewish life. The less reverend Drs. Albert Einstein or Stephen Wise[46] will invoke another set to justify their vital ones. Their compositions, their invocations, their demonstrations, their arguments are not revelations of the facts. Their compositions, their invocations, their demonstrations, and their arguments are only invidious uses, special applications of the facts. The facts themselves remain everlastingly neutral to all the causes that employ them, stubbornly elusive to all the meanings which are imposed on them.

We may get some inkling of the character and implications of the facts when the observer who studies them has no passionate concern about their use.

Thus, we may take it as being pretty close to the truth when George Foot Moore[47] tells us, in his magnificent *Judaism*, that the Judaistic tradition owns no theology in the Christian or Greek sense of the term; that its dynamic essence was the rule of life or the system of observances which were finally codified in the *Shulhan Arukh* and were the same wherever in the wide world Jews could be found; but that "basic human relations are without measure or norm and left to the conscience and right feeling of the individual"; that they are committed to heart.

But Moore was writing of what has sometimes been called "normative Judaism." He had also made a selection. He paid attention to nothing outside of this traditional historic complex which the generations kept on reliving until the middle of the last century. He ignored the variant, the new, the heretical, which had arisen and struggled to establish itself within the complex. But he knew he did so, and he did not endeavor to have anyone take the part for the whole. A complete science of Jewry cannot ignore those things. A complete science must include everything that any Jew has ever identified as Jewish in life and quality. But Jews laboring in their struggle for a life and a living, are prevented from dealing with this all-inclusive total. The time and place and circumstances of their struggle, its passions and its ideals dispose them to seek one item and reject another, so that their passions may be gratified and their ideals realized.

Thus, it is Dr. Einstein's necessity and his right to select from the Jewish inheritance that which seems to him pertinent to his struggle and his ideals. His opponents have the same necessity and right to make their own selections. But both he and they would be wrong if they treated their selections as accounts of the entire Jewish reality, as descriptions of the historic content of Judaism and Hebraism. In the nature of the case, such selections can be nothing of the sort. First and last, they are personal and class valuations, special pleas made by means of data lifted thus out of their original contexts, and employed to express the feelings and to realize the ideals of those who have so lifted them. Judaism or Hebraism is not any one of them by itself. It is all of them together—and then some.

Is there, then, a Jewish view of life? No. There is not *a* Jewish view of life. There are Jewish *views* of life. The views are many. Life, with all its conflicts and antagonisms and hates, indeed through them, makes itself somehow one.

MILTON STEINBERG

The Reasons for Religious Faith

The American conservative rabbi Milton Steinberg (1903–1950) was educated by the Jewish Theological Seminary, especially by Mordecai Kaplan, and by the naturalist philosopher Morris Raphael Cohen (1880–1947) of City College. From 1933 to his death he served as rabbi at New York's Park Avenue Synagogue. In *The Making of the Modern Jew* (1933) he analyzed the precarious status of the Jew in the modern world and examined the past for a better understanding of the present. He saw "the powers of dissolution struggle with the newer reinforcements of survival," without suggesting which would prevail. In *Basic Judaism* (1947) he posited a concise statement of Jewish faith for both Jews and inquiring Christians. Some of his writings were published posthumously: *A Believing Jew* (1951), *From the Sermons of Milton Steinberg* (1954), and *Anatomy of Faith* (1960). Yet, his real contribution resides not in what he wrote, said, or did, but in the man he was, in his love, his compassion, and his ability to listen and to help. The piece that follows is from *Anatomy of Faith*.

Religion's world outlook centers about God.

Before attempting to indicate what we mean by that word, let us first make clear what we do not mean.

"God" does not denote an old man on a throne somewhere up in the sky. That notion is in part a survival of the infancy of the human race, in part a hangover from our personal childhood, from those days when, having first heard about God and possessing only limited intellectual resources, we pictorialized Him according to our naïveté. However the conception is come by, it is far less innocent than is generally supposed. It impels many a person to regard himself as an atheist, simply because he does not believe that there really is an old man in the heavens. On the other hand, it condemns individuals capable of ripe spirituality to the stuntedness, perhaps lifelong, of puerile, unsatisfying, and undignified convictions.

To believe in God, maturely, intelligently, is to believe that reality did not just "happen," that it is no accident, no pointless interplay of matter and energy. It is to insist rather that things, including man's life, make sense, that they add up to something. It is to hold that the universe, physical and moral, is a cosmos, not an anarchy—made a cosmos instead of an anarchy, meaningful rather than mad, because it is the manifestation of a creating, sustaining, animating, design-lending Spirit, a Mind-will, or to use the oldest, most familiar and best word, a God.

Here at last we come to the crux of our investigation. Are there any reasons for maintaining that the world is of this character rather than that, that deity rather than nullity moves behind and through it?

There are such reasons, not one but a number, all good, indeed compelling.

God is the only tenable explanation for the universe.

Here we are, creatures of a day, in the midst of a vast, awesome world. Sometimes it strikes us as a big, blooming tumult. But through the seeming confusion some traits persist, constant and all-pervading.

Thus, the universe is *one*, an organic unity, subject everywhere to the same law, knitted together with interdependence.

Again, it is *dynamic*, pulsating with energy, movement, life.

It is *creative*, forever calling new things into being, from stars and solar systems to new breeds of animals, new ideas in the minds of men, new pictures on the artist's canvas.

It is *rational* in the sense that everything in it behaves according to law! Electrons and protons according to the rules of their being, plants in harmony with their nature, animals after the patterns of their respective kinds, and man in consonance with the mandates not only of chemistry, physics, and biology but of psychology and the moral order as well. Everywhere: form, design, predictable recurrence, law.

The universe, furthermore, is *purposive;* at least it is in some of its phases. An insect laying its eggs in a place where the larvae yet to be born will be assured of food as they will require it; a spider weaving its web, a bird building a nest, an engineer designing a bridge, a young man charting his career, a government drawing up a policy, a prophet blueprinting a perfected mankind—all these are instances, rudimentary or advanced, conscious or instinctual, of planning ahead. Purposiveness is indisputably an aspect of reality, and no theory can be said to explain the latter if it does not account for the former as well.

The universe further contains *consciousness.* It has produced man. At least in him it discloses intelligence, a thirst for truth, sensitivity to beauty, a desire for goodness. And man is a component of reality. Whence it follows that no explanation of the entirety can be acceptable if it does not illumine the existence and nature of this most complex, challenging and mysterious of its components.

This then is the world in which we live: one, dynamic, creative, rational, and inclusive of elements of purpose, consciousness, and goodness. For such a universe the religious theory is by far the best "fit." Only *it* accounts at all adequately for the striking features just enumerated. That is why men of all eras, cultures, and capacities, including most of the world's great philosophers, have tended so generally to arrive, no matter what their point of departure, at some kind of God-faith. For, once one begins to reflect on the nature of things, this is the only plausible explanation for them.

But what about the evil of the world? Can the God-idea account for *that?* Not entirely, and not to anyone's complete satisfaction. This fact unquestionably counts against faith. On the other hand, there are many interpretations of evil from the religious viewpoint whereby its existence can be reconciled, partially if not thoroughly, with the existence of God.

But even if evil were a total mystery on which theology could not make so much as a dent, the God-faith would still be indicated. For, at the worst, it leaves less unexplained than does its alternative. If the believer has his troubles with evil, the atheist has more and graver difficulties to contend with. Reality stumps him altogether, leaving him baffled not by one consideration but by many, from the existence of natural law through the instinctual cunning of the insect to the brain of the genius and heart of the prophet.

This then is the intellectual reason for believing in God: that, though this belief is not free from difficulties, it stands out, head and shoulders, as the best answer to the riddle of the universe.

The second reason for belief in God is that man cannot live joyously, hopefully, healthily, perhaps not at all, without it.

Consider what the universe and man look like under the assumption of atheism.

Reality appears totally devoid of point or purpose. Like everything else, man is seen as a by-product of a blind machine, his history a goalless eddy in an equally directionless whirlpool, his ideals random sparks thrown off by physiochemical reaction in the colloidal solution, compounded by chance, which is his brain. Everything adds up in the end to exactly nothing.

What is the consequence of such a view for man and society? Can it be other than discouragement, demoralization, despair? What else shall one say of it except that "that way madness lies." [. . .]

But is this fair to atheists? Have not some of them been among the most unselfish and self-forgetting of mortals? And on the other hand, are not many of the most bestial and least idealistic of human beings religionists?

No, what we have just said, had it been said of atheists, would have been grossly unfair. But it does no injustice whatsoever to atheism, the inescapable effects of which are to trivialize ideals, to present the human enterprise as a futility, and so to undermine the classic ethic of justice, mercy, and self-negation on behalf of moral principle and human welfare.

But, if so, how is one to account for the goodness of so many irreligionists? Very simply. Men often behave better than their philosophy. Only they cannot be expected to persist in doing so. In the end, how a man thinks must affect how he acts; atheism must finally, if not in one generation then in several, remake the conduct of atheists in the light of its own logic. [. . .]

CYNTHIA OZICK

On Living in the Gentile World

The native New Yorker Cynthia Ozick has been teaching English and fiction writing at American universities. In 1966 her novel *Trust* and in 1971 *The Pagan Rabbi and Other Stories* were published. In addition she has written essays and criticism that appeared in periodicals. In 1970 she presented a paper, "America: Toward Yavneh," at the America-Israel Dialogue at Rehovot (*Judaism* XIX, 3, Summer 1970). As a writer she has achieved almost complete freedom from the aspects that mark and often plague American Jewish authors, the "pull of nature," the gentile rhythm by which the world goes around, "Greek and pagan modes," and, in general, "Western Civilization and the religion of Art" and aesthetics. Instead, she hearkens back to the very sources of Judaism: Sinai that commands deed, conduct, act; the commandments against idols; the words of Rashi and Judah ha-Levi and Agnon, a literature "that touches on the liturgical" (liturgy as a type of perception); and Zion. Hers is a new, fresh voice.

The essay here reprinted was Cynthia Ozick's statement in a symposium on "Living in Two Cultures" (*Response*, Fall 1972).

Sometimes, when depressed or fatigued by a great deal of reading on Jewish subjects, I begin to wonder whether our gasping aspirations to make a Jewish literature in America are worthwhile. I become exhausted not by the task itself or even by the hope of it, because I hardly know whether I will ever be able to grapple with this task, but by the actual *formulation* of the task. I begin to think: is it necessary? and for what purpose? and for whom? I begin to feel irritation with so much emphasis on differentness, on marginality, on narrow dedication—on *survival*—and a kind of easeful sloth invades me, and I want to slide off into everydayness and everyone-ness. It is not so much that I am lured by the gentile world—this is for me by and large no longer true—as that I become worn out by the demands of thinking, thinking always about historical resonances, and by being always on the alert, and by always analyzing, and judging, and interpreting according to Jewish valuations.

Especially in diaspora we cannot be Jewish just by *being;* and that is the exhaustion and the difficulty. If we lapse even for a moment into "just being," then we have lapsed into the gentile world, into, from our point of view, triviality. So to remain Jewish is a *process*—something which is an ongoing and muscular thing, a progress or, sometimes, a regression, a constant self-reminding, a caravan of watchfulness always on the move; above all an unsparing *consciousness.* A friend of mine, a novelist, calls this labor—because it *is* a labor, and requires both stamina and steadfastness—she calls it a "peeling away."

My friend is a recent newcomer to Boston from New York's literary Upper West Side, and among the ways she has attempted to deal with the dislocation of losing her native city is by learning Hebrew and by attending the weekly colloquia at the New England seat of Rabbi [Joseph D.] Soloveitchik, the talmudic *ilui* and luminary. It is a curious thing that the means she chooses to get used to an untried part of America is a resumption of Jewish learning, as if growing more Jewish would somehow compensate for the daily sense of unfamiliarity in a new place. It is a miniaturization of our old habit; feeling homeless, we make a home in Torah. But it is only half her means; besides studying Hebrew and going to hear Rabbi Soloveitchik, my friend reads intensively in Emerson, and ends by teaching Emerson at Harvard. Torah is a home, but Emerson, she explains, is a traveler's keepsake. Recently she wrote me a letter about all this. Though the letter says "you," it is not the "you" of the alienated son in the *Haggadah;* it is clear that she means herself too, and all diaspora writers who are trying to think seriously about being Jews. She writes:

"More and more you are peeling away what seemed so attractive in the gentile world—that seemingly impeccable taste and style and rightness. You want, I think, to show the trivialness beneath the charisma of even the best gentiles. I gasp at the audaciousness of it when every once in a while it comes over me. Is it an either/or struggle? Must I melt down these little keepsakes I've lugged through the years? What a feeling of freedom that gives just to think about it! What a marvel it would be to come into some wholeness of mind after so many splintered years! Soloveitchik offers wholeness of mind, but I have to sit at a second-class table to get it."

(The reference to the second-class table is literal, not metaphoric. Wherever the master of *halakhah* presides, there looms the *mehitzah*.)

What I marveled at in my friend's letter was the word "audaciousness." Is it "audacious" to want to have what she herself calls "some wholeness of mind," or is it the very opposite, a desire for repose and relief, the surrender of the relaxed will? The splintered condition, it seems to me, is the more usual vessel of audaciousness. It takes nerve to attempt to live in two cultures which often conflict, and, even when they do not conflict, do not quite match; what it means is developing two distinct self-characterizations, one never quite at home with each other. But wholeness is a coming home to oneself, and it ought to be ease rather than daring we experience when we are knowingly and confidently at home. Why, then, does my friend suppose that it is necessary to be audacious—all spikes up and out and at the ready—in order to achieve a Jewish wholeness?

Before I have a try at what I think might be the answer, I would like to tell you what happened on a fragrant green lawn in the first explosion of Spring about two weeks ago. My little daughter is in the first grade of a suburban yeshivah. One afternoon, while visiting her school, I encountered the headmaster. We began to talk about the very things my novelist-friend had written in her letter. The headmaster, a Cambridge mathematician of radiant sophistication, explained his own "splintering." On the one hand, he said, he was a scientific rationalist, and on the other hand, he recognized the authority of, and paid homage to, every punctilio of Commandment. The rationalist was not disposed to accept authority, and had to work ideas through by every known test and proof. But the *halakhah*-abiding Jew bowed to the revelation on Sinai. To illustrate the paradox and to demonstrate his sense of things—that Sinai has authority over scholarship—he began to tell a *midrash*:[48]

Rabbi Akiva studied profoundly and was, more than other mortals, able to penetrate the most abstruse corners of the Law. Among his feats was his ability to unlock the meaning of the serifs, in the shape of tiny crowns, which adorn the heads of some of the letters that appear in the Scroll of the Law. These delectable flourishes the Master of the Universe, blessed be He, had added after giving Moses the Tablets; so Moses, poring disconsolately over the scrolls in heaven, was not familiar with them and could not decipher them. "What do the little crowns mean?" he asked God. God replied: "Only Akiva has entered into the heart of this puzzle." Moses was understandably resentful: he was the teacher, and his pupil, born centuries after him, had exceeded him. "Well then," he said to God, "how did Akiva get to be so wise?" God took pity on Moses and answered, "Because he received the Law from Moses on Sinai."

Here the headmaster stopped; his *midrash* hung in the air unfinished. The reason he stopped was this: a man was running wildly over the grass toward us. He wore a white shirt with the sleeves pushed up and a white apron. The apron was flapping around his legs as he ran, and his arms were flying out before him. When he came near I saw that one of his wrists had a row of tattooed numbers on it, and I recognized him as the school cook.

He told what had just happened. Two boys on bicycles had come through the school gates and were riding back and forth over a newly-seeded lawn, destroying it. The cook asked them to go away. They said: "You Jew, Hitler should have burned you too." Then they rode off beyond reach.

The headmaster stood and was silent. He looked at the cook.

The cook looked down at the grass. His fingers were shaking. I wondered what the headmaster would say. From a certain point of view the incident was a very small one. But for the cook, with his tattooed forearm, the incident was not small, only miniature. Quite suddenly the headmaster began again to speak. I was surprised; it was all at once plain that he had chosen to make no comment on what had just happened. Instead he merely resumed telling of the *midrash* as if there had been no interruption at all:

Then Moses said to God: "What happened to this man, who penetrated Torah beyond the reach even of Moses?" God replied, "Take eight steps backward." And Moses took eight steps backward, step by step, passing days and weeks and then years and then decades and then at last centuries, until he came to Rabbi Akiva. And there was Akiva in his martyrdom, bound before his torturers, who were combing his flesh with iron combs. And Moses cried to God, "Then was it all for nothing?" God answered: "That is the question that is not to be asked."

And so I understood one thing at least: that the headmaster, in choosing to make no comment but to resume the *midrash*, had after all given his comment. The resumption was itself the comment.

So we must resume; and it is the resumption that is the audacious thing. For the one certainty we can count on the world for is that it will interrupt us. The history of the Jews has always been a history of interruptions—sometimes in the form of eruptions, the fiery stake or the fiery oven, but now and then, in milder times, in the form of allure. Boys on bikes are more than a future pockmark in the eternal plague of anti-Semitism: they are also demonic disguises for voices in ourselves, those worldly voices which stir us now and again to think, Oh, oh, if only I were well out of this, if I too could be *other*, not subject to the irrational flaw endemic in the planet, well out of it, on the other side, the plunderer rather than the keeper of the grass, the careless cruel shouter rather than the man who barely escaped becoming ash. I do not say that we necessarily desire to be persecutors; but we desire to be free of the persecutor's breath, as the persecutor himself is free of his own breath, because he applies no consciousness to his breath, he breathes as simply as the predatory birds breathe upon living things.

And we want *not* to resume, but to go as simply and as freely as a pair of boys on a pair of bikes, or like the predatory birds who belong, after all, to the body of nature. At bottom what we want is to become ourselves an aspect of the natural, to be natural men and natural women—which (we know this intuitively) somehow feels different from being a Jew. To be natural: that way lies ease, and an energetic and athletic sort of sloth which is the worst sloth of all, and surrender, and, ultimately, worldliness and sentimentality. Worldliness: the gullibility that disbelieves everything. Sentimentality: the desire to escape history. Sentimentality means the urge to cover over, to make excuses for, to obscure with justification; it is a negative urge *not to clarify;* instead to choose an explanation that makes things seem easy rather than clear. History and nature are not friends. Nature offers ease: here you are, and what you need to be is only what your biology requires of you; all the rest is dream and imagination. History offers the hard life: history says, Beyond your biology stands Clarification. History says to us: Clarify, clarify! But what does it mean to clarify? Like Akiva, we must always look a little deeper, into the sense of the tiny crowns on the letters; but like Moses, we must not look too deeply, or a blind predatory nature will swallow us up. The question "Then it is all for nothing?" is of course not a question but an answer: "Look," goes the answer, "you see it is all for nothing." And that is nature's answer, the answer of the predatory birds and the predatory boys on bikes. It is all for nothing, so let us destroy the grass and let us burn the man, because you see it is all for nothing.

The Jew chooses against nature and in behalf of the clarifying impulse. He chooses in behalf of history. The terrible—and terrifying—difficulty is that it is truly against our natures to choose against nature. We do not want to do it. We do not want to make the trouble and the sorrow and the burden and the damn hard work of it. Why did Isaac Babel join the strenuous Cossacks? To rest from the fatigue of being a Jew. The self-righteous Jew who blames or despises the weak or self-hating Jew must remind himself how he, too, often dreams of riding off into naturalness and worldliness and sentiment, of escaping the reality-pain that clarification imposes. History is pain. From Egypt to the shame of the calf at the foot of Sinai to Treblinka is no natural road. One need not believe in God—in a sense, one *should* not—in order to see that ours has not been a natural road. The stopping-point at Sinai meant that the natural world would thereafter be differentiated from the holy. Among ancient peoples all the days of the week were alike, and that, of course, was only natural; to the trees and the fish and the molecules of air all the days *are* alike, nothing makes a week. Sinai made the Sabbath. The Sabbath is a made, invented, created, *given* thing; it is not a natural thing. What is holy is not natural, and what is natural is not holy. The God of the Jews must not be conceived of as belonging to nature—not in the image of anything we can know or recognize, not tree, not stone, not any heavenly body, least of all man. And so when the Jew chooses history instead of nature he is not thinking about a natural progression of days, event following event. If we left history to nature it would be a sort of bundle one generation hauls off its back to launch onto the next generation; every twenty-five years or so the bundle gets heavier and heavier, and the accumulation continues without conscience forever and ever. But history for the Jew is not like this; history for the Jew is not simply what has happened, it is a judgment on what has happened. History is to the continuum of events what the Sabbath is to the progression of days.

It is audacious to remember the Sabbath when day after ordinary day is what is natural. It is audacious to choose the judgment of history when the plain passage of events is what is natural. It is audacious to choose against nature. We are natural beings, every breath and bit of us is natural, the amino acids that drive us drive the stars, the galaxies share the dust beneath our fingernails. The earth is filled with other philosophies than ours, and they are all luring. Ours is the only philosophy which imposes a Sabbath on nature's loose equalities. The others invite us to let go, to succumb, to merge, to see God in everything around us, to see God in men or in one man, to confuse the natural with the holy, ourselves with God. How we want to join all those other philosophies which equalize and simplify! How freeing, how restful, to slide at last into nature and give up invention and observation, consciousness and conscience, judgment and justice! *That* is the real wholeness of mind: to accept nature's incontrovertible wholeness, to dismiss whatever is not in nature as dream and imagination, to dismiss as dream and imagination both the Sabbath and justice, because neither one is in nature.

It looks as if we cannot have wholeness of mind and live as Jews. Here my novelist-friend and I do not concur. "Is it an either/or struggle?" she cries, hoping for a Jewish wholeness. Presumably yes, it is an either/or struggle. Nature and holiness are not one, and somehow we mean to include them both. Nature we cannot exclude. But if we dare to dream and imagine holiness, we will have to wrestle until we are past exhaustion with denying nature its diurnal claims, and past self-despising too. It is easy to despise ourselves for choosing struggle instead of relief. It is easy and relieving to join the Cossacks. It is hard to be a Jew not only because we live from moment to moment with the smell of incipient pogrom—in Moscow the bureaucrats in the visa offices, in the suburbs of New York a pair of boys on bikes—but because we are engaged from moment to moment in separating ourselves from wanting the restful life of the Cossacks, who always come dressed as bureaucrats or boys. It is the unnatural Sabbath which separates us from the Cossacks. If we rest on the Sabbath, we do not rest in life, as the Cossacks do.

In literature too—I come back briefly to literature, as I briefly began with it—it is relieving to join the Cossacks, to write about Cossack life, to write naturally about what is most easily at hand. It gives wholeness of mind. But Jacob did not become Israel until he fought all night and was not left whole. The angel, you remember, struck him in the sinew of his thigh.[49] A Jewish literature is not a literature of wholeness; it too must have the angel's terrible mark left visibly in its sinew. A Jewish literature, like a Jewish life, should leave us with the sense of having been struck in the very meat of our being, altered by the blow.

ARTHUR A. COHEN

Human Fraternity:
The Liturgy of Theological Enmity

Arthur A. Cohen, born in 1928 in New York, studied at the University of Chicago and Columbia University (philosophy and history of religion) and at the Jewish Theological Seminary (medieval Jewish philosophy). From 1957 to 1961 he was consultant to the project "Religion and Free Society" of the Fund for the Republic. He founded Meridian Books, was an editor at Holt, Rinehart and Winston, and has been on the editorial advisory board of several periodicals. Among his writings are *Martin Buber* (1957), *The Natural and the Supernatural Jew* (1962), *The Myth of the Judeo-Christian Tradition* (1965).

Cohen's Judaism is rooted not in convention or family tradition but in theological conviction. He is representative of a small but determined group of younger American theologians who found their way back to a Judaism not restricted to convenient post-Emancipation formulations. To Cohen, "adjustment of the Jew to the natural conditions of his environment divests him of the only weapon, his supernatural vocation, which allows him to survive. The natural Jew as such has, we believe, no hope." He rejects "the myth of the Judeo-Christian tradition," yet, as evident from the passage here reprinted, he believes in the possibility of the emergence of a "Judeo-Christian humanism" based on the recognition by both Christian and Jew "of the magnitude of creation and the misery of man."

It is not enough to assert the reality of theological enmity nor to condemn human cruelty which issues from it. To invigorate the combat over truth is in itself no guarantee that men will not impose their absolutes by tyranny. But there is a process of learning and there is as well the willingness to do human work and leave divine work to God.

The hope which may be brought to the conflict over truth arises less from certainty that human beings are able to control the passions which accompany reflection and belief than from the conviction that whatever the temptations, Christians and Jews are aware of the demonism of which they are capable. It would be easier if we could disavow the enmity, if Jews could abandon their aristocratic *hauteur* before Jesus as Christ and Christians could acknowledge the legitimacy of Torah. But such accomodations are historical concessions which can balsam the abraded surface, but affect none of the deeper sources of the agitation. There are no resolutions possible in history other than the conversion of the Jews or the relapse of Christians into paganism. Assuming that Christians and Jews continue to believe as they have, we must, then, either reckon with the likelihood of a recrudescence of anti-Semitism (translating into social and political terms the ongoing anger of Christendom) or we must find a way of taking the contest of truth and making it a source of human community.

The humanist tradition of the Renaissance suggests certain possibilities which are relevant. It was a classicist humanism, and the concern for man arose less from an ideology of human equality than from the conviction that a common tradition of learning was available to Western man which civilizes the passions, educates the sensibilities, and transcends the borders of class, church, and nation. Learning was without boundaries, and community of learning, compassing the literature of Greece and Rome as well as that of Gospels and Church Fathers, supplied a coherence and commonalty to literary and intellectual activity which otherwise, limited either to theological pietism or to the contest with ideological heresy, would become repressive and deadly. The later humanism of the Enlightenment, regarded by both its supporters and its opponents as atheist and paganic, nevertheless focussed its critical and creative power upon the liberation of man from fanaticism, parochialism, superstition, irrationality. Both the Christian humanism of the Renaissance and the Enlightenment spirit of pagan humanism are parts of our historical legacy. The question that must be raised is whether, against the background of an essential theological enmity, it is possible to develop the resources of a Judeo-Christian humanism.

The enmity of Judaism and Christianity is founded upon the divergence of images of salvation. It is an appropriate issue upon which to define historical enmity, for the ultimate meeting of God and man in the fullness of time is salvation. But however the disunion of Jews and Christians is understood, before the End, both are incomplete. They are incomplete in their humanity, however virtual their assurance of redemption as believers. It is irrelevant to the condition of fulfillment in faith that Jews (amidst time and history) are already with God at the End or that Christians are redeemed in Christ, if the travail of history in which the humanity of both are tried continues. Elsewhere I have suggested that, theologically speaking, the Exile is the historical coefficient of being unredeemed.[50] What I intended then, referring to a specific condition of the Jews, is generally relevant here. The alienation of the humanity of the believer from God is witnessed to by the perpetuation of a whole variety of human, historical evils—war, poverty, racism, and that ongoing insensitivity, avarice, viciousness, cruelty which make them possible. The historical coefficient of the unredemption of Jews and Christians—whatever their redemption by faith and service—is that men continue to suffer from those evils which men can cure. Surely one acknowledges the need of grace that the hardened heart be relieved, that care, solicitude, the compassion possible even to the powerful be released, but the quietism which waits upon grace is not tolerable to the oppressed. The Negro no longer waits upon grace, nor does the Israeli, nor does the Latin American, nor do the Vietnamese. There is a weariness with the councils of quietism and whatever their relevance to the interior life, which may be ordered toward God; the world of suffering men and tormented institutions can no longer suffice with their conservative patience.

Jews and Christians have joined together, during these past decades, not alone as men in their naked humanity but as men bearing psalms and seeing visions to oppose the evils of history and to work toward the conditions of peace. They have joined against racism, they have labored against the war in Vietnam, they have been critical of all tyrannies and imperialisms, they have striven against poverty, dispossession, ignorance, disease. It could not be said that Judaism and Christianity have been wholehearted, that official declarations, official movements, official radicalism has defined their common militancy, but that is never and could only be under extraordinary conditions of leadership and spiritual regeneration. It is unquestionable, however, that now, as never before, Christians and Jews have managed to invest their enmity with a common love of the human person and his condition which brunts the hard intransigence of theological vindictiveness and makes of the quest for salvation—even over the chasm of a historical divison—an act of loving men. The natural Jew and the human Christian find a common means of incarnating their vision of the Kingdom of God by joining together as faithful to have faith in the historical man and his predicament.

The Judeo-Christian humanism is first and foremost conviction about the need to work within history to make the way smooth for the Kingdom. It matters not at all how God saves us. It is only that he saves us. Levi Yitzhak of Berditchev, seeing before him the destruction that followed in the aftermath of the Napoleonic wars, could pray that God save the gentiles, even if he delayed in saving the Jews. He intended that the love of man have precedence over theological promises. God will provide his redemption, but man must first offer his human love. The Judeo-Christian fraternity is in the love and service of man—and this in utmost radicality, in utmost criticism of the principalities and dominions of the world which immobilize fluidity of human address, deprive us of openness, deny us acess to one another.

The Jew and the Christian care for men, beyond loyalty to any contingent institution which pretends idolatrously to be eternal—whether such be a civil law, an economic doctrine, a society of privilege, a class, or a nation. The Jew and the Christian must come together, therefore, not only as common workers in causes and movements, but as thinkers who must grow to accommodate different conditions of history, whose obligation to reflect upon change and movement is as great as their obligation to preserve ancient prophecies. The prophets of Jerusalem could afford to be general in their search for justice and mercy since all who heard them knew the injustice and corruption to which they spoke. But our ears resonate to other injustices and more subtle corruptions—the racism, poverty, military-mercantile alliances of the ancient world were differently textured and the crimes of that time were differently regarded than the crimes of our own. The ancient Jews coped with the institution of slavery and xenophobic hostility to the pagan enemy, however coupled such were with calls to tolerance and generosity toward the stranger and alien. But then, unlike now, human care for the poor and the dispossessed was uncommonly pronounced, and charity for the orphan and the widow might serve the welfare agencies of our societies with models for moral fervor. In other words, the morality of the Bible can be our morality, but not as a closed codex transmitted without editorial revision. Morality—however we understand natural law—is always an instrumentality of history and must always be adjudicated to authentic needs.

Judeo-Christian humanism must be, then more than programmatic, speculative, more than directive, prophetic. We cannot raise up prophets who will announce to us what we must do and hear, but we can as men prepare history for the time of salvation, and, however our common action together or our coming to think together, our joining will be prophetic.

Lastly—and I think this aloud with tentativeness—both Jews and Christians in their human concern for human beings have need of the holy spirit, whether the holy spirit be the teaching voice, the *bat kol* of rabbinic times, the gift of grace. The bringing into our midst of the holy spirit is a task, not alone of prayer in singleness and within our historical liturgies, but in the formation of a liturgical expression of our humanism. The Jew need not learn to hear the Christian speak of the Christ nor must the Christian learn to hear the Jew speak of the dominion of Torah in the time of the Messiah; but both must come to hear in each other the sounds of truth—that the prayer of the Jew is not alone for Jew, but for all men, that the prayer of the Christian is not only for the faithful in Christ, but for all men. It is the commonalty of human suffering that is the commonalty of Christian and Jew; and there must come, as a miracle of grace, a means of expressing that shared experience. Such a liturgy must be a means of purgation—putting to rest the anger which has been the history of Jews and Christians and a liturgy of hope—making appeal to God for the wisdom and forbearance to join together, beyond the temptations of power and divisiveness to serve creation.

Upon one thing Jews and Christians agree: the magnitude of creation and the grandeur and misery of man. Out of such agreement an authentic community, a viable consensus, a meaningful cooperation can emerge—the Judeo-Christian humanism.

ELIE WIESEL

Yom Kippur:
The Day Without Forgiveness

Elie Wiesel was born in 1928 in Szighet, Transylvania, and grew up in the Judaic tradition. In 1944 the Jews of his town were deported to various concentration camps. Wiesel was rescued and lived first in Paris (attending the Sorbonne from 1948 to 1951), then, from 1956 to the present, in New York. Since 1947 he has been chief foreign correspondent for the Israeli *Yediot Aharonot*. He is Distinguished Professor of Jewish Studies at City College, New York and, starting in 1976, will teach at Boston University as Andrew W. Mellon Professor of the Humanities.

Wiesel is the most prominent spokesman for the survivors of the holocaust. His chief media of expression are novels, short stories, and essays, most of which first appear in French. *La Nuit* (1958; English edition, *Night*, 1960) documents his experiences in Auschwitz and the death of his father and of his God. *Les portes de la forêt* (1964; *The Gates of the Forest*, 1966) depicts the fate of the Jews in Hungary. Other works include *Le chant des morts* (1966; *Legends of Our Time*, 1968); *Les Juifs du silence* (1966; *The Jews of Silence*, 1968), an account of the plight of Soviet Jewry; *Célébration Hassidique* (1971; *Souls on Fire: Portraits and Legends of Hasidic Masters*, 1972); and *Zalmen, or the Madness of God* (a play, 1974). The piece that follows is taken from *Legends of Our Time*.

With a lifeless look, a painful smile on his face, while digging a hole in the ground, Pinhas moved his lips in silence. He appeared to be arguing with someone within himself and, judging from his expression, seemed close to admitting defeat.

I had never seen him so downhearted. I knew that his body would not hold out much longer. His strength was already abandoning him, his movements were becoming more heavy, more chaotic. No doubt he knew it too. But death figured only rarely in our conversations. We preferred to deny its presence, to reduce it, as in the past, to a simple allusion, something abstract, inoffensive, a word like any other.

"What are you thinking about? What's wrong?"

Pinhas lowered his head, as if to conceal his embarrassment, or his sadness, or both, and let a long time go by before he answered, in a voice scarcely audible: "Tomorrow is Yom Kippur."

Then I too felt depressed. My first Yom Kippur in the camp. Perhaps my last. The day of judgment, of atonement. Tomorrow the heavenly tribunal would sit and pass sentence: "And like unto a flock, the creatures of this world shall pass before thee."[51] Once upon a time—last year—the approach of this day of tears, of penitence and fear, had made me tremble. Tomorrow, we would present ourselves before God, who sees everything and who knows everything, and we would say: "Father, have pity on your children." Would I be capable of praying with fervor again? Pinhas shook himself abruptly. His glance plunged into mine.

"Tomorrow is the Day of Atonement and I have just made a decision: I am not going to fast. Do you hear? I am not going to fast."

I asked for no explanation. I knew he was going to die and suddenly I was afraid that by way of justification he might declare: "It is simple, I have decided not to comply with the law anymore and not to fast because in the eyes of man and of God I am already dead, and the dead can disobey the commandments of the Torah." I lowered my head and made believe I was not thinking about anything but the earth I was digging up under a sky more dark than the earth itself.

We belonged to the same Kommando. We always managed to

work side by side. Our age difference did not stop him from treating me like a friend. He must have been past forty. I was fifteen. Before the war, he had been *Rosh-Yeshivah*, director of a rabbinical school somewhere in Galicia. Often, to outwit our hunger or to forget our reasons for despair, we would study a page of the Talmud from memory. I relived my childhood by forcing myself not to think about those who were gone. If one of my arguments pleased Pinhas, if I quoted a commentary without distorting its meaning, he would smile at me and say: "I should have liked to have you among my disciples."

And I would answer: "But I am your disciple, where we are matters little."

That was false, the place was of capital importance. According to the law of the camp I was his equal; I used the familiar form when I addressed him. Any other form of address was inconceivable.

"Do you hear?" Pinhas shouted defiantly. "I will not fast."

"I understand. You are right. One must not fast. Not at Auschwitz. Here we live outside time, outside sin. Yom Kippur does not apply to Auschwitz."

Ever since Rosh ha-Shanah, the New Year, the question had been bitterly debated all over camp. Fasting meant a quicker death. Here everybody fasted all year round. Every day was Yom Kippur. And the book of life and death was no longer in God's hands, but in the hands of the executioner. The words *mi yichye umi yamut*, "who shall live and who shall die," had a terrible real meaning here, an immediate bearing. And all the prayers in the world could not alter the *gzar-din*, the inexorable movement of fate. Here, in order to live, one had to eat, not pray.

"You are right, Pinhas," I said, forcing myself to withstand his gaze. "You *must* eat tomorrow. You've been here longer than I have, longer than many of us. You need your strength. You have to save your strength, watch over it, protect it. You should not go beyond your limits. Or tempt misfortune. That would be a sin."

Me, his disciple? I gave him lessons, I gave him advice, as if I were his elder, his guide.

"That is not it," said Pinhas, getting irritated. "I could hold out for one day without food. It would not be the first time."

"Then what is it?"

"A decision. Until now, I've accepted everything. Without bitterness, without reservation. I have told myself: 'God knows what he is doing.' I have submitted to his will. Now I have had enough, I have reached my limit. If he knows what he is doing, then it is serious; and it is not any less serious if he does not. Therefore, I have decided to tell him: 'It is enough.' "

I said nothing. How could I argue with him? I was going through the same crisis. Every day I was moving a little further away from the God of my childhood. He had become a stranger to me; sometimes, I even thought he was my enemy.

The appearance of Edek put an end to our conversation. He was our master, our king. The Kapo. This young Pole with rosy cheeks, with the movements of a wild animal, enjoyed catching his slaves by surprise and making them shout with fear. Still an adolescent, he enjoyed possessing such power over so many adults. We dreaded his changeable moods, his sudden fits of anger: without unclenching his teeth, his eyes half-closed, he would beat his victims long after they had lost consciousness and had ceased to moan.

"Well?" he said, planting himself in front of us, his arms folded. "Taking a little nap? Talking over old times? You think you are at a resort? Or in the synagogue?"

A cruel flame lit his blue eyes, but it went out just as quickly. An aborted rage. We began to shovel furiously, not thinking about anything but the ground which opened up menacingly before us. Edek insulted us a few more times and then walked off.

Pinhas did not feel like talking anymore, neither did I. For him the die had been cast. The break with God appeared complete.

Meanwhile, the pit under our legs was becoming wider and deeper. Soon our heads would hardly be visible above the ground. I had the weird sensation that I was digging a grave. For whom? For Pinhas? For myself? Perhaps for our memories.

On my return to camp, I found it plunged in feverish anticipation: they were preparing to welcome the holiest and longest day of the year. My barracks neighbors, a father and son, were talking in low voices. One was saying: "Let us hope the roll-call does not last too long." The other added: "Let us hope that the soup is distributed before the sun sets, otherwise we will not have the right to touch it."

Their prayers were answered. The roll-call unfolded without incident, without delay, without public hanging. The section-chief hurriedly distributed the soup; I hurriedly gulped it down. I ran to wash, to purify myself. By the time the day was drawing to a close, I was ready.

Some days before, on the eve of Rosh ha-Shanah, all the Jews in camp—Kapos included—had congregated at the square where roll was taken, and we had implored the God of Abraham, Isaac, and Jacob to end our humiliation, to change sides, to break his pact with the enemy. In unison we had said *Kaddish* for the dead and for the living as well. Officers and soldiers, machine guns in hand, had stood by, amused spectators, on the other side of the barbed wire.

Now, we did not go back there for *Kol Nidre*. We were afraid of a selection: in preceding years, the Day of Atonement has been turned into a day of mourning. Yom Kippur had become *Tisha be-Av*, the day the Temple was destroyed.

Thus, each barracks housed its own synagogue. It was more prudent. I was sorry, because Pinhas was in another block.

A Hungarian rabbi officiated as our cantor. His voice stirred my memories and evoked that legend according to which, on the night of Yom Kippur, the dead rise from their graves and come to pray with the living. I thought: "Then it is true; that is what really happens. The legend is confirmed at Auschwitz."

For weeks, several learned Jews had gathered every night in our block to transcribe from memory—by hand, on toilet paper—the prayers for the High Holy Days. Each cantor received a copy. Ours read in a loud voice and we repeated each verse after him. The *Kol Nidre*, which releases us from all vows made under constraint, now seemed to me anachronistic, absurd, even though it had been composed in similar circumstances, in Spain, right near the Inquisition stakes. Once a year the converts would assemble and cry out to God: "Know this, all that we have said is unsaid, all that we have done is undone." *Kol Nidre?* A sad joke.

Here and now we no longer had any secret vows to make or to deny: everything was clear, irrevocable.

Then came the *Vidui*, the great confession. There again, everything rang false, none of it concerned us anymore. *Ashamnu*, we have sinned. *Bagadnu*, we have betrayed. *Gazalnu*, we have stolen. What? Us? *We* have sinned? Against whom? By doing what? *We* have betrayed? Whom? Undoubtedly this was the first time since God judged his creation that victims beat their breasts accusing themselves of the crimes of their executioners.

Why did we take responsibility for sins and offenses which not one of us could ever have had the desire or the possibility of committing? Perhaps we felt guilty despite everything. Things were simpler that way. It was better to believe our punishments had meaning, that we had deserved them; to believe in a cruel but just God was better than not to believe at all. It was in order not to provoke an open war between God and his people that we had chosen to spare him, and we cried out: "You are our God, blessed be your name. You smite us without pity, you shed our blood, we give thanks to you for it, O Eternal One, for you are determined to show us that you are just and that your name is justice!"

I admit having joined my voice to the others and implored the heavens to grant me mercy and forgiveness. At variance with everything my lips were saying, I indicted myself only to turn everything into derision, into farce. At any moment I expected the Master of the Universe to strike me dumb and to say: "That is enough—you have gone too far." And I like to think I would have replied: "You, also, blessed by your name, you also."

Our services were dispersed by the camp bell. The section-chiefs began to yell: "Okay, go to sleep! If God hasn't heard you, it's because he is incapable of hearing."

The next day, at work, Pinhas joined another group. I thought: "He wants to eat without being embarrassed by my presence." A day later, he returned. His face even more pale, even more gaunt than before. Death was gnawing at him. I caught myself thinking: "He will die because he did not observe Yom Kippur."

We dug for several hours without looking at each other. From far off, the shouting of the Kapo reached us. He walked around hitting people relentlessly.

Toward the end of the afternoon, Pinhas spoke to me: "I have a confession to make."

I shuddered, but went on digging. A strange, almost child-like smile appeared on his lips when he spoke again: "You know, I fasted."

I remained motionless. My stupor amused him.

"Yes, I fasted. Like the others. But not for the same reasons. Not out of obedience, but out of defiance. Before the war, you see, some Jews rebelled against the divine will by going to restaurants on the Day of Atonement; here, it is by observing the fast that we can make our indignation heard. Yes, my disciple and teacher, know that I fasted. Not for love of God, but against God."

He left me a few weeks later, victim of the first selection.

He shook my hand: "I would have liked to die some other way and elsewhere. I had always hoped to make of my death, as of my life, an act of faith. It is a pity. God prevents me from realizing my dream. He no longer likes dreams."

Nonetheless, he asked me to say *Kaddish* for him after his death, which, according to his calculations, would take place three days after his departure from camp.

"But why?" I asked, "since you are no longer a believer?"

He took the tone he always used when he explained a passage in the Talmud to me: "You do not see the heart of the matter. Here and now, the only way to accuse him is by praising him."

And he went, laughing, to his death.

EMIL L. FACKENHEIM

The Voice of Auschwitz

The philosopher Emil Ludwig Fackenheim (b. 1916) was ordained a liberal rabbi in 1939; in 1940 he left his native Germany and for many years has been affiliated with the department of philosophy at the University of Toronto. He has been an interpreter of Jewish faith in such books as *Paths to Jewish Belief* (1960) and *God's Presence in History* (1970), from which the following essay is taken, and has presented *The Religious Dimension in Hegel's Thought* (1968). His essays in Jewish theology are collected in *Quest for Past and Future* (1968); they deal with religious authority, Jewish-Christian-secularist dialogue, revelation, salvation. He gave deep thought to the possible meaning of the Nazi holocaust.

What does the Voice of Auschwitz command?

Jews are forbidden to hand Hitler posthumous victories. They are commanded to survive as Jews, lest the Jewish people perish. They are commanded to remember the victims of Auschwitz lest their memory perish. They are forbidden to despair of man and his world, and to escape into either cynicism or otherworldliness, lest they cooperate in delivering the world over to the forces of Auschwitz. Finally, they are forbidden to despair of the God of Israel, lest Judaism perish. A secularist Jew cannot make himself believe

by a mere act of will, nor can he be commanded to do so. . . . And a
religious Jew who has stayed with his God may be forced into new,
possibly revolutionary relationships with Him. One possibility,
however, is wholly unthinkable. A Jew may not respond to Hitler's
attempt to destroy Judaism by himself cooperating in its destruction. In ancient times, the unthinkable Jewish sin was idolatry,
Today, it is to respond to Hitler by doing his work. [52]

Elie Wiesel has compared the holocaust with Sinai in revela-
tory significance—and expressed the fear that we are not listening.
We shrink from this daring comparison—but even more from not
listening. We shrink from any claim to have heard—but even more
from a false refuge, in an endless agnosticism, from a Voice
speaking to us. I was able to make the above, fragmentary statement [. . .] only because it no more than articulates what is being
heard by Jews the world over—rich and poor, learned and ignorant, believing and secularist. I cannot go beyond this earlier
statement but only expand it.

1. The First Fragment

In the murder camps the unarmed, decimated, emaciated survivors often rallied their feeble remaining resources for a final,
desperate attempt at revolt. The revolt was hopeless. There was no
hope but one. One might escape. Why must one escape? To tell
the tale. Why must the tale be told when evidence was already at
hand that the world would not listen?[53] Because not to tell the
tale, when it might be told, was unthinkable. The Nazis were not
satisfied with mere murder. Before murdering Jews, they were
trying to reduce them to numbers; after murdering them, they
were dumping their corpses into nameless ditches or making them
into soap. They were making as sure as was possible to wipe out
every trace of memory. Millions would be as though they had
never been. But to the pitiful and glorious desperadoes of Warsaw,
Treblinka, and Auschwitz, who would soon themselves be as
though they had never been, not to rescue for memory what could
be rescued was unthinkable because it was sacrilege. [54]

It will remain a sacrilege ever after. Today, suggestions come from every side to the effect that the past had best be forgotten, or at least remain unmentioned, or at least be coupled with the greatest and most thoughtless speed with other, but quite different, human tragedies. Sometimes these suggestions come from Jews rationalizing their flight from the Nazi holocaust. More often they come from non-Jews, who rationalize their own flight, or even maintain, affrontingly enough, that unless Jews universalize the holocaust, thus robbing the Jews of Auschwitz of their Jewish identity, they are guilty of disregard for humanity. But for a Jew hearing the commanding Voice of Auschwitz the duty to remember and to tell the tale, is not negotiable. It is holy. The religious Jew still possesses this word. The secularist Jew is commanded to restore it. A secular holiness, as it were, has forced itself into his vocabulary.

2. The Second Fragment

Jewish survival, were it even for no more than survival's sake, is a holy duty as well. The murderers of Auschwitz cut off Jews from humanity and denied them the right to existence; yet in being denied that right, Jews represented all humanity. Jews after Auschwitz represent all humanity when they affirm their Jewishness and deny the Nazi denial. They would fail if they affirmed the mere *right* to their Jewishness, participating, as it were, in an obscene debate between others who deny the right of Jews to exist and Jews who affirm it. Nor would they deny the Nazi denial if they affirmed merely their humanity-in-general, permitting an anti-Semitic split between their humanity and their Jewishness, or, worse, agreeing to vanish as Jews in one way, in response to Hitler's attempt to make them vanish in another. The commanding Voice of Auschwitz singles Jews out; Jewish survival is a commandment which brooks no compromise. It was this Voice which was heard by the Jews of Israel in May and June 1967 when they refused to lie down and be slaughtered.

Yet such is the extent of Hitler's posthumous victories that

Jews, commanded to survive as Jews, are widely denied even the right. More precisely—for overt anti-Semitism is not popular in the post-holocaust world—they are granted the right only on certain conditions. Russians, Poles, Indians, and Arabs have a natural right to exist; Jews must earn that right. Other states must refrain from wars of aggression; the State of Israel is an "aggressor" even if it fights for its life. Peoples unscarred by Auschwitz ought to protest when any evil resembling Auschwitz is in sight, such as the black ghettoes or Vietnam. The Jewish survivors of Auschwitz have no right to survive unless they engage in such protests. Other peoples may include secularists and believers. Jews must be divided into bad secularists or Zionists, and good—albeit anachronistic—saints who stay on the cross.

The commanding Voice of Auschwitz bids Jews reject all such views as a monumental affront. It bids them reject as no longer tolerable every version—Christian or leftist, gentile or Jewish—of the view that the Jewish people is an anachronism, when it is the elements of the world perpetrating and permitting Auschwitz, not its survivors, that are anachronistic. A Jew is commanded to descend from the cross and, in so doing, not only to reiterate his ancient rejection of an ancient Christian view but also to suspend the time-honored Jewish exaltation of martyrdom. For after Auschwitz, Jewish life is more sacred than Jewish death, were it even for the sanctification of the divine Name. The left-wing secularist Israeli journalist Amos Kenan writes: "After the death camps, we are left only one supreme value: existence."[55]

3. The Third Fragment

But such as Kenan, being committed and unrepentant lovers of the downtrodden, accept other supreme values as well, and will suspend these only when Jewish existence itself is threatened or denied. Kenan has a universal vision of peace, justice, and brotherhood. He loves the poor of Cuba and hates death in Vietnam. In these and other commitments such left-wing secularists share the ancient Jewish religious, messianically inspired

refusal to embrace either pagan cynicism (which despairs of the
world and accepts the *status quo*) or Christian or pseudo-Christian
otherworldliness (which despairs of the world and flees from it).
The commanding Voice of Auschwitz bids Jews, religious and
secularist, not to abandon the world to the forces of Auschwitz, but
rather to continue to work and hope for it. Two possibilities are
equally ruled out: to despair of the world on account of Auschwitz,
abandoning the age-old Jewish identification with poor and persecuted humanity; and to abuse such identification as a means of
flight from Jewish destiny. It is precisely *because* of the uniqueness of Auschwitz, and *in* his Jewish particularity, that a Jew must
be at one with humanity. For it is precisely because Auschwitz has
made the world a desperate place that a Jew is forbidden to despair
of it. The hero of Wiesel's *The Gates of the Forest* asserts that it is
too late for the Messiah—and that for exactly this reason we are
commanded to hope.[56]

4. The Fourth Fragment

The Voice of Auschwitz commands the religious Jew after Auschwitz to continue to wrestle with his God in however revolutionary ways; and it forbids the secularist Jew (who has already,
and on other grounds, lost Him) to use Auschwitz as an additional
weapon wherewith to deny Him.

The ways of the religious Jew are revolutionary, for there is no
previous Jewish protest against divine Power like his protest.
Continuing to hear the Voice of Sinai as he hears the Voice of
Auschwitz, his citing of God against God may have to assume
extremes which dwarf those of Abraham, Jeremiah, Job, Rabbi
Levi Yitzhak. (You have abandoned the covenant? We shall not
abandon it! You no longer want Jews to survive? We shall survive,
as better, more faithful, more pious Jews! You have destroyed all
grounds for hope? We shall obey the commandment to hope which
You Yourself have given!) Nor is there any previous Jewish compassion with divine powerlessness like the compassion required by
such a powerlessness. (The fear of God is dead among the nations?
We shall keep it alive and be its witnesses! The times are too late

for the coming of the Messiah? We shall persist without hope and recreate hope—and, as it were, divine Power—by our persistence!) For the religious Jew, who remains within the midrashic framework, the Voice of Auschwitz manifests a divine Presence which, as it were, is shorn of all except commanding Power. *This* Power, however, is inescapable.

No less inescapable is this Power for the secularist Jew who has all along been outside the midrashic framework and this despite the fact that the Voice of Auschwitz does not enable him to return into that framework. He cannot return; but neither may he turn the Voice of Auschwitz against that of Sinai. For he may not cut off his secular present from the religious past: the Voice of Auschwitz commands preservation of that past. Nor may he widen the chasm between himself and the religious Jew: the Voice of Auschwitz commands Jewish unity.

As religious and secularist Jews are united in kinship with all the victims of Auschwitz and against all the executioners, they face a many-sided mystery and find a simple certainty. As regards the minds and souls of the victims of Auschwitz, God's presence to them is a many-sided mystery which will never be exhausted either by subsequent committed believers or by subsequent committed unbelievers, and least of all by subsequent neutral theorists—psychological, sociological, philosophical, theological— who spin out their theories immune to love and hate, submission and rage, faith and despair. As regards the murderers of Auschwitz, however, there was no mystery, for they denied, mocked, murdered the God of Israel six million times—and together with Him four thousand years of Jewish faith. For a Jew after Auschwitz, only one thing is certain: he may not side with the murderers and do what they have left undone. The religious Jew who has heard the Voice of Sinai must continue to listen as he hears the commanding Voice of Auschwitz. And the secularist Jew, who has all along lost Sinai and now hears the Voice of Auschwitz, cannot abuse that Voice as a means to destroy four thousand years of Jewish believing testimony. The rabbis assert that the first Temple was destroyed because of idolatry. Jews may not destroy the Temple which is the tears of Auschwitz by doing, wittingly or unwittingly, Hitler's work.

5. The Clash Between the Fragments

Such is the commanding Voice of Auschwitz as it is increasingly being heard by Jews of this generation. But how can it be obeyed? Each of the four fragments described—and they are mere fragments, and the description has been poor and inadequate—is by itself overwhelming. Taken together, they seem unbearable. For there are clashes between them which tear us apart.

How can the religious Jew be faithful to both the faith of the past and the victims of the present? We have already asked this question, but are now further from an answer than before. For a reconciliation by means of willing martyrdom is ruled out by the duty to Jewish survival, and a reconciliation by means of refuge in otherworldly mysticism is ruled out by the duty to hold fast to the world and to continue to hope and work for it. God, world and Israel are in so total a conflict when they meet at Auschwitz as to seem to leave religious Jews confronting that conflict with nothing but a prayer addressed to God, yet spoken softly lest it be heard: in short, with madness.

But the conflict is no less unbearable for the secularist Jew. To be sure, the space once occupied by God is void for him or else occupied by a question mark. Only three of the four fragments effectively remain. Yet the conflict which remains tears him asunder.

Søren Kierkegaard's "knight of faith" was obliged to retrace the road which led Abraham to Mount Moriah, where Isaac's sacrifice was to take place.[57] A Jew today is obliged to retrace the road which led his brethren to Auschwitz. It is a road of pain and mourning, of humiliation, guilt, and despair. To retrace it is living death. How suffer this death *and also* choose Jewish life which, like all life, must include joy, laughter, and childlike innocence? How reconcile *such* a remembrance with life itself? How dare a Jewish parent crush his child's innocence with the knowledge that his uncle or grandfather was denied life because of his Jewishness? And how dare he *not* burden him with this knowledge? The conflict is inescapable, for we may neither forget the past for the sake of present life, nor destroy present life by a mourning without relief—and there is no relief.

Nor is this all. The first two fragments above clash with each other: each clashes with the third as well. No Jewish secularist today may continue to hope and work for mankind as though Auschwitz had never happened, falling back on secularist beliefs of yesterday that man is good, progress real, and brotherhood inevitable. Yet neither may he, on account of Auschwitz, despair of human brotherhood and cease to hope and work for it. How face Auschwitz and not despair? How hope and work, and not act as though Auschwitz had never occurred? Yet to forget and to despair are both forbidden.

Perhaps reconciliation would be possible if the Jewish secularist of today, like the Trotskys and Rosa Luxemburgs of yesterday, could sacrifice Jewish existence on the altar of future humanity. (Is this in the minds of "progressive" Jews when they protest against war in Vietnam but refuse to protest against Polish anti-Semitism? Or in the minds of what Kenan calls the "good people" of the world when they demand that Israel hand over weapons to those sworn to destroy her?) This sacrifice, however, is forbidden, and the altar is false. The left-wing Israeli secularist Kenan may accept all sorts of advice from his progressive friends, but not that he allow himself to be shot for the good of humanity. Perhaps he has listened for a moment even to this advice, for he hates a gun in his hand. Perhaps he has even wished for a second he could accept it, feeling, like many of his pious ancestors, that it is better to be killed than to kill. Yet he firmly rejects such advice, for he is *commanded* to reject it; rather than be shot, he will shoot first when there is no third alternative. But he will shoot with tears in his eyes. He writes:

> Why weren't the June 4 borders peace borders on the fourth of June, but will only become so now? Why weren't the UN Partition Plan borders of 1947 peace borders then, but will become so now? Why should I return his gun to the bandit as a reward for having failed to kill me?
>
> I want peace peace peace peace, peace peace peace.
>
> I am ready to give everything back in exchange for peace. And I shall give nothing back without peace.
>
> I am ready to solve the refugee problem. I am ready to accept an

independent Palestinian state. I am ready to sit and talk. About
everything, all at the same time. Direct talks, indirect talks, all this
is immaterial. But peace.

Until you agree to have peace, I shall give back nothing. And if you
force me to become a conqueror, I shall become a conqueror. And if
you force me to become an oppressor, I shall become an oppressor.
And if you force me into the same camp with all the forces of
darkness in the world, there I shall be.[58]

Kenan's article ends:

> . . . if I survive . . . , without a god but without prophets either, my
> life will have no sense whatever. I shall have nothing else to do but
> walk on the banks of streams, or on the top of the rocks, watch the
> wonders of nature, and console myself with the words of
> Ecclesiastes, the wisest of men: "For the light is sweet, and it is
> good for the eyes to see the sun" [Ecclesiastes 11:7].[59]

The conclusion, then, is inescapable. Secularist Jewish existence after Auschwitz is threatened with a madness no less extreme than that which produces a prayer addressed to God, yet
spoken softly lest it be heard.

*The Voice of Auschwitz commands Jews not to go mad. It
commands them to accept their singled out condition, face up to its
contradictions, and endure them. Moreover, it gives the power of
endurance, the power of sanity. The Jew of today can endure
because he must endure, and he must endure because he is
commanded to endure.*

We ask: whence has come our strength to endure even these
twenty-five years—not to flee or disintegrate but rather to stay,
however feebly, at our solitary post, to affirm, however weakly,
our Jewishness, and to bear witness, if only by this affirmation,
against the forces of hell itself? The question produces abiding
wonder. It is at a commanding Voice without which we, like the
Psalmist (Psalm 119:92), would have perished in our affliction.

JOSEPH DOV SOLOVEITCHIK

The Lonely Man of Faith

Born in Poland in 1903, Joseph Dov Soloveitchik, scion of a rabbinical family, received a thorough talmudic training which was supplemented by studies at Berlin University, concentrating on the philosophy of Hermann Cohen. In 1932 he came to the U.S.A. and settled in Boston. Soon he was recognized as the final authority in rabbinic learning (he is popularly called "the Rav") and the center of Orthodoxy, especially of the younger Orthodox theologians. In 1941 he succeeded his father as professor of Talmud at the rabbinical school of Yeshiva University. He also served as professor of Jewish philosophy at the university's graduate school.

Being a perfectionist, Rabbi Soloveitchik dislikes publishing his thinking. Among the few writings he has allowed to be printed is *"Ish ha-Halakhah"* (The Halakhic Personality), 1944, and "The Lonely Man of Faith" (1965). He developed a philosophy of Halakhah (Jewish law). In his view observance of the law vouchsafes a sanctified life and nearness to God. Not the essence of God is to be defined but his will as directed to man. "We are committed to God and his laws, but God also wills us to be committed to mankind." In 1959, Soloveitchik declined to be considered as successor to Isaac Herzog as Ashkenazi chief rabbi of the State of Israel. In the 1960s, he voiced opposition to Judeo-Christian theological dialogues, while welcoming cooperation in the social-philanthropic realm.

The passage that follows is the introductory section from "The Lonely Man of Faith," a paper whose basic ideas were formulated in lectures to the students of the program "Marriage and Family—

National Institute of Mental Health Project, Yeshiva University, New York." The body of the paper is a searching analysis of the two types of man, based on the two biblical accounts of the creation of Adam: Adam the first (Genesis 1) is "aggressive, bold, creative, this worldly, finitude-oriented"; Adam the second (Genesis 2) wants to know "Why is it?" "What is it?" "Who is it?" "What is the message imbedded in organic and inorganic matter?" The analysis leads to a profound understanding of man.

It is not the plan of this paper to discuss the millennium-old problem of faith and reason. Theory is not my concern at the moment. I want instead to focus attention on a human life situation in which the man of faith as an individual concrete being, with his cares and hopes, concerns and needs, joys and sad moments, is entangled. Therefore, whatever I am going to say here has been derived not from philosophical dialectics, abstract speculation, or detached impersonal reflections, but from actual situations and experiences with which I have been confronted. Indeed, the term lecture is, in this context, a misnomer. It is rather a tale of a personal dilemma. Instead of talking theology, in the didactic sense, eloquently and in balanced sentences, I would like, hesitantly and haltingly, to confide in you, and to share with you some concerns which weigh heavily on my mind and which frequently assume the proportions of an awareness of crisis.

I have no problem-solving thoughts. I do not intend to suggest a new method of remedying the human situation which I am about to describe; neither do I believe that it can be remedied at all. The role of the man of faith, whose religious experience is fraught with inner conflicts and incongruities, who oscillates between ecstasy in God's companionship and despair when he feels abandoned by God, and who is torn asunder by the heightened contrast between self-appreciation and abnegation, has been a difficult one since the times of Abraham and Moses. It would be presumptuous of me to attempt to convert the passional antinomic faith-experience into a eudaemonic-harmonious one, while the biblical knights of faith lived heroically with this very tragic and paradoxical experience.

All I want is to follow the advice given by Elihu the son of Berachel of old who said, "I will speak that I may find relief" [Job 32:20]; for there is a redemptive quality for an agitated mind in the spoken word and a tormented soul finds peace in confessing.

The nature of the dilemma can be stated in a three-word sentence. I am lonely. Let me emphasize, however, that by stating "I am lonely" I do not intend to convey to you the impression that I am alone. I, thank God, do enjoy the love and friendship of many. I meet people, talk, preach, argue, reason; I am surrounded by comrades and acquaintances. And yet, companionship and friendship do not alleviate the passional experience of loneliness which trails me constantly. I am lonely because at times I feel rejected and thrust away by everybody, not excluding my most intimate friends, and the words of the Psalmist "My father and my mother have forsaken me" [Psalm 27:10] ring quite often in my ears like the plaintive cooing of the turtledove. It is a strange, alas, absurd experience engendering sharp, enervating pain as well as a stimulating, cathartic feeling. I despair because I am lonely and, hence, feel frustrated. On the other hand, I also feel invigorated because this very experience of loneliness presses everything in me into the service of God. In my "desolate, howling solitude" I experience a growing awareness that, to paraphrase Plotinus' apothegm about prayer, this service to which I, a lonely and solitary individual, am committed is wanted and gracefully accepted by God in His transcendental loneliness and numinous sotitude.

I must address myself to the obvious question: why am I beset by this feeling of loneliness and being unwanted? Is it the Kierkegaardian anguish—an ontological fear nurtured by the awareness of non-being threatening one's existence—that assails me, or is this feeling of loneliness solely due to my own personal stresses, cares and frustrations? Or is it perhaps the result of the pervasive state of mind of western man who has become estranged from himself, a state with which all of us as westerners are acquainted?

I believe that even though all three explanations might be true to some extent, the genuine and central cause of the feeling of loneliness from which I cannot free myself is to be found in a different dimension, namely, in the experience of faith itself. I am lonely because, in my humble, inadequate way, I am a man of faith for whom to be means to believe, and who substituted "credo" for "cogito" in the time-honored Cartesian maxim.* Apparently, in this role, as a man of faith, I must experience a sense of loneliness which is of a compound nature. It is a blend of that which is inseparably interwoven into the very texture of the faith gesture, characterizing the unfluctuating metaphysical destiny of the man of faith, and of that which is extraneous to the act of believing and stems from the ever-changing human-historical situation with all its whimsicality. On the one hand, the man of faith has been a solitary figure throughout the ages, indeed millennia, and no one has succeeded in escaping this unalterable destiny which is an "objective" awareness rather than a subjective feeling. On the other hand, it is undeniably true that this basic awareness expresses itself in a variety of ways, utilizing the whole gamut of one's affective emotional life which is extremely responsive to outward challenges and moves along with the tide of cultural-historical change. Therefore, it is my intent to analyze this experience at both levels: at the ontological, at which it is a root awareness, and at the historical, at which a highly sensitized and agitated heart, overwhelmed by the impact of social and cultural forces, filters this root awareness through the medium of painful, frustrating emotions.

As a matter of fact, the investigation at the second level is my prime concern since I am mainly interested in contemporary man of faith who is, due to his peculiar position in our secular society, lonely in a special way. No matter how time-honored and time-hallowed the interpenetration of faith and loneliness is, and it certainly goes back to the dawn of the Judaic covenant, contemporary man of faith lives through a particularly difficult and agonizing crisis.

*This is, of course, a rhetorical phrase, since all emotional and volitional activity was included in the Cartesian *cogitatio* as *modi cogitandi*. In fact, faith in the existence of an intelligent *causa prima* was for Descartes an integral part of his logical postulate system, by which he proves the existence of the external world.

Let me spell out this passional experience of contemporary man of faith.

He looks upon himself as a stranger in modern society which is technically minded, self-centered, and self-loving, almost in a sickly narcissistic fashion, scoring honor upon honor, piling up victory upon victory, reaching for the distant galaxies, and seeing in the here-and-now sensible world the only manifestation of being. What can a man of faith like myself, living by a doctrine which has no technical potential, by a law which cannot be tested in the laboratory, steadfast in his loyalty to an eschatological vision whose fulfillment cannot be predicted with any degree of probability, let alone certainty, even by the most complex, advanced mathematical calculations—what can such a man say to a functional utilitarian society which is *saeculum*-oriented and whose practical reasons of the mind have long ago supplanted the sensitive reasons of the heart?

It would be worthwhile to add the following in order to place the dilemma in the proper focus. I have never been seriously troubled by the problem of the biblical doctrine of creation vis-à-vis the scientific story of evolution at both the cosmic and the organic levels, nor have I been perturbed by the confrontation of the mechanistic interpretation of the human mind with the biblical spiritual concept of man. I have not been perplexed by the impossibility of fitting the mystery of revelation into the framework of historical empiricism. Moreover, I have not even been troubled by the theories of biblical criticism which contradict the very foundations upon which the sanctity and integrity of the Scriptures rest. However, while theoretical oppositions and dichotomies have never tormented my thoughts, I could not shake off the disquieting feeling that the practical role of the man of faith within modern society is a very difficult, indeed, a paradoxical one.

The purpose of this paper, then, is to define the great dilemma confronting contemporary man of faith. Of course, as I already remarked, by defining the dilemma we do not expect to find its solution, for the dilemma is insoluble. However, the defining itself is a worthwhile cognitive gesture which, I hope, will yield a better understanding of ourselves and our commitment. Knowledge in general and self-knowledge in particular are gained not only from discovering logical answers but also from formulating logical, even though unanswerable, questions. The human logos is as concerned with an honest inquiry into an insoluble antinomy which leads to intellectual despair and humility as it is with an unprejudiced true solution of a complex problem arousing joy and enhancing one's intellectual determination and boldness.

Before beginning the analysis, we must determine within which frame of reference, psychologico-empirical or theologico-biblical, should our dilemma be described. I believe you will agree with me that we do not have much choice in the matter; for, to the man of faith, self-knowledge has one connotation only,—to understand one's place and role within the scheme of events and things willed and approved by God, when He ordered finitude to emerge out of infinity and the universe, including man, to unfold itself. This kind of self-knowledge may not always be pleasant or comforting. On the contrary, it might from time to time express itself in a painful appraisal of the difficulties which man of faith, caught in his paradoxical destiny, has to encounter, for knowledge at both planes, the objective-natural and subjective-personal, is not always a eudaemonic experience. However, this unpleasant prospect should not deter us from our undertaking.

Before I go any further, I want to make the following reservation. Whatever I am about to say is to be seen only as a modest attempt on the part of a man of faith to interpret his spiritual perceptions and emotions in modern theologico-philosophical categories. My interpretive gesture is completely subjective and lays no claim to representing a definitive *Halakhic* philosophy. If my audience will feel that these interpretations are also relevant to their perceptions and emotions, I shall feel amply rewarded. However, I shall not feel hurt if my thoughts will find no response in the hearts of my listeners.

ABRAHAM JOSHUA HESCHEL

Reflections on Being a Jew

Scion of old and venerable Hasidic families, A. J. Heschel (1907–1972) combined the Hasidic tradition with the learning of the West in addressing himself to the problems of both the Jewish community and modern society. He lectured in Berlin, Frankfurt am Main, London, and Warsaw, prior to his coming to the U.S.A. in 1940. He first taught at the Hebrew Union College; from 1945 on, he was professor of Jewish ethics and mysticism at the Jewish Theological Seminary. He was an influential lecturer and prodigious author. Among his books are *Man Is Not Alone*, 1951; *Man's Quest for God*, 1954; *God in Search of Man*, 1955; *The Prophets*, 1962; *The Insecurity of Freedom*, 1966; *Israel: An Echo of Eternity*, 1967; and *A Passion for Truth*, 1973.

Heschel is deeply aware of the crises in the life of contemporary man; he approaches the task of a guide with the knowledge that faith is the answer, faith understood as "living in a holy dimension." He objects to religion being reduced to an institution and a formal theology; he rejects intellectual self-righteousness and smugness. He teaches inwardness and personal concern, and evokes a sense of wonder and awe. God is in need of man, he writes. The religious commandments *(mitzvah)* express reverence and awareness of God's eternal presence.

Heschel translated his religious views into practice: he participated in the struggle for civil rights in the U.S., addressed himself to issues of youth and old age at White House conferences, took a stand in the Vietnam controversy, and represented world Jewry as consultant to the Vatican on the hotly debated declaration on Jews.

Pope Paul VI and Heschel met on March 17, 1971. The selection that follows is taken from an interview.

I was trained as a child to live a life, or to strive to live a life, which is compatible with the mystery and marvel of human existence.

Throughout history, as seen by the Bible, there is one disappointment for God after another. But He's still waiting, waiting, waiting for mankind that will live by justice and compassion. He's in search of man.

Prayer may not save us. But prayer may make us worthy of being saved. Prayer is not requesting. There is a partnership of God and man. God needs our help. I would define man as a divine need. God is in need of man.

What is the meaning of God? I would have to use a number of sentences. One is the certainty that there is a meaning beyond mystery. That holiness conquers absurdity. And without holiness, we will sink in absurdity.

I don't believe in a monopoly. I think God loves all men. He has given many nations, He has given all men an awareness of His greatness and of His love. And God is to be found in many hearts all over the world. Not limited to one nation or to one people, to one religion.

What is the greatest concern in the Bible? Injustice to the fellow man, bloodshed. What is the greatest dream of the prophets and of the Bible? Peace.

In a very deep sense, religion is two things. First of all, it's an answer to the ultimate problems of human existence. And it also has another side. It is a challenge to all answers. It is living in this polarity of these two points.

Let me say to you the following: The central problem in the Bible is not God, but man. The Bible is a book about man. Rather than man's book about God. And the great problem is how to answer, to respond to the human situation.

God is the meaning beyond absurdity. Wherever I go, I encounter absurdity.

You see, there is an old idea in Judaism found in the Bible, strongly developed by the rabbis and very little known. And that is that God suffers when man suffers.

Remember that life is a celebration or can be a celebration.

One of the most important things is to teach man how to celebrate.

Notes

Mendelssohn

1. Sanhedrin 59a; Maimonides, *Mishneh Torah*, Hilkhot Melakhim VIII, 10.

2. The "seven Noahide laws" include prohibition of idolatry, adultery, incest, bloodshed, robbery, social injustice, and eating flesh from a living animal. Cf. Abodah Zarah 64b.

3. Maimonides, Hilkhot Teshuvah III, 5; Hilkhot Melakhim VII, II.

4. Maimonides, Hilkhot Issure Biah XIII, XIV.

Zunz

5. Johann Andreas Eisenmenger (1654–1704), German anti-Semitic writer on classical Judaism.

6. Johann Jacob Schudt (1664–1722), Christian orientalist and writer on Jewish folklore.

7. Johannes Buxtorf (1564–1629), Christian hebraist; his son, Johannes Buxtorf Jr. (1599–1664), published his father's works.

8. At the beginning of the Second Temple period.

Krochmal

9. Megillah 29a.

Graetz

10. The period from the destruction of the Second Temple in 70 C.E. down to 1850.

Hess

11. Adolphe Crémieux (1796–1880), French statesman and Jewish communal leader
12. In 1840 the Jews of Damascus were falsely accused of slaying a Capuchin friar, Father Thomas, for ritual purposes ("Damascus Affair").
13. "And saviors shall come up on Mount Zion to judge the mount of Esau; and the kingdom shall be the Lord's."
14. Ernest Laharanne: private secretary of Napoleon III.

Geiger

15. Sanhedrin 89a.
16. Hagigah 13b.
17. Simeon bar Kokhba, leader of the Jewish rebellion of 132–135.
18. Makkot 24a.
19. Shabbat 92a.
20. *Kuzari* II, 36–44.
21. *Guide to the Perplexed* II, 38–39.

Hirsch

22. Circumcision, garment with fringes, inscription on the doorpost, Sabbath, benedictions.

H. Cohen

23. "One," lower case, stands for a numerical concept, while "One," upper case, will be used throughout the text to convey a qualitative concept, as in the German "einzig"—one and only, singular, unique. *Translator*.

Bialik

24. Sages of the Talmud.

25. Sections on "How Torah Is Rescued," "The Discipline of Feeling," "Variety of *Halakhah*," and "Epic and Lyric" are here omitted.

26. Authoritative code of Jewish law, compiled by Joseph Karo in the 16th century.

Kook

27. Berakhot 28b ff.

Ahad Haam

28. The anti-Jewish riots of April 1920 in which many lives were lost. In a footnote at this point the author recalls that as far back as 1891 he drew attention to the Arab question. *Translator.*

Magnes

29. Sanhedrin 37a.

Kaufmann

30. Representatives of Jewish communities who argued their cause before the ruling powers.

31. Lay leaders of Jewish communities.

Rathenau

32. See introduction to Mendelssohn's "Letter to Johann Caspar Lavater" in this volume.

33. The reference is to Deuteronomy 6:4.

34. Pirke de Rabbi Eliezer XLI.

35. Sections on "Church and Religion," "The State Church," "Catholicism and Protestantism," and "State Religion" are here omitted.

Baeck

36. Makkot 23b f.

Buber

37. John the Baptist; Matthew 3:10.

Rosenzweig

38. Cicero.
39. "Lord, where shall I find Thee?
   High and hidden is Thy place;
   And where shall I not find Thee?
   The World is full of Thy glory."
             (Translated by Nina Salaman.)
40. Marcion, Christian gnostic of the second century.
41. Adolf von Harnack (1851–1930), German Protestant theologian.
42. Karl Barth (1886–1968), Swiss Protestant representative of dialectic theology.

Kallen

43. Prayerbook.
44. Authoritative code of Jewish law.
45. Elohist–Yahwist: hypothetical documents underlying the Pentateuch.
46. Stephen S. Wise (1874–1949), Prominent leader, Zionist, and reform rabbi.
47. George Foot Moore (1851–1931), Christian Judaic scholar; author of *Judaism in the First Centuries of the Christian Era* (3 vols., Cambridge, Mass., 1927–30), a study of rabbinic Judaism.

Ozick

48. Menahot 29b.
49. See Genesis 32:25–33.

A. Cohen

50. *The Natural and the Supernatural Jew,* New York, 1962, p. 6.

Wiesel

51. From the liturgy of Rosh ha-Shanah and Yom Kippur.

Fackenheim

52. See E. Fackenheim, *Quest for Past and Future,* Bloomington and London, 1968, pp. 17–20.
53. See especially Elie Wiesel, "A Plea for the Dead," *Legends of Our Time,* New York, 1968, pp. 174–97.
54. See especially Yuri Suhl, *They Fought Back,* New York, 1967.
55. "A Letter to All Good People—To Fidel Castro, Sartre, Russell and All the Rest," *Midstream,* October 1968.
56. P. 225.
57. See *Fear and Trembling,* New York, 1954.
58. Amos Kenan, "A Letter to All Good People," p. 35.
59. *Ibid.,* p. 36.

Sources and Acknowledgments

Thanks are due to the authors and publishers referred to in the list which follows, for permission to include in this volume material copyrighted in their name.

AHAD HAAM, After the Balfour Declaration. *Nationalism and the Jewish Ethic. Basic Writings of Ahad Haam,* ed. Hans Kohn, New York, 1962, pp. 157–64 (tr. Leon Simon). By permission of Schocken Books, Inc.

LEO BAECK, The Tension of Jewish History. *This People Israel: The Meaning of Jewish Existence,* tr. by Albert H. Friedlander, Philadelphia, 1965, pp. 392–95. Copyright © 1964 by the Union of American Hebrew Congregations. Reprinted by permission of the Union of American Hebrew Congregations, the book's publisher.

HAYYIM NAHMAN BIALIK, *Halakhah and Aggadah.* English version published anonymously in *Contemporary Jewish Record VII,* 1944, pp. 663–67, 677–80. Copyright © 1944 by *Commentary;* reprinted by permission.

MARTIN BUBER, I, Judaism and Civilization. *On Judaism,* ed. N. N. Glatzer, New York, 1967, pp. 193–201. Copyright © 1967 by Schocken Books, Inc. and reprinted by permission. II, Thoughts on Jewish Existence, culled from *The Way of Response: Martin Buber,* ed. N. N. Glatzer, New York, 1966, pp. 179–95, 199–201. Copyright © 1966 by Schocken Books, Inc.; reprinted by permission.

of America, copyright 1973, reprinted by permission of the National Broadcasting Company, Inc.

MOSES HESS, Political Rebirth. *Rome and Jerusalem*, tr. by M. Waxman, New York, 1918, pp. 145–50. Reprinted by permission of Bloch Publishing Company.

SAMSON RAPHAEL HIRSCH, The Jewish Calendar. Tr. by Isidor Grunfeld in his edition of *Judaism Eternal I*, London, 1956, pp. 3–6, 15–19. Copyright 1956 by Isidor Grunfeld; reprinted by permission.

HORACE M. KALLEN, A Jewish View of Life. *"Of Them Which Say They Are Jews" and Other Essays on the Jewish Struggle for Survival*, ed. Judah Pilch, New York, 1954, pp. 104 ff. Copyright 1954 by American Association for Jewish Education; reprinted by permission.

MORDECAI M. KAPLAN, The Principles of Reconstructionism and Some Questions Jews Ask. *Questions Jews Ask: Reconstructionist Answers*, New York, 1956, pp. xi–xiii, 117–20, 128f.,)92f. Copyright © 1956, by The Jewish Reconstructionist Foundation, Inc.; reprinted by permission.

YEHEZKEL KAUFMANN, On the Fate and Survival of the Jews. Tr. by Michael A. Meyer, in his *Ideas of Jewish History*, New York, 1974, pp. 277–83. Copyright 1974 by Michael A. Meyer; reprinted by permission of Professor Meyer and Behrman House.

ABRAHAM ISAAC KOOK, On Prayer. *Commentary on the Prayer Book;* selections in *Judaism* ii, 1 (1953), tr. Ben Halpern. Reprinted by permission of *Judaism*.

NAHMAN KROCHMAL, The Cycles of Jewish History. *Guide of the Perplexed of the Time*, tr. by Michael A. Meyer in his *Ideas of Jewish History*, New York, 1974, pp. 202f. Copyright 1974 by Michael A. Meyer; reprinted by permission of Professor Meyer and Behrman House.

JUDAH L. MAGNES, A Letter to Gandhi. *In the Perplexity of the Times*, Jerusalem, 1946, 117–28. Copyright 1946 by Magnes Press; reprinted by permission.

MOSES MENDELSSOHN, Letter to Johann Caspar Lavater. Tr. and ed. by Alfred Jospe, in *Jerusalem and Other Jewish Writings by Moses Men-*

delssohn, New York, 1969, pp. 113–22. Copyright © 1969 by Schocken Books, Inc.; reprinted by permission.

CYNTHIA OZICK, On Living in the Gentile World. Symposium, "Living in Two Cultures," *Response,* Fall 1972 pp. 87–93; reprinted by permission.

WALTHER RATHENAU, Of Faith: A Polemic. English version published anonymously in *Contemporary Jewish Record VII,* 1944, pp. 434–37, 445–47. Copyright © 1944 by *Commentary;* reprinted by permission.

SIMON RAWIDOWICZ, Israel: The Ever-Dying People. *Studies in Jewish Thought,* ed. N. N. Glatzer, Philadelphia, 1974, pp. 219–24. Originally published in *Judaism* xvi (1967), pp. 423–33. Copyright © 1974 by The Jewish Publication Society of America,; reprinted by permission.

FRANZ ROSENZWEIG, Two Theological Considerations. "The Nations and Their States," *The Star of Redemption, Part III,* in *Franz Rosenzweig: His Life and Thought,* ed. N. N. Glatzer, New York, 1953, pp. 336–39. "Remote and Near," *Jehuda Halevi,* pp. 188–90, *ibid.,* 278–81. Copyright 1953 by Schocken Books, Inc.; reprinted by permission.

JOSEPH DOV SOLOVEITCHIK, The Lonely Man of Faith. *Tradition* vii (1964–65), pp. 3–10. Reprinted by permission.

MILTON STEINBERG, The Reasons for Religious Faith. *Anatomy of Faith.* Copyright 1960 by Edith A. Steinberg and A. A. Cohen; reprinted by permission of Harcourt Brace Jovanovich, Inc.

ELIE WIESEL, Yom Kippur: The Dey Without Forgiveness. *Legends of Our Time,* New York, 1968, pp. 53–61. Copyright © 1968 by Elie Wiesel; reprinted by permission.

LEOPOLD ZUNZ, Scholarship and Emancipation. Introduction to *The Liturgical Addresses of the Jews,* tr. Harry Zohn. *The Judaic Tradition,* ed. N. N. Glatzer, Boston, 1969, pp. 515–18. Copyright © 1969 by Nahum N. Glatzer. Reprinted by permission of Beacon Press.

Selected Bibliography**

General

Agus, Jacob B. *Modern Philosophies of Judaism.* New York, 1941.

———. *The Meaning of Jewish History,* Vol. II. London, New York, and Toronto, 1963

Altmann, Alexander. "Theology in 20th Century German Jewry." *Year Book I, Leo Baeck Institute.* London, 1956.

———. ed. *Studies in Nineteenth-Century Jewish Intellectual History.* Cambridge, Mass., 1964.

Baron, Salo W. "Ghetto and Emancipation." *Menorah Journal* xiv (1928).

Bein, Alex. *Theodor Herzl: A Biography.* Philadelphia, 1956.

Bergman, S. H. *Faith and Reason: An Introduction to Modern Jewish Thought,* tr. and ed. Alfred Jospe. New York, 1966.*

Berkovits, Eliezer. *Major Themes in Modern Philosophies of Judaism.* New York, 1974.

Blau, Joseph. *Modern Varieties of Judaism.* New York, 1966.

Borowitz, Eugene B. *A New Jewish Theology in the Making.* Philadelphia, 1968.

Chazan, Robert and Marc Lee Raphael, eds. *Modern Jewish History: A Source Reader.* New York, 1975.*

Cioran, E. M. "A People of Solitaries" in *The Temptation to Exist,* tr. Richard Howard. Chicago, 1970.

---

*An asterisk indicates paperback edition.
**Only works in the English language are listed.

Davis, Moshe. *The Emergence of Conservative Judaism.* Philadelphia, 1963.

Dawidowicz, Lucy S. *The War Against the Jews, 1933–1945.* New York, 1975.

Deutscher, Isaac. *The Non-Jewish Jew and Other Essays.* London, 1968.

Fishbane, Michael. "Freedom and Belonging: A Personal Encounter with Judaic Study" in *The New Jews,* ed. James A. Sleeper and Alan L. Mintz. New York, 1971.

Friedman, Philip. *Martyrs and Fighters: An Epic of the Warsaw Ghetto.* New York, 1954.

Glatzer, Nahum N., ed. *The Dynamics of Emancipation: The Jew in the Modern Age.* Boston, 1965. (Also as part III of *The Judaic Tradition,* Boston, 1969).

Glazer, Nathan. *American Judaism.* Chicago, 1957.

Halpern, Benjamin. *The Idea of the Jewish State.* Cambridge, Mass., 1961.

Hertzberg, Arthur. *The Zionist Idea: A Historical Analysis and Reader.* New York, 1960.*

Himmelfarb, Milton. *The Condition of Jewish Belief.* New York, 1966.*

Howe, Irving and Eliezer Greenberg, eds. *Voices from the Yiddish: Essays, Memoirs, Diaries,* New York, 1975.*

Jacobs, Louis. *Jewish Thought Today.* New York, 1970.

Janowsky, Oscar, ed. *The American Jew: A Reappraisal.* Philadelphia, 1964.

Jung, Leo, ed. *Guardians of Our Heritage (1724–1953).* New York, 1958.

Katz, Jacob. *Exclusiveness and Tolerance: Jewish-Gentile Relations in Medieval and Modern Times.* New York, 1962.*

———. *Out of the Ghetto: The Social Background of Jewish Emancipation.* Cambridge, Mass., 1973.

Katz, Steven T., ed. *Jewish Philosophers.* New York, 1975.

Laqueur, Walter. *A History of Zionism.* New York, 1972.

Leftvich, Joseph. *The Way We Think: Essays from Yiddish.* New York and London, 1969.

Lewisohn, Ludwig. *The American Jew.* New York, 1950.

Liptzin, Solomon. *The Jew in American Literature.* New York, 1966.

———. *Germany's Stepchildren.* Philadelphia, 1944.

Malin, Irving, and Irwin Stark. *Breakthrough. A Treasury of Contemporary American-Jewish Literature.* Philadelphia, 1963.

Meyer, Michael A. *The Origins of the Modern Jew: Jewish Identity and European Culture in Germany, 1749–1824.* Detroit, 1967.

————. ed. *Ideas of Jewish History*. New York, 1974.

Neusner, Jacob. *Fellowship in Judaism*. London, 1963.

————. *History and Torah*. New York, 1967.*

Noveck, Simon, ed. *Contemporary Jewish Thought: A Reader*. New York, 1973.*

Pinson, Koppel, ed. *Essays on Antisemitism*. New York, 1942.

Plaut, Gunther. *The Rise of Reform Judaism*. New York, 1963.

————. *The Growth of Reform Judaism*. New York, 1965.

Rotenstreich, Nathan. *Jewish Philosophy in Modern Times*. New York, 1968.

————. *Tradition and Reality: The Impact of History on Modern Jewish Thought*. New York, 1972.

Sachar, A. L. *Sufferance is the Badge*. New York, 1940.

Sachar, Howard M. *The Course of Modern Jewish History*. Cleveland and New York, 1958.

Schwarz, Leo W. *The Redeemers: A Sega of the Years 1945–1952*. New York, 1953.

Senesh, Hannah. *Her Life and Diary*, tr. Marta Cohn. New York, 1973.*

Sklare, Marshall. *Conservative Judaism*. New York, 1972.*

Sleeper, James A., and Alan Mintz, eds. *The New Jews*. New York, 1971.

Spiegel, Shalom. *Hebrew Reborn*. Philadelphia, 1962.*

Spiro, Melford E. *Kibbutz: Venture in Utopia*. New York, 1970.*

Syrkin, Marie. *Blessed Is the Match (On Hannah Senesh)*. New York, 1947.

Veblen, Thorstein. "The Intellectual Pre-eminence of Jews in Modern Europe." *Political Science Quarterly*, March 1919.

Ahad Haam

WRITINGS

Ahad Haam. *Selected Essays*, tr. Leon Simon. Philadelphia, 1962.*

————. *Nationalism and the Jewish Ethic: Basic Writings*, ed. Hans Kohn. New York, 1972.*

STUDIES

Bentwich, Norman. *Ahad Haam and His Philosophy*. Philadelphia, 1927.

Hertzberg, A. "Ahad Haam" in *The Zionist Idea*. New York, 1960.*

Simon, Leon. *Ahad Haam: A Biography.* Philadelphia, 1960.
Spiegel, Shalom. "The Thinker of the Jewish Renaissance" in *Hebrew Reborn.* New York, 1962.*

Baeck

WRITINGS

Baeck, Leo. *The Essence of Judaism.* New York, 1961.*
――――. *God and Man in Judaism.* New York, 1958.
――――. *Judaism and Christianity: Essays,* tr. Walter Kaufmann. New York, 1958.
――――. *The Pharisees and Other Essays.* New York, 1966.*
――――. *This People Israel: The Meaning of Jewish Existence,* tr. A. H. Friedlander. New York, 1965.

STUDIES

Bamberger, Fritz. *Leo Baeck: The Man and the Idea* (The Leo Baeck Memorial Lecture 1). New York, 1958.
Friedlander, A. H. *Leo Baeck: Teacher of Theresienstadt.* New York, 1959.
Kaufmann, Fritz. "Baeck and Buber." *Conservative Judaism.* Winter, 1958.

Bialik

WRITINGS

Bialik, H. N. *Selected Poems,* tr. Maurice Samuel. New York, 1926.

STUDIES

Hertzberg, A. "H. N. Bialik" in *The Zionist Idea.* New York, 1960.*
The New Palestine. Bialik issue. Vol. X, 1926.
Spiegel, Shalom. "The Mouthpiece of the Folk," *Hebrew Reborn.* New York, 1962.*

Brandeis

WRITINGS

Fraenkel, O. K., ed. *Curse of Bigness: Miscellaneous Papers of Louis D. Brandeis.* New York, 1934.

STUDIES

Konvitz, Milton. "Louis D. Brandeis." *Molders of the Jewish Mind.* A B'nai B'rith Book. Washington, 1966.

Mason, Alpheus Thomas. *Brandeis, A Free Man's Life.* New York, 1946.

Rabinowitz, E. *Justice Louis DX. Brandeis, the Zionist Chapter of His Life.* New York, 1968.

Buber

WRITINGS

Buber, Martin. *Between Man and Man,* tr. R. G. Smith. London, 1947.

————. *Eclipse of God: Studies in the Relation Between Religion and Philosophy.* New York, 19571*

————, *Good and Evil,* tr. M. Bullock and R. G. Smith. New York, 1953.

————. *Hasidism.* New York, 1948.

————. *I and Thou,* tr. R. G. Smith. New York, 1958.*

————. *I and Thou,* tr. Walter Kaufmann. New York, 1970.*

————. *Israel and the World: Essays in a Time of Crisis.* New York, 1963.*

————. *The Knowledge of Man,* tr. Maurice Friedman and R. G. Smith. New York, 1965.*

————. *On the Bible,* ed N. N. Glatzer. New York, 1968.

————. *On Judaism,* ed. N. N. Glatzer. New York, 1972.

————. *On Zion: The History of an Idea,* tr. Stanley Goldman. London, 1973.

————. *Pointing the Way,* tr. Maurice S. Friedman. New York, 1974.*

————. *The Tales of the Hasidim,* 2 vols., tr. Olga Marx. New York, 1961.*

————. *Ten Rungs: Hasidic Sayings.* New York, 1962.*

————. *The Way of Response,* ed. N. N. Glatzer. New York, 1966.*

STUDIES

Balthasar, Hans Urs von. *Martin Buber and Christianity: A Dialogue Between Israel and the Church*, tr. A. Dru. London, 1961.

Bergman, S. H. "Martin Buber" in *Faith and Reason: Modern Jewish Thought*. New York, 1966.*

Cohen, Arthur A. *Martin Buber*. New York, 1957.

Diamond, Malcolm L. *Martin Buber: Jewish Existentialist*. New York, 1960.

Friedman, Maurice S. *Martin Buber: The Life of Dialogue*. Chicago, 1955.

Schaeder, Grete. *The Hebrew Humanism of Martin Buber*, tr. Noah J. Jacobs. Detroit, 1973.

Schilpp, Paul A. and Maurice Fiedman, eds. *The Philosophy of Martin Buber*. Le Salle, Ill., 1967.

A. A. Cohen

WRITINGS

Cohen, Arthur A., ed. *Arguments and Doctrines: A Reader in Jewish Thinking in the Aftermath of the Holocaust*. New York, 1970.

———. "The Jewish Intellectual in an Open Society," in *Confrontations with Judaism*, ed. Philip Longworth. London, 1967.

———. *The Myth of the Judeo-Christian Tradition*. New York, 1970.*

———. *The Natural and the Supernatural Jew*. New York, 1962.

———. "Why I Choose to Be a Jew" in *Breakthrough: A Treasury of Contemporary American-Jewish Literature*, ed. Irving Malin and Irwin Stark. Philadelphia, 1963.

H. Cohen

WRITINGS

Cohen, Hermann. *Reason and Hope. Selections from the Jewish Writings of Hermann Cohen*, tr. Eva Jospe. New York, 1971.

———. *Religion of Reason*, tr. Simon Kaplan. bnew York, 1972.

STUDIES

Bergman, S. H., "Hermann Cohen" in *Faith and Reason & Modern Jewish Thought*. New York, 1966.*

Guttmann, Julius. "Hermann Cohen" in *Philosophies of Judaism*. New York, 1973.*

Kaplan, M. M. *The Purpose and Meaning of Jewish Existence*. New York, 1964.

Melber, Jehuda. *Hermann Cohen's Philosophy of Judaism*. New York, 1968.

Rotenstreich, Nathan. "From the Ethical Idea to the True Being: Hermann Cohen" in *Jewish Philosophy in Modern Times*. New York, 1968.

Weiss-Rosmarin, Trude. *Religion of Reason. Cohen's System of Religious Philosophy*. New York, 1936.

Dubnow

WRITINGS

Dubnow, Simon. *History of the Jews*, tr. M. Spiegel, 5 vols. South Brunswick, N.J., 1967–73.

———. *History of the Jews in Russia and Poland*, 3 vols. Philadelphia, 1916–19⁰fi

———. *Nationalism and History: Essays on Old and New Judaism*, ed. Koppel S. Pinson. Philadelphia, 1958. [Includes Pinson's essay on Dubnow.]

Einstein

WRITINGS

Einstein, Albert. *About Zionism: Speeches and Letters*, ed. Leon Simon. New York, 1931.

———. *The World as I See It*. New York, 1934.

STUDIES

Frank, P. *Einstein, His Life and Times*. New Yorf, 1947.

Schilpp, Paul Arthur, ed. *Albert Einstein, Philosopher-Scientist*. La Salle, Ill., 1951.
Schmidt, H. D. "Einstein's Concept of God." *Judaism* viii, 3 (Summer 1959).
Seelig, K. *Albert Einstein: A Documentery Biography*. New York, 1956.

Fackenheim

WRITINGS

Fackenheim, Emil L. *Encounters Between Judaism and Modern Philosophy: A Preface to Future Jewish Thought*. New York, 1973.
———. *God's Presence in History*. New York, 1960.*
———. *Paths to Jewish Belief*. New York, 1960.
———. *Quest for Past and Future: Essays in Jewish Theology*. Boston, 1970.*

Fichman, Rachel, Lamdan, Broides, Amichai

WRITINGS

Burnshaw, Stanley, T. Carmi, and Ezra Spicehandler, eds. *The Modern Hebrew Poem Itself*. New York, 1966.

STUDIES

Alter, Robert. "Poetry in Israel." *Commentary* xl, 6 (December 1965).
———. *After the Tradition: Essays on Modern Jewish Writing*. New York, 1969.
Bargad, Warren. "Children and Lovers: On Yehuda Amichai's Poetic Zorks." *Midstream*, October, 1975.
Halkin, Simon. *Modern Hebrew Literature: Trends and Values*. New York, 1970.*
Wallenrod, Reuben. *The Literatüre of Modern Israel*. New York and London, 1956.

Geiger

WRITINGS

Geiger, Abraham. *Judaism and Its History,* tr. Charles Newburgh. New York, 1911.

STUDIES

Petuchowski, Jakob H., ed. *New Perspective on Abraham Geiger.* Cincinnati, 1975.
Wiener, Max, ed. *Abraham Geiger and Liberal Judaism: The Challenge of the 19th Century,* tr. E. J. Schlochauer. Philadelphia, 1962.

Graetz

WRITINGS

Graetz, Heinrich. *History of the Jews,* 6 vols., tr. Bella Loewy. Philadelphia, 1891–92.
———. "The Construction of Jewish History," tr. Michael A. Meyer in *Ideas of Jewish History.* New York, 1964.
———. *The Structure of Jewish History and Other Essays,* tr. and ed. Ismar Schorsch. New York, 1975.

STUDIES

Abrahams, Israel. "H. Graetz, the Jewish Historian." *Jewish Quarterly Review,* 1892.
Baron, Salo W. "Heinrich Graetz" in *History and Jewish Historians: Essays and Addresses.* Philadelphia, 1964.
Bloch, Philipp. "Memoir" in Heinrich Graetz, *History of the Jews VI* (1927).
Deutsch, Gotthard, "Heinrich Graetz, A Centenary." *Central Conference of American Rabbis Year Book XXVII,* 1917.

Heschel

WRITINGS

Heschel, Abraham Joshua. A Conversation with Doctor Abraham Joshua Heschel. The National Broadcasting Company and the Jewish Theological Seminary of America. February 4, 1973.

——. God in Search of Man: A Philosophy of Judaism. New York, 1966.*

——. The Insecurity of Freedom: Essays on Human Existence. New York, 1972.*

——. Israel: An Echo of Eternity. New York, 1969.*

——. Man is Not Alone. A Philosophy of Religion. New York, 1966.*

——. Man's Quest for God. Studies in Prayr and Symbolism. New York, 1954.

——. A Passion for Truth. New York, 1973.

STUDIES

Rothschild, Fritz A., ed. Between God and Man: An Interpretation of Judaism. From the Writings of Abraham J. Heschel. New York, 1959.

Sherman, Franklin. The Promise of Heschel. Philadelphia, 1970.*

Hess

WRITINGS

Hess, Moses. Rome and Jerusalem, tr. Meyer Waxman. New York, 1918.

STUDIES

Berlin, Isaiah. The Life and Opinions of Moses Hess. Cambridge, 1959.

Carlebach, Julius. "The Problem of Moses Hess's Influence on the Young Marx." Year Book XVIII, Leo Baeck Institute. London, 1973.

Hertzberg, A. "Moses Hess." The Zionist Idea I. New York, 1960.*

Weiss, John. Moses Hess: Utopian Socialist. Detroit, 1960.*

S. R. Hirsch

WRITINGS

Hirsch, Samson Raphael. *Horeb: A Philosophy of Jewish Laws and Observances*, tr. Isidor Grunfeld, 2 vols. London, 1972.
————. *Judaism Eternal: Selected Essays*, ed. I. Grunfeld. London, 1956.
————. *The Nineteen Letters of Ben Uziel, Being a Spiritual Presentation of the Principles of Judaism*, tr. B. Drachman. New York, 1942.

STUDIES

Breuer, Mordecei. "Samson Raphael Hirsch" in *Guardians of Our Heritage*, ed. L. Jung. New York, 1958.
Grunfeld, Isidor. *Three Generations: The Influence of S. R. Hirsch on Jewish Life and Thought*. London, 1958.
Rosenbloom, N. H. *Tradition in an Age of Reform. The Religious Philosophy of S. R. Hirsch*. Philadelphia, 1976.

Kallen

WRITINGS

Kallen, Horace M. *Judaism at Bay*. New York, 1932.
————. *"Of Them Which Say They Are Jews" and Other Essays on the Jewish Struggle for Survival*, ed. Judah Pilch. New York, 1954.

STUDIES

Hertzberg, Arthur. "Horace Mayer Kallen" in *The Zionist Idea*. New York, 1960.*
Ratner, S., ed. *Vision and Action: Essays Presented to Horace M. Kallen*. New York, 1947.

Kaplan

WRITINGS

Kaplan, Mordecai M. *The Future on the American Jew*. New York, 1948.

――――. *The Greater Judaism in the Making: A Study of the Modern Evolution in Judaism.* New York, 1960.

――――. *Judaism as a Civilization.* New York, 1967.*

――――. *Questions Jews Ask: Reconstructionist Answers.* New York, 1956.

Kaplan, Mordecai M. and Arthur A. Cohen. *If Not Now When?* New York, 1973.

STUDIES

Borowitz, Eugene B. "Mordecai Kaplan: The Limits of Naturalism." *A New Jewish Theology in the Making* II, 5. Philadelphia, 1968.

Eisenstein, I. and E. Kohn, eds. *Mordecai M. Kaplen: An Evaluation.* New York, 1957.

Kaufmann

WRITINGS

Kaufmann, Yehezkel. *The Religion of Israel,* tr. and abridged by Moshe Greenberg. New York, 1972.*

STUDIES

Koffler O'dea, Janet. "Israel With and Without Religion." *Judaism* xxv, 1 (Winter 1976), pp. 85–97.

Silberstein, Laurence. *History and Ideology: The Writings of Yehezkel Kaufmann.* Ph.D. dissertation, Brandeis University, 1971.

Kook

STUDIES

Agus, Jacob B. *Banner of Jerusalem.* XNew York, 1948.

Bergman, S. H. "Abraham Isaac Kook" in *Faith and Reason: Modern Jewish Thought.* New York, 1963.*

Epstein, I. *Abraham Yitzhak Hacohen Kook: His Life and Times.* London, 1951.

Hertzberg, A. "Rabbi Abraham Isaac Kook" in *The Zionist Idea.* New York, 196...*

Rotenstreich, Nathan. "Harmony and Return: *Rav Kook*" in *Jewish Philosophy in Modern Times.* New York, 1968.

Krochmal

STUDIES

Guttmann, Julius. "Nachman Krochmal" in *Philosophies of Judaism,* New York, 1973.*

Rawidowicz, Simon. "Was Nachman Krochmal a Hegelian?" in *Studies in Jewish Thought,* ed. N. N. Glatzer. Philadelphia, 1974.

Spiegel, Shalom. "A Galician Socrates" in *Hebrew Reborn.* New York, 1962.*

Taubes, Jacob, "Nachman Krochmal and Modern Historicism." *Judaism* xii, 2 (Spring, 1963).

Magnes

WRITINGS

[Magnes, Judah L.] *Addresses by the Chancellor of the Hebrew University.* Jerusalem, 1936.

————. *In the Perplexity of the Times.* Jerusalem, 1946.

STUDIES

Bentwich, Norman. *For Zion's Sake: A Biography of Judah L. Magnes.* New York, 1954.

Bergman, S. H. "J. L. Magnes: The Conquest of Pessimism by Faith" in *Faith and Reason: Modern Jewish Thought.* New York, 1966.*

Mendelssohn

WRITINGS

Jospe, Alfred, ed. *Jerusalem and Other Jewish Writings by Moses Mendelssohn.* New York, 1969.

STUDIES

Agus, Jacob B. "The Age of Reason" in *The Evolution of Jewish Thought*. New York, 1959.

Altmann, Alexander. "Moses Mendelssohn on Leibnitt and Spinoza" in *Studies in Rationalism, Judaism and Universalism*, ed. R. Loewe. London, 1966.

———. *Moses Mendelssohn: A Biographical Study*. University, Ala., 1973.

Guttmann, Julius. "Moses Mendelssohn" in *Philosophies of Judaism*, New York, 1973.*

Patterson, David. "Moses Mendelssohn's Concept of Tolerance" in *Between East and West*, ed. A. Altmann. London, 1958.

Rawidowicz, Simon. "Moses Mendelssohn: The German and Jewish Philosopher" in S. Rawidowicz, *Studies in Jewish Thought*, ed. N. N. Glatzer. Philadelphia, 1974.

Rotenstreich, Nathan. "On Mendelssohn's Political Philosophy" in *Yearbook XI, Leo Baeck Institute*. London, 1966.

———. "The Rule of Ethics: Moses Mendelssohn" in *Jewish Philosophy in Modern Times*. New York, 1968.

Walter, Hermann. *Moses Mendelssohn: Critic and Philosopher*. New York, 1930.

Ozick

WRITINGS

Ozick, Cynthia. "All the World Wants the Jews Dead." *Esquire*, November, 1974.

———. "America: Toward Yavneh." *Judaism* xix, 3 (Summer, 1970).

———. *The Pagan Rabbi and Other Stories*. New York, 1976.*

———. Statement in a symposium on "Living in Two Cultures." *Response*, Fall, 1972.

Rosenzweig

WRITINGS

Rosenzweig, Franz. *On Jewish Learning*, ed. N. N. Glatzer. New York, 1955.
————. *The Star of Redemption*, tr. William Hallo. Boston, 1972.*
————. *Understanding the Sick and the Healthy: A View of World, Man, and God*, ed. N. N. Glatzer. New York, 1954.
Rosenzweig, Franz and Eugen Rosenstock-Huessy. *Judaism Despite Christianity. Letters on Christianity and Judaism*, ed. Eugen Rosenstock-Huessy. New York, 1971.*

STUDIES

Altmann, Alexander. "Rosenzweig on History" in *Studies in Religious Philosophy and Mysticism*. London, 1969.
Bergman, S. H. "Franz Rosenzweig: Beyond Liberalism and Orthodoxy" in *Faith and Reason: Modern Jewish Thought*. New York, 1966.*
Glatzer, Nahum N. "The Frankfurt Lehrhaus" in *Year Book I, Leo Baeck Institute*. New York, 1956.
————. *Franz Rosenzweig: His Life and Thought*. New York, 1961.*
Guttmann, Julius. "Franz Rosenzweig" in *Philosophies of Judaism III*. New York, 1973.*
Rotenstreich, Nathan. "The Road Back: S. L. Steinheim and Franz Rosenzweig" in *Jewish Philosophy in Modern Times*. New York, 1968.
Schwarzschild, S. *Franz Rosenzweig: Guide for Reversioners*. London, 1960.

Soloveitchik

WRITINGS

Soloveitchik, Joseph Dov. "Confrontation." *Tradition* vi, 2 (1963–64).
————. "The Lonely Man of Faith." *Tradition* vii 1–3 (1964–65).

STUDIES

Borowitz, Eugen. "The Typological Theology of Joseph Baer Soloveitchik." *Judaism* xv, 2 (Spring 1966).
Lichtenstein, Aharon. "R. Joseph Soloveitchik" in *Great Jewish Thinkers
of the Twentieth Century*, ed. S. Noveck. Philadelphia, 1963.

Steinberg

WRITINGS

Steinberg, Milton. Anatomy of Faith: Theological Essays, ed. Arthur
Cohen. New York, 1960.
————. *Basic Judaism*. New York, 1947.*
————. *The Making of the Modern Jew*. Indianapolis, 1963.
————. *A Partisan Guide to the Jewish Problem*. New York, 1945.

Wiesel

WRITINGS

Wiesel, Elie. *A Beggar in Jerusalem*, tr. Lily Edelman and Elie Wiesel.
New York, 1970.
————. *The Jews of Silence: A Firsthand Report on Jews in Russia*, tr.
Neal Kozodoy. New York, 1966.*
————. *Legends of Our Time*. New Yorf, 1970.*
————. *The Oath: A Novel*, tr. Marion Wiesel. New York, 1973.
————. *One Generation After*. New York, 1970.
————. *Souls on Fire: Portraits and Legends of Hasidic Masters*, tr.
Marion Wiesel. New York, 1972.

STUDIES

Daiches, David. "After Such Knowledge." *Commentary* xl, 6 (December,
1965).
Jewish Heritage, VIII (19..6). Issue devoted to Elie Wiesel.

Zunz

STUDIES

Arendt, Hannah. "The Jew as Pariah: A Hidden Tradition." *Jewish Social Studies* vi (1944).

Bamberger, Fritz. "Zunz's Conception of History." *Proceedings of the American Academy for Jewish Research* xi (1941).

Glatzer, Nahsm N. "The Beginnings of Modern Jewish Studies" in *Studies in Nineteenth Century Intellectual History*, ed. A. Altmann. Cambridge, Mass., 1964.

————. *Leopold and Adelheid Zunz: An Account in Letters.* London, 1958.

————. "Leopold Zunz and the Jewish Community." *Living Legacy* (Hugo Hahn Volume). New York, 1963.

————. "Leopold Zunz and the Revolution of 1848." *Year Book V, Leo Baeck Institute.* London, 1960.

Wallach, Luitpold. *Liberty and Letters: The Thoughts of Leopold Zunz.* London, 1959.

Wiener, Max. "The Ideology of the Founders of Jewish Scientific Research." *Yivo Annual of Social Science,* v (1950).

Index